NO MORE GOODBYES

NO MORE GOODBYES

Circling the Wagons around Our Gay Loved Ones

CAROL LYNN PEARSON

Pivot Point Books • Walnut Creek • 2007

"The Story She Couldn't Tell" by "Melissa Johnson" and "Tumbling Down" by Tracy Duvalis Kriese were originally published at www.ldsfamilyfellowship.org and are used by permission here.

No More Goodbyes was printed on acid-free paper and meets the permanence of paper requirements of the American National Standard for Informations Sciences. This book was composed, printed, and bound in the United States of America.

Library of Congress Cataloging-in-Publication Data
   No more goodbyes : circling the wagons around our gay loved ones / by Carol Lynn Pearson.
      p. cm.
   ISBN 0-9638852-4-3 (alk. paper)
   1. Family—Religious aspects—Church of Jesus Christ of Latter-day Saints. 2. Marriage—Religious aspects—Church of Jesus Christ of Latter-day Saints. 3. Homosexuality—Religious aspects—Church of Jesus Christ of Latter-day Saints. 4. Church of Jesus Christ of Latter-day Saints—Doctrines. I. Title
   BX8643.F3P42 2006
   261.8'357660882893—dc22
                                                     2006047180

To
the families of every faith
whose love
lights the way for all

Contents

Foreword, *Robert A. Rees* xi

1. FIRST STEPS

This New Pioneer Journey 3
An Enemy Is Someone Whose Story You Do Not Know 11
Goodbye, I Love You: Then and Now 23

2. THAT FINAL, DESPERATE ACT

Driving Them to the Brink 35
More Than a Person Can Bear 41
Bobby Gave up on Love 46
I Would Really Rather Be Dead 50
Moving toward the Light 57
All Our Sons 62

3. STAR-CROSSED LOVES

I Speak for Romantic Love 67
Sad Harvest 71
When It's Your Daughter 79
There Are So Many Kinds of Love 85
Music Up: Cello, Sad 90
Planning the Wedding 98
Choosing and Keeping the Star-Crossed Love 101
I'll Walk with You 109

4. CIRCLING THE WAGONS (ONE)

When There's Love at Home 117
I Drew a Circle That Took Him In 122
Nothing Could Stop Me from Flying to His Side 128
Your Tear in My Eye 133

You Don't Know Him 141

The Story She Couldn't Tell 143

Healing at Christmas 147

Importance of "The One" 156

This Story Has Taken a Wrong Turn 159

Pieces of Eugene: Navajo, Mormon, and Gay 165

Snapshots for the Family Album 169

Religion, Politics, Sex, and Chocolate 179

My Voice Will Not Be Silenced 181

I Am So Blessed 191

Hatred Saddens Mom of Gay Son 194

5. CIRCLING THE WAGONS (TWO)

I Never Would Have Dreamed 203

Is She Still My Daughter? 209

It Has Become Our Universe 214

The Blessing 220

Thank You for Not Leaving Me Out 222

You Just Have to Love 226

Our Children's Vows: Ben and Clare, Brett and Jeff 235

Rod's Other Family 237

He Just Cried with Me 241

Tumbling Down 244

On the Inside 250

Gary's Protectors 257

My Son Is More Important Than My Prejudice 260

Life Is a Song 262

My Family Is Not Like That 268

6. THE ROAD AHEAD

Filling Our Wagons 273

Special Thanks

I am deeply appreciative to the individuals and families who so generously shared the stories included in this book. I am also very grateful to the following:

Don Wright, brother extraordinaire, whose good mind and heart have steadied this project from the beginning.

Marie Cheever, my sister, whose enthusiasm, good ideas, and careful reading have been a great blessing.

Warren Wright, my brother, whose generous support in numerous ways continues to make life easier.

David Wright, my brother, whose constant prayers and good wishes are felt.

Emily Pearson, my daughter, who has surprised herself as a splendid writer, surprised me as an excellent editor, and surprises no one with her ongoing wisdom and wit.

Connie Disney, for her artistic cover, interior design, and devoted book midwifery.

Robert Rees, for his sensitive foreword and for being a fine traveling companion on the plains.

Ron Scott, Connell O'Donovan and Hugo Salinas, for reading, responding, and enriching this book.

John-Charles Duffy for his careful editing eye.

Scott Sorenson, for instant, unsung, important aid.

My friends, who, gratefully, are too numerous to mention, for continually keeping me within the circle of their love and support.

Foreword

Carol Lynn Pearson is a pioneer. With her book, *Goodbye, I Love You* (1986), she was among the first to address the issue of homosexuality in Mormon family life with boldness and compassion. The wide reception of that book revealed how ready Mormons and many others were for someone to speak personally and compassionately about a subject that was essentially taboo. Until then, homosexuality in Mormon culture was spoken of, when it was spoken of at all, as "the sin of the ages" and "the abominable and detestable crime against nature." Even today for people of many religions, just knowing that homosexuality exists calls up the worst images of Sodom and Gomorrah. As Stuart Matis, a gay Mormon man who took his own life over his inability to resolve the conflict he experienced between self and religion, wrote in a letter published in Brigham Young University's *The Daily Universe*:

> I read a recent letter to the editor [of your newspaper] with great regret. The author compared my friends and me to murderers, Satanists, prostitutes, pedophiles and partakers of bestiality. Imagine having to live with this rhetoric constantly being spewed at you.

Stuart, like so many others who have committed suicide over this issue, eventually came to feel he couldn't live in such a world.

Goodbye, I Love You was powerful because it was an honest account of a family dealing with homosexuality in that dangerous terrain between cultural/religious expectations and personal experience. What's more, it was written by a faithful, committed Latter-day Saint. For many, it was the first compassionate voice they had ever heard on the subject. But it wasn't the last. Carol Lynn's story emboldened others—both homosexual and heterosexual, both leader and lay member, both those inside Mormon culture and beyond—to begin speaking out, to begin telling their stories, to begin challenging conventional thinking. *No More Goodbyes* is in many ways a necessary extension of *Goodbye, I Love You*—necessary because in spite of the earlier book's clear message, in spite of the progress made since its publication, we are still—as Mormons and as people of all religions—far from where we need to be when it comes to understanding homosexuality and relating to homosexual people.

Goodbye, I Love You was published the year I became bishop [local ecclesiastical leader] of the Los Angeles First Ward [congregation], serving single members of the LDS Church. Like almost everyone of my generation, I was terribly misinformed about homosexuality. Although I had shed the deep-seated prejudices and even hostility toward gay people that I had learned at home, at church, and practically everywhere else, I still had little understanding of what it meant to be gay in a church culture that condemned homosexuality as among the most perverse of human conditions. All I really knew was that I had a number of homosexuals in my congregation and that I had been called to minister to them. Doing so was one of the most meaningful and sacred experiences of my life.

During the more than five years I served as bishop, I had the privilege not only of ministering to the gay and lesbian members of my congregation but of being ministered to by them. Their patience with and charity toward me, their deep devotion to the gospel, in spite of the pain it caused them to try and be faithful, indeed constituted a kind of ministry. As we met together, I became aware that their attempts to reconcile their sexual orientation with their church were a sacrament of faith and courage, of sacrifice and love. Most of them had endured years of anguish and alienation, were plagued with tremendous doubts about their own self-worth, and yet their love of God and the Church motivated them to continue to find resolution. Often I felt that I was in the presence of something holy as I witnessed their attempts to find harmony between desire and devotion. During those years and since, I felt my humanity broadened, my discipleship deepened, by these remarkable people.

It was while I served as a bishop that I learned of the various ways that families respond to having a homosexual member. Some, feeling they have to choose between their family member and the Church, choose the Church. Others, pained by what they experience as the ecclesiastical rejection of their loved one, choose to leave the Church in support of their child or spouse. Still others find a way to choose both. When I was told by a church leader in another area that a number of young men he was aware of had died of AIDS and that in some instances the families refused to come to the funeral, I was shocked. I could not understand how, under any circumstance, familial bonds could become so cold and broken. I have since known of instances where parents, siblings, spouses, and children have renounced their association with homosexual members of their families, sometimes for a lifetime. But I also know of increasing numbers of families in which the gay or lesbian member is embraced, his or her partner and perhaps children are welcomed wholeheartedly into the family circle, even when this results, as it sometimes does, in the disapproval of extended family, friends, and fellow congregants.

My experience as bishop plus the number of years since then working with homosexual people have taught me that there can be no room in a Christian's life for un-Christlike treatment of anyone, no matter how we may regard his or her life choices. In fact, according to what Christ teaches, we are under greater obligation to those whom we consider "the least" (Matthew 25). The way some Christians and some Christian churches speak of and treat homosexual people cannot be defended from the teachings of Jesus. He invites all—without exception—to come unto him, and he commands those of us who have taken upon ourselves his name to love one another without condition. As John says, "Beloved, let us love one another: for love is of God; and every one that loveth is born of God, and knoweth God" (1 John 4:7).

The Mormon pioneers who set out on the treacherous journey to their promised land did so because they were misunderstood, persecuted, and at times even murdered for their beliefs, including their very unorthodox beliefs about marriage. They went to escape social ostracism and political tyranny that sought to deprive them of their right to live according to their beliefs. What sustained them was their faith and their fellowship with one another and their belief that they would find a place, "far away in the West, / Where none shall come to hurt or make afraid," where they would not only be free of persecution but free as well to build a better kingdom for themselves and for those who would come after.

I dream of such a place for our homosexual brothers and sisters. But rather than traveling to it over plains and mountains, rather than carving it out of a desert wilderness, I believe we have to make it where we are, here and now, in our homes, in our communities, and in our congregations. It is the courage of people like Carol Lynn Pearson that gives me hope that we can—heterosexual and homosexual together—build the Zion we are called to build.

Carol Lynn's new book is a testament to the power of personal stories. The stories told and summarized in this collection stand against the deeply entrenched and strongly defended status quo, which has insisted, often with angry self-righteousness, that homosexuality is a choice, that it is a manifestation of selfishness, that it can be repented of, and that it can be changed through faith, righteousness, and the atonement of Jesus Christ —or through heterosexual marriage. Some of these stories are heartbreaking, some even tragic, but many are warming and inspiring. Together they are hopeful, for they testify that care and compassion are more transformative than prejudice and persecution, that faith and courage are stronger than ignorance and cowardice, and that goodness and love are more powerful than anything.

If *Goodbye, I Love You* was a wake up call to understand homosexuality, *No More Goodbyes* is a clarion call to action. Its central message is: we can't allow what is happening to homosexuals in our churches to continue. We can't accept one more disowned child, one more failed homosexual-heterosexual marriage, one more suicide.

We can't accept one more goodbye.

Robert A. Rees, PhD

Director of Education and Humanities
The Institute of HeartMath

1
FIRST STEPS

Where there is an open mind,
there will always be a frontier.

—CHARLES F. KETTERING

This New Pioneer Journey

I don't pay much attention to the television reality show, *Survivor*. But when I read recently that one of the final six contestants in Guatemala was Rafe Judkins, an Ivy League graduate and wilderness guide, I decided to tune in. He had a reputation as the sweetheart of this cutthroat show, playing the game without deceit. He was honest and loyal and even shed tears for a broken-hearted teammate voted out of the game. But the dichotomy that really intrigued me was the fact that Judkins is a gay Mormon.

Half my life—it has often seemed like more—had been spent with gay men, like my former husband, who had been raised Mormon, members of the Church of Jesus Christ of Latter-day Saints. Still, it was a novelty to have one of them "out" in a major public way, right there on network television, acknowledging his Mormon-ness and his gayness for the world to see.

Rafe was indeed irresistible as he navigated the difficult physical and psychological terrain of the show. He was smart and charming. Any family would be proud to call him son, brother, cousin, friend. Wouldn't they? Did his? Imagine my smile when I read in the papers that a relative, speaking of their sprawling family of devout Mormons, including more than 50 cousins and 20 aunts and uncles, who learned of Rafe's homosexuality not long before the show aired, admitted that it was a shock but said to him, "Rafe, we're circling the wagons around you."

Writing those words months later still brings a surge of pride. "Circling the wagons." What a splendid, Mormon thing to say! That early pioneer, crossing-the-plains trek is still in our blood, that awareness of danger, that efficient determination to protect the loved ones. We Mormons do it quite spectacularly and often. But sometimes we fail. Sometimes we don't quite know how to do it, or even if we should do it, particularly those sometimes when the loved one is a homosexual.

In this we are not unique. Many religious communities today, as they confront homosexuality, find themselves up against one of the most difficult issues they've faced in a very long time. The Episcopal Church's split over homosexuality is getting worldwide attention. A U.S. denomination of about the same size and stature—the Presbyterian Church—is similarly torn. Catholic, Protestant, Orthodox, Jewish, and Latter-day Saint leaders signed a petition encouraging a constitutional amendment to prevent gay marriage. The emotion inherent in the discourse around religion and homosexuality can intensify the confusion and distress of families as they strive to find the "right" way to relate to their gay loved ones.

I have seen families in my own church, like Rafe's family, respond to the challenge of discovering a family member is gay with certitude of love and loyalty. However, I have also seen families, and much of the religious community, circle the wagons around their fears, their beliefs, their judgments and condemnations, leaving the gay person outside the warmth, abandoned to the wolves and the weather.

I have also sometimes seen families gather firmly around their gay loved one, only to discover that the larger community, often without meaning to, has circled the wagons in a way that places the family outside as well, leaving them in a wilderness of isolation.

I have seen glimpses, too, of gay individuals, their Mormon families, and the larger community together accepting the daunting task of finding new and creative ways to configure the wagons, managing somehow to share the safety and the warmth.

I see pain that rips my heart out. And I see healing.

That is why I wrote this book.

⌒

I write primarily of the Mormon experience, but I don't write only *to* Mormons. I write to all who find themselves walking that challenging territory where religion and sexuality collide. We are an interesting bunch, we Latter-day Saints. Politically we hold a significant place on the national scene, and I think we offer a fine microcosm of all conservative religions as they address this unavoidable subject. Everyone can learn a lot from our pain, our confusion, our failures, our learning, and our successes.

I am a fourth-generation Mormon. My own grandmother, Sarah Oakey Sirrine, walked across the plains to Utah when she was eight years old, leaving her treasured collection of dolls in Nottingham, England, and settling finally in Dingle Dell, Idaho. My great-great-grandfather, Thomas Morris, in the short-lived war with Mexico in 1847, crossed the country in our nation's longest recorded infantry march, with a group of U.S. soldiers known as the Mormon Battalion. He boiled his leather shirt and ate it to stay alive. Another great-grandfather, George Warren Sirrine, holding a pickax, was lowered over the sides of the ship *Brooklyn* to break off the ice so the voyage could continue around Cape Horn and arrive at what would become San Francisco. He was one of the first vigilantes to bring law and order to that city, later becoming a founder of Mesa, Arizona.

I love my Mormon pioneer ancestors.

And I do not believe our pioneering is finished.

~

Some of you know me. I wrote a book that was published in 1986, *Goodbye, I Love You*. It was the story of my life with my husband, Gerald, a very dear man who was also a homosexual man. We married in the Salt Lake Mormon temple in 1966, buoyantly determined to create a happy eternal marriage in spite of the challenge his sexual orientation presented. He had repented. He knew and I knew that we would be blessed. Homosexuality wasn't a "real" thing, it was something Gerald fell into because of the temptations of this imperfect world. A good woman who loved him was the answer, along with faithfulness to the gospel, prayer, scripture study, church attendance, and loving the Lord.

Nine years and four children later, we were dealing with a greater anguish than I'd ever believed possible. Gerald was not "cured." Despite his love for me and for our children, despite his rigorous spiritual discipline, he was still a man whose need for intimate love was not with a woman, but with another man. This need, I learned, was far more than sex; it related to every aspect of his personality.

After all the cards were on the table, we struggled for four years—two in Provo, Utah, and two in Walnut Creek, California—trying to find a way to maintain our family. Finally, we ended the marriage and kept the friendship. Gerald relocated to nearby San Francisco to live what he felt was a more authentic life and to find his true love. He never found him. "Oh, Carol Lynn," he said to me more than once, "if I could just find a man like you, I'd be in seventh heaven." In 1984, Gerald died of AIDS in my home, where I was taking care of him. I read his favorite Walt Whitman poems, I sang accompanied by the three guitar chords that I knew, and I said as I held him, "It's okay, Gerald, you can fly now."

In the twenty years since I shared my story so publicly, I have had the privilege of serving as a safe place where a large number of people, especially Mormons, have been able to bring their stories and their tears. Yesterday morning I received an email from a woman who said, "Thanks for giving a voice to families of gay people. We are aching, and aching to be heard." And today an email from David, a Brigham Young University student, saying, "I do not eat. I do not sleep. I cannot focus. I cannot study. I cannot breathe. Will I ever figure this out?"

Recently in sacrament meeting (Sunday service) in my ward (local congregation), our visiting high councilman, Brother Marostica, spoke about callings. He reminded us that in early Christianity, a calling was something different from the callings we receive today from the bishop to serve as a teacher or work in the nursery or in the Cub Scouts. "That larger kind of calling," he said, "is one you receive directly from God, one you are guided to by the Holy Spirit, designed specifically for you to bless the world."

I have a calling. I don't remember asking for it, but Gerald assured me that I must have. "You know, don't you," he said, "that you've been set up to do something more than write nice little poems. Somehow you and I volunteered to do a really hard project together. I'm sorry it's so painful, but I know you've got an important work to do."

I accept my calling. I don't do it perfectly, but I do it as well as I can, and I do it with reverence. I see myself as one of the advance scouts who have been assigned to walk a rough landscape and come back to report.

This is my report. We are not yet in the promised land. We cannot proclaim, "This is the right place," as Brigham Young did in 1847 at the mouth of Emigration Canyon above Salt Lake City. You and I may not agree on what the promised land will look like when and if we finally get there, but let us agree on one thing. We are not yet there.

We—people of all religions and of no religion—are called to be one in love, but very often we trample love in our rush to the familiar comfort of fear and judgment.

We are called to create relationships that are enduring, but we allow our beliefs about homosexuality to bring the most agonizing disruptions. As we circle the wagons around our fears and misunderstandings, with our gay loved ones on the outside, we say too many goodbyes. I report here on three kinds of goodbyes that I see all too often in my culture. I also offer suggestions of a map brought to me in pieces by many courageous families and individuals who share their part in charting the way we must go.

Too many goodbyes are said due to the final, desperate act of suicide.

Too many goodbyes are said due to ill-fated marriages, which are contracted under unrealistic expectations of change and then explode, leaving behind enormous devastation.

Too many goodbyes are said due to families being torn apart by beliefs that seem more important than people.

Paradoxically, and to our great shame, the beliefs that prompt these awful goodbyes are attributed to the will of God.

~

I want to tell you a few things about my own beliefs and

position on the subject at hand. My favorite description of our Creator is, "God is love." I enjoy singing the little song in my own church, *"Where love is, there God is also."* I believe we can learn a great deal from scriptures of the past, but I believe we need to add to them the light of the present, especially the light that comes to each of us from our own godly hearts. I'm reluctant to accept the precision of some as to what God considers an abomination. I note, in the fourteenth chapter of Deuteronomy, it was believed that God considered it an abomination to eat the meat of swine, or rabbit, or shellfish. For lunch today I had a bowl of delicious ham and lentil soup. And in the seventeenth chapter of the same book, I note it was believed that God considered it an abomination to offer an animal sacrifice that contained a blemish. I am comfortable with the thought that we, like the ancients, continue to seek God, continue to stumble in our seeking, continue to find truth that is consistent with the one secure touchstone, "God is love."

A strong belief of mine is that sexuality is an awesome gift and should be treasured. I am impressed with the words of American publisher Margaret Anderson, who said, "In real love you want the other person's good. In romantic love you want the other person." I wholeheartedly believe that intimate access to the body of another person is the most supreme of privileges, that being in love—real love—wanting both the other person and the other person's highest good—is a breathtaking experience that brings us about the closest we mortals ever get to heaven.

I have several gay friends who have chosen lifelong celibacy. It is not easy. They believe this to be the right choice for them. I respect that choice, and I wish them well.

I have gay friends who have married heterosexual partners.

Most of those marriages have ended in extreme sorrow. A few of the marriages are still intact, with the partners experiencing some satisfaction along with significant difficulty. They believe this is the right choice for them. I respect that choice, and I wish them well.

Most of my gay friends are in gay relationships or are navigating the territory toward establishing them. Many are happy in their relationships. They believe this is the right choice for them. I respect that choice, and I wish them well.

And so our journey begins.

An Enemy Is Someone Whose Story You Do Not Know

It's not that some of us have to cross these particular plains and some of us, thank goodness, do not. The turns of history insist that we can travel them either reluctantly or travel them as deliberate pioneers, setting out to find a better life for us and our loved ones than the life we're leaving behind. There's most likely a homosexual in your family, whether you know it or not. The conservative estimate of five percent of the population means that if you can fill a room for Thanksgiving with twenty relatives, chances are that at least one person at the table is gay. And without question, there are homosexual people just up the street. The 2000 Census showed gay couples living in 99.3 percent of the counties in the United States.

"But—but they're not *really* gay, are they?" is the hope of many of us. "They're really just 'so-called gays' who are actually heterosexuals suffering from same-sex attraction that can be healed, aren't they?" That was the hope with which I went into my marriage. That was the hope with which Gerald entered the marriage and fathered four children he dearly loved. That was the hope that has led large numbers of people in the past to undergo shock therapy, allowing electrodes to burn their genitals, and today to fast and pray until they're near to madness.

Yes. Yes, they're *really* gay. How all of this will work out in

11

the eternities, I am comfortable leaving in the hands of God. But for this lifetime, there is a small but significant minority of people who are truly homosexual, meaning that they fall in love only with people of their own sex and desire with them emotional and physical intimacy.

My personal beliefs, formed after decades of experience and study, are that there is a continuum on which we all find ourselves relative to sexual orientation, that there is some fluidity in our placement at given times in our lives, as well as a wide variety in our need for sexual expression as individuals and at various stages of life. There are a small number of people who find themselves in the center of that continuum, who are truly bisexual and can relate intimately and comfortably with either sex. A dear friend is in this category. Most of these people assimilate into the heterosexual world, though their feelings of sexual attraction continue in varying degrees to include members of their own gender. A small but significant number, perhaps five percent of the population, experience themselves firmly and wholly as homosexual, can make various choices around this fact, but find that their physical/emotional desire for a partner of the same gender never goes away.

Some people's natural sexuality, gay or straight, is deeply wounded by abuse. Therapy and spiritual guidance can help many of them to sexual health. Some people, especially at the height of adolescent hormonal frenzy, can find themselves sexually interested in anyone within reach. I am aware that these days some young people find being gay sort of "hip" and try on the identity. But sleeping in the garage does not make you a car. Nor does sleeping with a heterosexual spouse make a gay person straight. The large number of gay people I know who have slept for years with their straight spouses without it making the slightest impact on their sexual orientation leads me to believe it would be an impossible assignment to take a truly heterosexual person and turn him or her into a gay person. Which brings us to a major point that must be understood. Both straights and gays *discover* rather than decide their sexual feelings. In the words of one Mormon man who emailed me,

> Your characterization of the challenges I/we face as a "strange frontier" is accurate. I'm feeling quite worn down by my trek on this frontier. I didn't ask to be a pioneer; I just woke up and found myself on the plains one day pulling my homosexual handcart.

There are still mysteries in how our sexual orientation is formed, but today some significant facts are in. Recently *60 Minutes* aired a fascinating segment called "The Science of Sexual Orientation." Lesley Stahl reported that while the final answer of what makes a person gay or straight may be a long way off, "scientists . . . are already yielding tantalizing clues." Michael Bailey, a psychology professor at Northwestern University and a leading researcher in the field of sexual orientation, commented on the extremely different gender behaviors of a set of boy twins. "To me, cases like that really scream out, 'Hey, it's not out there, it's in here,'" he said, pointing to his heart. He said he doesn't think nurture is a plausible explanation, as in what he called the largely disproved theory that homosexuality is caused by overbearing mothers and distant fathers.

"Today," reported Ms. Stahl, "scientists are looking at genes, environment, brain structure, and hormones." The report went on to demonstrate that gay and straight people move differently and talk differently, suggesting that their brains work somewhat differently. Also that homosexuality runs in families. After introducing two identical twins, one gay and one straight, Dr. Bailey suggested that the environment he's most interested in is "the environment that happens to us while we're in the womb," which is an environment that is "much more important than we ever thought it was." Adding to the mystery is that "the more older brothers a man has, the greater that man's chance of being gay," a finding that has been "demonstrated in study after study." *60 Minutes* concluded that the scientists they spoke to are "increasingly convinced that genes, hormones, or both . . . determine sexual orientation before birth."

Leaders and members of the Mormon Church are traditionally very open to the discoveries of science. We quote a statement of the founding prophet of the Church, Joseph Smith, asserting that "one of the grand fundamental principles of Mormonism is to receive truth, let it come from whence it may." The statements of church leaders on sexual orientation in recent years are not unaffected by scientific findings.

Many Mormon scientists are coming to conclusions that match those of *60 Minutes*. In a talk in 2004, Dr. William Bradshaw, of Brigham Young University's biology department, discussed scientific data that he felt "proved homosexuality is a result of biological orientation." In addition to some of the findings also cited by *60 Minutes*, Dr. Bradshaw presented the results of studies that show homosexuals have a 39 percent greater probability of being left-handed than right-handed, and that homosexual men go through puberty significantly earlier than heterosexual men do. As reported in BYU's *The Daily Universe*, Dr. Bradshaw

> expressed his deep concern about the harmful opinions and actions of the LDS community. "In our LDS community there is not much discourse on this issue," Bradshaw said. When there

is, it is "not usually civil and it's not always informed." Bradshaw said the LDS community must reach out and include those who are homosexual, because no encouraging evidence suggests the possibility of behavioral and biological changes . . .

Bradshaw referred to an article in the *Ensign* [an official LDS Church periodical] that says the atonement is a sufficient means to resolve the problems of this world. Bradshaw said though he is absolutely committed to the atonement of Jesus Christ, he feels this attitude is detrimental to those who will cope with homosexuality for the remainder of their lives.

Another BYU professor, Dr. Duane E. Jeffery of the zoology department, observes:

> The best synthesis of available data suggests that specific combinations of genes . . . make the fetus susceptible to influence by the interacting fetal/maternal hormones. . . . Homosexuality is far more profitably understood as a phenomenon of biology than of the schoolyard. . . . [It is] "hard-wired"—i.e., inherent and "natural"; it is not the result of learning or training.

He continues:

> [To] see real emotional hell due to gender variations, observe the devout, conscientious parents of persons who are homosexual. Too many of us convince ourselves that we understand this one, and that we are therefore free—or even called upon—to denigrate, revile, and persecute. . . . And who is it, exactly, that we pain and persecute? Homosexuality knows no ethnic boundaries, it occurs among all cultures, religions, and social strata. Homosexuals are among, or are family members of, our most respected and contributive citizens.

Another Latter-day Saint scientist, Dr. R. Jan Stout, a psychiatrist who began his study of homosexuality with the firm conviction that it was "a learned behavior, an illness to be treated and corrected," learned over the years that his earlier position had been "wrong and simplistic." He came to believe that "the crucial factor is the timing and amount of testosterone released in utero by the developing embryo," that apparently after birth "environment fine tunes the instrument of sexuality but neither creates nor organizes its direction."

Science has also broadened our understanding by documenting that homosexual behavior has been observed in more than 450 species of mammals, birds, reptiles, and insects. I have followed the charming story of Roy and Silo, two male penguins who met in a zoo holding tank in 1998 in New York's Central Park. They became inseparable, built a nest, defended it from others, and "engaged in what zookeepers euphemistically call 'ecstatic display.'" They showed signs of wanting to be parents, so the zookeepers gave them a dummy egg, which they successfully incubated, then gave them an actual egg. When the baby chick was born, Roy and Silo cared for it, fed it, kept it warm, and successfully launched it into maturity. Years later, the couple is still going strong and is regarded as just another couple by their heterosexual penguin peers.

Today's science should also relieve us of the fear that our children are at great risk to be recruited into homosexuality. I believe that if the gay community sent missionaries door to door like we Mormons do, spreading the good news of homosexuality, they would get pitifully few converts, probably only a small sliver of the terminally confused. "Join us and very possibly break your parents' hearts, throw the family into chaos, run the risk of intense self-loathing, especially if you are religious, invite the disgust of much of society, give up the warmth and benefits of marriage and probably of parenthood." I know many gay people who are very happy with who they are and who would not take a magic heterosexuality pill if such a thing were suddenly available. But I can't think of one who, when he knew which direction his feet were pointing, would not have given a great deal (and many have given more than you can imagine) to be able to travel the other road, that utterly unavailable and so much easier road not taken.

And the "gay lifestyle"—what is this? We can check out *Lifestyles of the Rich and Famous* and get a fair idea of what that world looks like. But "gay lifestyle"? I don't think we know yet, nor will we know for a few more decades. It has been a relatively short time that gay people have been visible in modern society, following a very lengthy time in which they were assigned to dark alleyways and lived in fear of discovery, ostracized, sent to the concentration camps along with the Jews in the Holocaust, and otherwise killed. Darkness and fear can do something to us, can make us behave in strange ways. My husband Gerald lived and died in the great excess of the 1980s, when so many gay people behaved much like tipsy teenagers at their first all-nighter, unchaperoned even by good judgment.

For many of us, it is hard to fathom what we judge to be excessive and bizarre sexual behavior, such as having hundreds of relationships with anonymous partners, as some, but not all, gay men and very few lesbians do. Sexuality, I am convinced, is the life force itself—and not just the reproductive life force. When a power so great is not allowed a respectable stage upon which to dance, it will nearly always come out in twisted and tortuous ways. We have sadly learned from our Catholic friends, through the news of case after case of sexual molestation by priests, that celibacy is a calling for some but clearly not for all. I am beginning to understand why some gay people have expressed their sexuality in ways that have shocked us. I recently heard a very articulate gay man on *Oprah* say he is convinced that the promiscuity of many gay men is due to the shame they have absorbed. With absolutely no societal, family, or spiritual support, with few role models, and under layers of learned self-loathing, I believe that many have been left one by one to re-invent the wheel of relationship, even to some extent the wheel of life. I firmly believe that what they will do with societal, family, and spiritual support, excellent role models, and layers of self-respect is surely something that will bless us all. I am reminded of a statement of early feminist writer Sarah Moore Grimke: "I ask no favors for my sex. . . . All I ask of our brethren is that they will take their feet from off our necks."

Will gay culture ever look precisely like straight culture? I'm remembering a comment by a gay hairdresser standing behind me at last year's Gay Pride Parade in San Francisco, the first I had ever attended. When a few particularly underdressed and overflabbed marchers came by, he groaned and said, "Where's the pride in *that*?" What the "gay lifestyle" will look like in years to come will likely not be radically different from the non-gay lifestyle.

We Mormons understand about being reviled and hated. In 1839, the governor of Missouri issued an "extermination order" against us, declaring that the Mormons must be destroyed, "as their outrages are beyond all description." Subsequently, in 1847, led by Brigham Young, we were forced to leave Illinois and made a long trek west, settling in the desert territory of Utah. Interesting, I think, that one of the crimes we were accused of was our sexual lifestyle, which included the oddity of polygamy. Fear can put us on edge, can make us do things we wouldn't ordinarily do. In the history of early Utah, stemming from community paranoia and blind obedience to authority, there is a bloody and highly aberrant incident of which we are not proud, known as the Mountain Meadows Massacre. But the enduring characteristics of the Mormon people are wholesomeness and helpfulness, and if you have Mormon neighbors today, the worst you probably have to fear is that they'll invite you to a church activity or that they'll shovel the snow from your driveway without even asking.

Back to the homosexuals: who are "these people" anyway? They can be obnoxious, narcissistic, contentious, promiscuous, selfish, annoying. Just like the rest of us. They can also be delightful, sensitive, faithful, generous, brilliantly creative, and the best friends you will ever find. They can be easy to identify, exhibiting physiological and behavioral attributes that go against gender stereotypes, or they can look as typically "masculine" or "feminine" as their heterosexual counterparts. (Conversely, not every man who displays feminine characteristics is homosexual, nor is every woman who appears masculine a lesbian.)

I thought of gay people as I read a section in Eckhart Tolle's *A New Earth*. I love Tolle's insistence that the core teachings of the great spiritual masters all point toward an awareness of our oneness, our divinity. If we choose to follow them, we are poised for radical and universal enlightenment. Yet too often the religions that sprang from those teachings have contributed to darkness because to a large extent, they

> became divisive rather than unifying forces. Instead of bringing about an ending of violence and hatred through a realization of the fundamental oneness of all life, they brought more violence and hatred, more divisions between people as well as between different religions and even within the same religion. They became ideologies, belief systems people could identify with and

so use them to . . . make themselves "right" and others "wrong" and thus define their identity through their enemies, the "others," the "nonbelievers" or "wrong believers" who not infrequently they saw themselves justified in killing. . . .

By far the greater part of violence that humans have inflicted on each other is not the work of criminals or the mentally deranged, but of normal, respectable citizens in the service of the collective ego. . . . You construct a conceptual identity for an individual or group and you say: "This is who he is. This is who they are." . . . All this . . . strengthens the sense of separation between yourself and the other, whose "otherness" has become magnified to such an extent that you can no longer feel your common humanity, nor the rootedness in the one life that you share with each human being, your common divinity.

We make someone "the other" virtually in the twinkling of an eye. Consider this story sent to me by Don Holsinger, professor at Brigham Young University and father of a gay son:

Lest anyone doubt that total rejection by LDS families of gay family members is commonplace, let me pass along a recent personal experience. At a Salt Lake City meeting of gay university students, a former student of mine at BYU recognized my wife and me. We asked him about his experience at BYU and how he was getting along in his life now that he had come out to his parents. He told us that he was the first of nine children and beloved of his parents. He was gifted academically, a talented musician, and a returned missionary. However, when he told his mother that he was gay, he said that she told him to gather his belongings immediately, leave the house, and never return.

That an *idea*—my child is gay—could be so powerful a shock that, within minutes, years of love, devotion, service, and admiration are transformed into horror and condemnation is astonishing. That a belief should invade the sacred space of a mother's love like a poison dart and suddenly turn a loved son into "the other," a *despised* other, leaves me reeling.

If, in your mind, homosexual feelings are so abhorrent and homosexual behavior so sinful that you cannot move beyond repugnance, I include as part of the invitation this statement by the prophet Joseph Smith:

> Nothing is so much calculated to lead people to forsake sin as to take them by the hand, and watch over them with tenderness. When persons manifest the least kindness and love to me, O what power it has over my mind, while the opposite course has a tendency to harrow up all the harsh feelings and depress the human mind. . . . All the religious world is boasting of righteousness: it is the doctrine of the devil to retard the human mind, and hinder our progress, by filling us with self-righteousness. . . . [If] you would have God have mercy on you, have mercy on one another.

"Sin" is an interesting word. At its root it is an archery term that means "missing the mark." If you and I were taking an archery class together and you missed the target by a yard, I would not turn away in horror and judgment. I would say, "Oh, oh. Try it again. Bet you can get closer this time." And if I, in my turn, missed the bull's eye, I think you might say, "Good try! Come on! Give it another shot!"

What if we are in that archery class, all of us, practicing for perfection, rehearsing for heaven? And what is the bull's eye, that desired center point for which we aim? No secret there. Love. That is made clear in every sacred text that has graced this planet. Jesus said that the center point, the greatest commandment, is to love God and your neighbor (as well as yourself). "Love one another, as I have loved you." Missing the bull's eye—sinning—is missing the mark of love. Perhaps many of us respond to our fellow students' learning with a righteous zeal that causes us to miss love and land on judgment, fear, hate. Perhaps some of us strain at a gnat and swallow a camel. Perhaps some of us see the mote that is in our brother's eye and are not aware of the beam that is in our own. Perhaps our Teacher would like us to be one another's cheerleaders rather than one another's judges.

One of my favorite texts is *A Course in Miracles*. It tells me that "everything that comes from love is a miracle" and brings about oneness. Whatever does not come from love comes from fear and contributes to the illusion of "separation," separation from God and from one another.

Can we be "kind" to others when we see them as a different "kind"? We can be polite to our homosexual brothers and sisters, but we are not being "kind" unless we acknowledge them as "kin," not as "the other," but as our very own kind.

In this book I introduce you to your kin, your own kind. There's an old Jewish saying: *An enemy is someone whose story you do not know.* Storytelling is part of my calling, and as you read the following stories, I have full confidence that your understanding and compassion will increase, that you will respond from the place of love, of kindness, and that together we will create miracles.

Goodbye, I Love You: *Then and Now*

I can still remember how I felt the day my editor at Random House called to tell me that Deseret Book, the Mormon Church-owned publishing house in Salt Lake City, had asked for a preview copy of *Goodbye, I Love You*. Panic hit. *No!* I wasn't *ready* for this! It had become clear to me soon after Gerald's death that telling our story was important. On the national scene, I was hearing again and again of young men abandoned by their families, left to die of AIDS alone. And on the closer ground of my own religious culture, I knew that we had enormous misunderstandings about homosexuality and that Gerald himself had helped put me in a position to have a voice that would be heard. Still, it was frightening, and I was not sure what to expect.

Two weeks after the call just mentioned, my editor telephoned to tell me that Deseret Book had ordered one thousand copies of *Goodbye, I Love You* and had also requested that I come for a book signing at their Salt Lake store during the Church's October general conference. I hung up the phone and burst into tears.

I described that book signing in the diary I have kept since high school:

Saturday was an amazing day. . . . When we got to the downtown store, there was a line of at least twenty people waiting for me. And for about three hours there was not a letup. Such a stream of grateful people—a woman whose son died of AIDS, more gay married men, former wives, and people who didn't let on but I knew they were in pain. . . . The Deseret Book people told me they checked their computer and found that my book has broken every sales record they've ever had for the sale of one book in one month.

My file holds only four or five letters received from people critical of me for writing the book. It also holds hundreds and hundreds of letters from people deeply grateful for finally feeling not alone on what they had felt was a desperately solitary journey. A Mormon woman from New York was very distressed and disappointed in me. She felt I was "adding fodder to today's immorality." How could I say something like, "Gerald, you can fly now"? Didn't I know he gave up the right to fly when he broke his temple covenants? But the very next letter was one of the most beautiful I've ever received, from a Jewish man in New York, thanking me and blessing me. I filed the letters in categories, and to my surprise the largest file of them all was the one marked "LDS General," Mormon people who were not gay and did not have a gay family member, but were so grateful to be able to better understand a difficult subject.

I've selected a few other excerpts from my diary to give a glimpse into that remarkable time in 1986:

Saturday morning I was on KTLK radio. . . . [The] first one to call was a crazy lady, who assured us if we had the right kind of laws that would let us execute a few of those homos the others would never do it again. A few calls later I heard Gerald's father's voice on the line. . . . He challenged the first caller, saying, "If you saw a bunch of those homos lined up and you saw one of your loved ones among them, would you say, 'Pull the trigger'?" Then he identified himself. . . . It was, of course, a very emotional thing. My kids were listening to this at [my brother] Donald's house and were amazed.

~

At the first event in Detroit [on a publicity tour] . . . I had a message to call Lenore Romney, the wife of the former governor of Michigan, George [and mother of Mitt Romney]. . . . She said she wanted me to know how proud of me she was. She had seen me on *Good Morning, America* and . . . she knew this was a subject we all needed to know more about, even she needed to know more about it.

~

So many families have called to thank me, especially mothers of gay sons. Night before last, one called me from L.A. to tell me how thrilled she was with the book . . . and how she feels the Church has to address this more realistically. Last night her son called me, just ecstatic, saying "I can't believe the change in my mother since she read your book. She's called me twice today as I've been reading it, saying, 'How far are you now?' and is so anxious to talk about things. It is a huge, huge change, and I'm so *grateful* to you."

~

[After a talk at a Mormon study group in Pasadena,] a man asked, sincerely . . . if the final answer to this was not just a healing blessing of the priesthood to relieve one of this problem. . . . A woman then rose and commented . . . that maybe what we should be doing is rather than looking for the priesthood to heal them, to instead call on the healing powers of the priesthood to heal us of our attitudes and our prejudices.

~

Yesterday afternoon I got a call from Senator Orrin Hatch, Republican from Utah. . . . He said "I loved your book. It is a wonderful contribution to the Church and to everyone else." He went on to tell me that as he has worked with homosexual people in his government work and earlier as a bishop, he found that he could not condemn them. "I know what the Bible says and all that, but there's something else going on here. These people did not choose to be homosexual." . . . He told me to let him know if ever he could do anything for me.

~

A couple of weeks ago I got a letter from Gordon B. Hinckley [then in the Quorum of the Twelve; at this writing, president and prophet of the Church]. I had sent him a very good article on how the Catholic Church is dealing with AIDS, suggesting we could have a similar approach. His letter was a thank-you note, and at the end he said, "I appreciate the good you have done and are doing."

~

I had an hour with Alan Gundry, the head of the new [Church] Department of Homosexual Concerns in Social Services. . . . He is a very good and kind person, who realizes we do not have the answers. He said, "Ten years ago I would have said all these guys can be changed, but I know now that's not true." His goal for the department is to help everyone love one another and to realize that we're all brothers and sisters. He's just going to be collecting data right now, listening to people's stories.

~

My children received great support from church members and others during the time that I was traveling. As I called home, I continued to ask if they had been receiving negative comments at school or at church. To my great relief, they had not. However, I was distressed by an experience that my son Aaron, then 17, had at a BYU Youth Conference:

> [At his first workshop, the teacher] got onto homosexuality, saying it was the most evil of all the evils and that Satan had figured out how to destroy the family, etc. Aaron was very upset. He got up and left. But he waited until noon when all her workshops were done and then went back in and talked to her. I have encouraged my children to speak up when they feel it is

right, but especially Aaron has not yet learned the kind of tact that lets him do it kindly. Anyway, he let her know that she was "the most bigoted and ignorant woman" he had ever met. "Would you like to talk about it?" she asked, smiling and inviting him to sit down. He told her she didn't know what she was talking about regarding homosexuals. She continued to smile and said, "This is the Church's position. They can change and that is expected of them." Aaron argued that they cannot change, that they're just that way. He began to cry in front of her and she continued to smile and quote the Church's position. He said, "Wipe that smile off your face and listen to me." By the end of the conversation she knew who he was, and he asked if she had read my book. No, she hadn't. He told her that maybe she should. And he left.

I feel bad about this. You would think that the woman would have enough compassion that when speaking to the child of a man who was a homosexual, a man whom the child loved, she would make some kind of gesture of understanding or encouragement or at least say, "Well, there are a lot of things we don't quite have figured out." But she just smiled and quoted the Church's position. Her smile was what Aaron was most furious with. And I can see it now. I don't know the woman. But I know Mormons who have that self-satisfied smile that never goes away. It rides them through everything.

~

The lay of the land was very clear regarding homosexuality in the 80s. Like all conservative religions, Mormonism explained the subject in terms that were unambiguous. Spencer W. Kimball, a member of the Quorum of the Twelve Apostles for thirty years, was in charge of homosexual concerns for the Church for some years prior to becoming prophet and president, which office he held from 1973 to 1985. He counseled with hundreds if not thousands of church members who came to him or were referred to him because of their homosexuality. In a book that he wrote, published in 1969, *The Miracle of Forgiveness*, he wrote a chapter called "Crime Against Nature," which became the standard reference on the subject throughout the Mormon Church. A few excerpts from that chapter are:

> Masturbation often leads to grievous sin, even to that sin against nature, homosexuality . . . an ugly sin . . . repugnant . . . embarrassing . . . detestable . . . perversion . . .
>
> Thus it is that through the ages, perhaps as an extension of homosexual practices, men and women have sunk even to seeking sexual satisfactions with animals. . .
>
> [The abominable practice] can be overcome. . . . [To] those who say that this practice or any other evil is incurable, I respond: "How can you say the door cannot be opened until your knuckles are bloody, till your head is bruised, till your muscles are sore? It can be done."
>
> . . . [Some] totally conquer homosexuality in a few months, others linger on with less power and require more time to make the total comeback. The cure is as permanent as the individual makes it. . . . Satan will not readily let go . . .

I know Mormon gay people who have practically memorized the above language and have used it to flagellate themselves year after year. I recall my husband assuring me between sobs that his "knuckles were bloody," his "head bruised" and his "muscles sore," and that no door to healing had opened.

Much of President Kimball's description of homosexuality is consistent with other things that were being written at the time in the national press. Additionally, Edward L. Kimball writes in a 2005 biography of his father, *Lengthen Your Stride*:

> Like other Americans at mid-century, President Kimball's

strongly negative attitude toward homosexuality was shaped in large part by his fervent acceptance of chastity before marriage and fidelity after marriage, as the Lord's standard for sexual activity, by his belief that a major purpose of marriage was bearing and rearing children, and by an abhorrence for what sexual conduct struck him as unnatural.

~

Here we are, twenty years after the publication of *Goodbye, I Love You*. A lot has happened in those years, both in society and in our churches, as we have continued to struggle with the difficult issue of homosexuality. Pain is still very much with us. Unfortunate and unnecessary goodbyes are still being said. Many of our gay brothers and sisters receive stones of ignorance when they ask for bread. Families of gay people sometimes feel they have impossible choices to make. The current national political climate, especially around the "Protection of Marriage" issue, has intensified some feelings and raised some stakes. Daily I sense the urgency of placing this subject where we can see it in better light.

Leaders of the LDS Church do not generally use the same language in speaking of homosexuality as they did twenty years ago. Rather than seeing it as simply an evil choice, they acknowledge that its causes may be complex. In an interview with the current church president, Gordon B. Hinckley, in 2004, Larry King asked if being gay was "a problem they caused, or they were born with?" President Hinckley answered, "I don't know. I'm not an expert on these things." In the same year, the First Presidency of the Church issued the following statement:

> We . . . reach out with understanding and respect for individuals who are attracted to those of the same gender. We realize there may be great loneliness in their lives.

A lengthy statement that appeared on the Church's official website (www.lds.org) in August 2006, framed by two high-ranking church leaders, Elder Dallin H. Oaks and Elder Lance B. Wickman, contains the following excerpts:

> The distinction between feelings or inclinations on the one hand, and behavior on the other hand, is very clear. It's no sin to have inclinations that if yielded to would produce behavior that would be a transgression. The sin is in yielding to temptation. Temptation is not unique. Even the Savior was tempted. . . . Everyone has some challenges they have to struggle with. . . . We expect celibacy of any person that is not . . . [in] a marriage recognized by God as well as by the law of the land. . . . Why someone has a same-gender attraction . . . who can say? But what matters is the fact that we know we can control how we behave, and it is behavior which is important.
>
> The good news for somebody who is struggling with same-gender attraction is this: . . . if I can keep myself worthy here [in mortality], if I can be true to gospel commandments . . . the blessings of exaltation and eternal life that Heavenly Father holds out to all of His children apply to me. . .

As I listen to the leaders of the Mormon Church today, I hear less about "change" and more about "control." The harsh language that was used in Spencer W. Kimball's *The Miracle of Forgiveness* is not generally repeated in new commentary. However, those earlier words laid the foundation for deeply held attitudes of revulsion around the subject of homosexuality.

President Kimball's son wrote:

> *The Miracle of Forgiveness* set a demanding standard, and Spencer later seemed to wish he had adopted a gentler tone. In 1977 he invited Lyle Ward, the former bishop of his home ward, and

Lyle's wife, Virginia, to his office. . . . In the course of the visit, he showed them many interesting gifts and artifacts. . . . Coming to a bookshelf holding the many translations of *The Miracle of Forgiveness*, he paused and pulled a copy out to the edge of the shelf, saying, "Sometimes I think I might have been a little too strong about some of the things I wrote in this book." His manner, according to Bishop Ward, indicated he had given the matter considerable thought.

Believing that the harshest language in that book occurs in the section on homosexuality, I contacted Edward Kimball and asked if he had any more information on his father's feelings around that subject. He responded:

I wish I could add something to the statement on page 80 of *Lengthen Your Stride* about misgivings Dad had concerning the tough language in *The Miracle of Forgiveness*, but I cannot. If I ever had a discussion with him about homosexuality (aside from expressions of regret that individuals with whom he had counseled had been unable to succeed in their efforts to change), I have forgotten it.

For decades, the "tough language" around which President Kimball later had misgivings found its way into the conversation, the condemnation, the anguish, the abject despair, and sometimes the final abandonment of hope of large numbers of Mormon gay people and their families. *The Miracle of Forgiveness*, with its original language, is still being published and sold by Deseret Book. By 1998, it had sold approximately 1.6 million copies in seventeen languages.

To me, it is sad comfort to know that President Kimball wished he had used more gentle language in addressing the profoundly important topic of homosexuality, as well as, perhaps, other topics in his book. I wish that in 1977, eight years after the book came out, when he voiced his regret in private, he would also have done it in public. Thousands of Mormon gay people and their families would have considered even the modest statement that he "might have been a little too strong" in some of the things he wrote to be news that was worthy of a press conference.

For many, his words on this subject were all they had.

2
THAT FINAL, DESPERATE ACT

*Each one of them
is Jesus in disguise.*

—MOTHER TERESA

Driving Them to the Brink

"Why would a sixteen-year-old, tall, slender, good-looking boy drink ant poison? Why would he even *think* of suicide? I didn't know, not then. Only later, when he and his twin brother confessed to me they both were gay. He was airlifted to Primary Children's Hospital."

Over the nearly two decades since *Goodbye, I Love You* was published, I had grown accustomed to people, especially mothers, approaching me with tears in their eyes, hugging me tightly as they told me their own stories. So I was not surprised that at a book signing in southern Utah—ironically, during the writing of this book in early 2006—a woman approached and opened her heart, telling me the story above.

Only minutes earlier, another mother had told me her experience. Her son, now in his twenties, had been in anguish as a youth, convinced he was condemned by God and by his church. "A year ago he couldn't take it any longer," his mother told me. "He gave himself HIV, his choice of suicide. He deliberately injected himself with a dirty needle. He's cut off all contact with the family, even though we've tried so hard to support him. I think it's just too hard for him to see us."

I have received hundreds of letters and emails from anguished families, real mothers and fathers with real children very much like your own. If you are LDS, perhaps it was your own son who wrote this note to me:

> I have a dear friend who will commit suicide very soon. I met him in the mission field. We live 2,000 miles apart. He has a beautiful wife and six wonderful children. They were married in the temple and are active in the Church (although he recently stopped attending Sunday meetings). He has served as a bishop and has never acted on his same sex attraction. He is empty inside. . . . He has sought professional counseling. . . . He is on medication for depression. . . . He does not draw strength and hope and the will to go on from his relationships. . . . Please let me know if you have any thoughts that might help me help my friend.

In April of 2006, the Church-owned *Deseret Morning News*, in a remarkable week-long series on suicide in Utah, reported: "A former surgeon general who recently spoke in Utah about suicide prevention said he was impressed with the state's warm and friendly people. . . . But, he added, 'In New York, we kill each other. In Utah, you kill yourselves.'" The newspaper gave the shocking statistic that Utah leads the entire nation in suicides among men aged 15 to 24. Utah also has the 11th highest suicide rate over all age groups.

All sorts of people kill themselves. That homosexual people would commit suicide, then, should not surprise us. But what should surprise, shock, and distress us is to realize that, according to the U.S. Department of Health and Human Services, up to 30% of completed youth suicides are committed by gay and lesbian youth. The *LDS Church News*, in a 1994 article titled "Suicide Rates Increasing—Church Members Not Immune," reinforced that statistic, stating that "the largest single group of teen suicides, about one-third of the total," consists of those who have "gender identity problems." As gays compose somewhere around 5% of the general population, the disproportion is remarkable.

Numerous complex phenomena are responsible for suicide: mental health, personal traumas, economics all play a role. But to me it is clear that many suicides among young Mormon homosexuals, as well as gay people in other religions, can be traced directly to a hostile social and religious environment.

According to statistics, males commit suicide four times more often than females do; however, females attempt suicide three times more often than males. The discrepancy is evidently due to women choosing less violent and therefore less successful methods. And, too, I believe that—at least in the very patriarchal culture of Mormondom—the pressures on men are much more severe than they are on women.

However, I have occasionally received a story of the suicide attempt of a lesbian. The year after *Goodbye, I Love You* came out, I wrote in my diary of a Mormon lesbian who called me from Chico, California. Her name was Jo, and she told me if I ever spoke of her I was to use her real name. She loved the Church, had gone on a mission, determined to change her sexual orientation. As her missionary time was coming to a close, she spent the night with another sister missionary, the two of them just holding each other. The next morning she knew that her yearning to be with another woman emotionally and physically would never go away, and knowing what this would mean for her life in the Church, she swallowed rat poison. It did not kill her. Later she developed a long-term relationship with a woman she dearly loved, a wonderful singer who performed throughout the Church. However, guilt and the excommunication of both women took their toll. They broke up but remained friends. I wrote in my diary:

> Two years ago Jo's friend shot herself. But she did not die; she's in a rest home in San Jose unable to talk or to do anything. Jo had to decide to give up the Church or to end her own life, so she gave up the Church. But there is a "huge ache" there for all the things she loves so much and still believes.
>
> Her first question to me was, "Sister Pearson, what do you think God's point of view is on people like Gerald, people like me?"
>
> My heart just broke. I told her I was sure God loved them dearly.
>
> She said that when she lived in San Jose there were in the same ward four lesbians, including the bishop's wife, who met secretly to comfort each other.

I have communicated with an evangelical Christian woman, Mary Lou Wallner, whose daughter hung herself. She wrote about this tragedy in *The Slow Miracle of Transformation*:

> Four days ago would have been my daughter's 35th birthday. But she is dead. She committed suicide nearly six years ago. She was a Christian, and a lesbian, and I did not accept her sexual orientation. I did not love Anna unconditionally . . . I miss her unspeakably and feel so sad and broken about my own poor choices that contributed to her pain. . . . Now she is dead, and I can do nothing to bring her back. Anna is dead because of . . . the untruth I was taught by the church.

In addition to those who attempt or commit suicide, there are many who are resigned to complete their lives in extreme suffering, people like "Mark," a 35-year-old Mormon man in Australia who, after praying and fasting to be made normal, began to cut himself. He wrote me, "I was mowing the lawn and mowed alongside a barbed wire fence, pushing my forearm into the wire as I walked." Or "Jason," a man who has been celibate all his life and attends church every Sunday, who wrote to me:

> My own ward members mostly look at me as an individual who doesn't belong. My fellow elders avoid me at church. The single sisters receive a lot of attention for being alone and struggling to manage their need for love, but I feel that homosexual men are looked at as unworthy of love.
>
> I wish that I had more people to share my life with. I wish that I could have a social life in the Mormon Church where I could invite others over to my home for dinner and I could talk to other members about my struggles. I wish that someone knew me. It's a real sacrifice to not go see *Brokeback Mountain* because it's rated R.
>
> I wish that I had kids. I wish that I had a best friend to come home to each night. I wish that my parents were proud of me.
>
> I wish I knew more of what my Heavenly Father thinks of me. The talks at church are geared toward heterosexual family relationships, and I feel left out. I wish that I was allowed to think of myself as a worthy male in the Church even though I find myself fond of other men and don't act on those feelings.
>
> I look forward to the day I die, when I am called to kneel in front of my Maker and ask him if he has the power to take away this terrible pain.

And yes, goodbyes still are said because of AIDS. These days the disease is largely preventable. However, along with our bewilderment as to how some people still put themselves at risk through promiscuous and careless behavior, should come, I believe, another thought. When our gay loved ones are left outside the circle of our comfort and protection, open to the wolves and the weather, they are likely to make bad choices in their search for warmth.

In John 1 we read, "Whosoever hateth his brother is a murderer." Some of us are guilty of feeling hatred toward our homosexual brothers and sisters. Words kill the spirit. A thoughtless mother spoke to her lesbian daughter, saying, "I have to get a blessing every day so I don't hate you." Another mother said to her gay son who had survived an auto accident, "It would have been better for God to have taken you from the earth rather than leave you here to be gay." A bishop who had a gay son at home watched carefully as a young gay man in his university ward explained to his brothers and sisters in the congregation that he was homosexual, was keeping the standards of the Church, and did not know where the future would take him. He asked for their understanding and their support. The bishop described the faces of those who listened as looking as if they were watching a horror show.

Maya Angelou said, "I've learned that people will forget what you said, people will forget what you did, but people will never forget how you made them feel."

How you made them feel.

In every human interaction, we give out either life or death. When we hate we become murderers, at the least by extinguishing the light in someone's eyes and at the most by driving them a little closer to the brink of self-destruction.

More Than a Person Can Bear

Carol Lynn about
Brad Adams

It was the first time I had spoken in public since *Goodbye, I Love You* was published. The audience was Affirmation, the association for gay and lesbian Mormons and ex-Mormons, at their annual conference in San Francisco. When I finished my talk and took my seat at the round dinner table, the young man to my left touched my arm and looked at me with the saddest and most guileless brown eyes I had ever seen.

"Sister Pearson," he said. "Do you know what breaks my heart and makes me want to give up?"

"What, Brad?" We had just met and had made light conversation over our meal.

"In the next life, I want to be where people like you are—where God and Jesus are. And to know that I can never be there makes me just want to give up."

I stared at him. He was serious. "Brad! How can you *say* that?"

"Well, it's true."

I was at a loss for words. "How—? Who—? Brad, that's—awful! That's *not true!*"

My heart began to pound. How *dare* they? How dare *anyone* make this sweet young man at my side feel so unworthy, feel

41

forever barred from the presence of God and of Christ? And even, absurdly, from *me!*

"No, Brad," I said vehemently, "we've got it all wrong, no one can make a judgment like that. Your relationship with God is a private, sacred thing, and God loves you and has a place for you!"

As the evening ended, Brad and I hugged and he said, "I wish I had a friend like you."

"I'll be your friend, Brad!" I kissed his cheek and gave him my phone number and said goodnight.

～

So Brad and I became friends. I had just received my first computer—you'll read that story later in this book—and Brad became my computer teacher. But mostly he was just my friend. The first time he called and asked if he could drive out to see me, he said, "You know what I want to do?"

"What, Brad?"

"I want to go to church."

Brad had not been inside a Mormon chapel for eight years. He sat there and sang the hymns and said "Amen" to the prayers and the talks and smiled and sighed. You may find this next statement strange, but it is true. I have never known anyone who loved the Mormon Church more than Brad loved it. He would cry when he spoke of how much he loved the Church.

That afternoon at my home, after eating dinner with me and my children, Brad told me his story. He was converted to the Church in his early teens. He had never known such warmth, such good people, such love as he found there. He drank it in, a thirsty true believer. But—he was gay.

"I'm one hundred percent gay, not just ninety-nine percent," he told me. "I have never had the slightest sexual feeling toward a woman. When I was baptized—I knew I would change. I knew Jesus would heal me. But it didn't happen, and I didn't understand why. I loved the Lord, I loved the Church, I loved the gospel, I studied the scriptures, I paid my tithing, I fasted, I obeyed all the commandments. But I was still gay. I went on a mission. I came home and—I was still gay. I was terrified. I knew the next step was marriage. God wanted me to marry, and the Church wanted me to marry. Just thinking about it would terrify me.

"I talked to my bishop in Provo. He was such a good man, wanted so much to help me. He gave me a blessing. It didn't help. Carol Lynn—" Tears came, and it was hard for Brad to continue. "Every Sunday for *one whole year*, every Sunday I went into my bishop's office and he laid his hands on my head and gave me a blessing, asking the Lord to help me, to heal me, to comfort me. All that happened was that during that year I pretty much succeeded in feeling nothing for anyone. My emotions were dead. And at the end of the year I thought to myself, it's never going to happen. I am never going to change. I'm destined to go to the lowest place in God's kingdom, and I'd just as well go now.

"So I figured out how to get a lot of pills; I collected them for weeks. One evening I took them all. I knew I would have about fifteen minutes until the effects set in, so—" Tears again. "So I drove up to the Provo Temple. I figured that would be the place I wanted to die. I believed there would be kind and helpful spirits around the temple, and that when I passed over, there would be someone willing to help me.

"I sat there on the temple grounds, and I felt the waves of blackness coming toward me. I lost consciousness. Two weeks later, when I woke up from the coma, they told me what had happened. That next morning, a BYU professor on his way to work had found me in a field, spread-eagle on the ground. The doctor said it had been so cold that my metabolism had slowed and the pills had not finished their work.

"I guess God didn't want me to die. I came to San Francisco to start a new life. I went to see the bishop here, then the stake president. [A stake is a geographical unit composed of 5-12 wards.] They were both so kind to me. I told them to excommunicate me. They refused. They said, 'It would do the Church no good to excommunicate you, and it would do you no good either.' But I knew I couldn't stay in the Church. I knew I didn't fit, could never fit, no matter how hard I tried. And I couldn't bear spending the rest of my life not feeling. So I dropped out. But I go to the Mormon Church every day in my heart. And I go to the temple every day in my heart."

Brad's social life had never been wild, but he did have several partners, and a few months into our friendship he told me he had tested positive for HIV. It added to his negative feelings, the conflict he dealt with daily over his self-worth. On several occasions during those difficult days, Brad and I prayed together, and I used those times to give him assurance of God's love for him, to tell him that the anguish he had felt for so many years over his unworthiness had caused the heavens to grieve. I told him that the Lord walked beside him and that his body and spirit were in the hands of One wiser than us.

Once he said, "It's so hard not to be part of the Church. Sometimes when I'm really, really low, I give myself a blessing. I put my hands on my head and I give myself a blessing." He broke into sobs and couldn't speak for a while. Then he went on, and these are his exact words, which I copy now from my diary. "The Mormons have got to stop being so rejecting. To be rejected by something so wonderful as the Mormon Church is nearly more than a person can bear."

As long as Brad was able, we continued to spend time together, talking, walking, going out to dinner, salvaging documents I had nearly lost to the dark oblivion of my computer, ushering at plays in San Francisco. I helped him pack when he had to leave his apartment and move to Santa Barbara, where friends took care of him. Once I visited him there when he was growing weaker. Several times we prayed together over the phone. And then he was gone.

I miss Brad. I have invited him to be on my welcoming committee when my time comes to enter the next world. I want to thank him for sharing his story with me so that I could share it with you. I want to thank him for painting in my mind one of the images that haunts me still and always will, an image that has broken my heart and that may have broken yours, too—a dear young man who believed he was unworthy of life, of God's love, and of fellowship in the church he loved, taking handfuls of pills and driving to a Mormon temple to die, believing that around that holy place he would find kind spirits to take him in.

Bobby Gave up on Love

Carol Lynn about
Bobby Griffith

Mary Griffith is a Presbyterian who lives near me in Walnut Creek, California. When the book about her son Bobby was published, a lengthy article in our local paper told of a mother who had lost her twenty-year-old son to suicide and laid responsibility for the tragedy at the foot of her church. She had been a devout member all her life. Mary had become a reluctant activist, racing around to television appearances, speaking to government committees, and devoting herself to promoting PFLAG (Parents and Friends of Lesbians and Gays, a national support and advocacy organization of over 200,000 members). I remember thinking as I read her story: religion again; yes, religion and homosexuality in that deadly dance. Recently I drove over to Mary's house. Again we sat at her kitchen table, a Mormon woman and a Presbyterian woman, discussing the dark side of religion as it is often practiced by members and leaders of our congregations.

Between us on the table were the two diaries she had located from her storage, small hardback books very much like the diaries I wrote in when I was Bobby's age, one grey with maroon stripes, the other green. I had read the very compelling book written by journalist Leroy Aarons, *Prayers for Bobby*, but I wanted to see for myself the words Bobby had written.

I opened the first book and glanced at a few pages, then the second book. I wanted to read the ending first. His final entry was nothing unusual, a mundane list of purchases, a glued-in photo of an admired cousin. Across from the last page, in different handwriting, the hand of his mother, an entry written much later. "August 27, 1983. Bobby gave up on love. He jumped off a freeway overpass into the path of a semi-truck. There were two witnesses. As Bobby approached the guard rail, he took a hop and skip and with his hands grasping the rail, did a back flip over."

Mary watched me read, a steely calm on a face now textured with harsh experience. The faith that Mary had given her religion had been total. She knew that God rewarded righteousness and condemned sin. Learning in Bobby's early teenage years that he was gay was heartbreaking to her. Family was everything, and the prospect of losing a child for eternity was unbearable. "I always counted noses before I turned the lights out," she told me. "How could I bear the pain of going to heaven and counting noses and seeing that Bobby was not there?"

Mary had done everything a good, believing mother could do. She sang in church, "Trust and obey for there's no other way." Every day she admonished her children, "God cannot protect you from Satan if you are disobedient." Bobby was obedient, gentle, and lovable. He loved nature, telling his mother at age three, "Mom, when I woke up this morning, I said good morning to all the trees and the forest." He organized carnivals in his backyard for the neighborhood kids. He won a prize in school for an essay on local naturalist John Muir. He was shy but loved to laugh.

All that changed in adolescence. Bobby's awareness of being different began to take a frightening shape in his mind. Near his sixteenth birthday, Bobby wrote in his diary:

I can't ever let anyone find out that I'm not straight. It would be so humiliating. My friends would hate me. They might even want to beat me up. And my family? I've overheard them. They've said they hate gays, and even God hates gays, too. Gays are bad and God sends bad people to hell. It really scares me when they talk that way because now they are talking about me.

But the family did discover Bobby's awful secret. Believing she was doing God's will, Mary constantly told Bobby that God could heal him through prayer. She placed Bible verses clearly targeted to Bobby around the house and over the bathroom mirror. "Everyone who does what is right is righteous. . . . Everyone who commits sin is a child of the devil." She turned up the volume on the Christian radio station, making sure Bobby could hear it in his room. She tiptoed into his bedroom while he was asleep to pray over him. When her son assured her no healing was taking place, she told him he was not trying hard enough, not praying hard enough. Bobby's homosexuality had become a family obsession. Mary believed that Bobby's intense personal anguish was a sign that he was close to being cured, for her church taught that God uses misery to convince a person of his sin. Bobby was becoming more and more unhappy. Surely that meant he was soon to see the light and be released.

That light seemed never available to Bobby. His diaries tell of a mental state that took him toward deeper and deeper darkness. Even though he worked with a Christian counselor and did a church program of daily prayer and guided Bible study that included doing an unselfish daily good deed, he found himself in despair, writing, "My life is over as far as I'm concerned. I hate living on this earth." One month later, Bobby leapt from the overpass to his death.

As we sat together at her kitchen table, her son's diaries between us, I listened to Mary's indictment of her church and herself. "If only I'd known then what I know now. It's an awesome thing to know the mind of God, and that's what they claim about our kids. That's what destroyed Bobby, and I was part of it. God did not cure our son. Why? Because there was nothing to cure."

The kitchen walls were covered with pinned-up pieces of artwork of Mary's grandchildren and other pictures. I found myself staring at a familiar photograph, Dorothy and her three friends dancing down the yellow brick road. Remembering that on the first page of Bobby's diary, I had read a reference to Judy Garland, I said, "Mary, tell me something. Why do you have that picture from *The Wizard of Oz* on your wall?"

Mary chuckled at my question. "Oh, that's my favorite movie. I saw it the first time when I was five. But it's more than that. The story is so relevant to my life. That big, wise Wizard, you know. He's nothing. You pull back the curtain, it's just a man. I went through my whole life looking at the men at church as the Wizard, practically as God. I believed every word they said, every way they interpreted the Bible, every condemning judgment on my gay son. After Bobby died, I started to study on my own, and I see the Bible through my own eyes now, not through theirs. I pulled back the curtain, and it was not God, just men. The tin man, he had a heart all along. The lion had courage all along. I knew the truth about Bobby all along, but I didn't listen inside, I listened outside. Most of us go on dancing down that yellow brick road to find the Wizard and be told the secret. But the secret is, the kingdom of God is within, inside every one of us. That picture, I keep it there to remind me."

I Would Really Rather Be Dead

Carol Lynn about
Stuart Matis

"The scary truth of matters is that I would really rather be dead than living outside of the Church."

So it was written, and so it was done. The suicide of Stuart Matis, a life-long celibate gay Mormon man, is, I think, the most well publicized of many similar stories. Stuart lived only miles from me here in northern California, and I remember that when I heard of his death from a self-administered gunshot wound on the steps of the LDS stake center in Los Altos in the early morning hours of February 25, 2000, I felt that I had lost someone close to me. I had never met this man, but in very real ways I knew him. I had come to know intimately the workings of the mind, the workings of the heart of the devout, gay Mormon man. As I read bits of his story—in the newspapers, in *Newsweek*, on the Internet, in the very moving account written by his parents and published by Mormon Church-owned Deseret Book, *In Quiet Desperation*—I could only sigh and say: Of course, of course.

He was thirty-two years old before he told his parents about the cross he had carried since age seven. He had been certain that with obedience and faith his attraction for the same gender would pass—at age twelve when he was ordained to the priesthood, a rite of passage for most Mormon boys—then when he received his patriarchal blessing, an individualized, special guide for one's life—then when he attended the temple for the first time, making serious covenants with God and the Church —then when he went on a mission. Surely God would approve of his life *now* and work for him the miracle of becoming normal, taking away the torment of his homosexual feelings.

Of course.

He fasted and prayed, and he went to the temple every week. He wept as night after night he prayed until morning, begging and pleading with a God he knew could help him if he was only worthy enough. As a child he would deny himself a favorite television program as punishment for a homosexual thought, or he wouldn't allow himself to attend a friend's birthday party.

Of course.

His mother wrote:

> Stuart's entire life was spent striving for perfection. He reasoned that if he were perfect, then he would find God's approval. His efforts became a never-ending cycle: effort—perceived failure— effort—perceived failure. The harder Stuart strove for perfection, the more he hated himself. . . . he believed that he not only *could* change, but *should* change. When no change in his feelings occurred, no matter how hard he worked at it, he came to the conclusion that he was not worthy and that God did not accept his efforts. His self-loathing became . . . intense. . . . Once Stuart said to me, "Mother, all my life I have tried to do what is right. I just can't pass the test."

Of course.

In the suicide note that Stuart left on his bed that morning, along with love and appreciation to his family, were the words: "I am free, I am no longer in pain, and I no longer hate myself . . . my life was actually killed long ago."

Stuart's bishop, with whom he had been counseling for months, aware of his suicidal thoughts, had pled with him, "Stuart, if this is a choice between the Church and your life, choose your *life!*" How I wish Stuart had done that, had grabbed his soul and run for his life, out the chapel door never to look back. How I wish he had listened to the voice inside that surely witnessed to God's unconditional love for him. But—of course —I know so well how that voice was silenced in childhood by the voices that came from outside, speaking with authority and spelling out the conditions under which God's love would be available.

The final straw that drove Stuart to suicide was the intense distress he felt around the politics of California's "Protection of Marriage" initiative, Proposition 22, for which the Mormon Church was perhaps the leading proponent. The time of his suicide—two weeks before the voters went to the polls—and the place of his suicide—the steps of a Mormon building in which he had worshiped for years—give a clear indication that he hoped his death would bring attention to the issues about which he felt so passionate and so helpless.

After all the reports of others, I was yearning to get a better glimpse into Stuart's mind, and I found it on the website of Affirmation. Earlier in February, the month of his death, Stuart wrote a very long letter to a cousin who had asked Stuart to give him information and opinion for a paper he was writing on California's "Protection of Marriage" proposal. There, along with a picture of this very handsome and endearing young man, were some impassioned personal and political statements, fragments of which I share here.

~

Feb. 2000

Clay,

At the outset, I'll tell you that the events surrounding this initiative have been painfully difficult for me to endure. Last July, I read online that the Church had instructed the bishops to read a letter imploring the members to give of their time and money to support this initiative. . . . I cried for hours in my room, and I could do very little to console the grief of hearing this news.

Furthermore, I read that the Church had supported similar measures in Hawaii and in Alaska. In Alaska, the supporters of the measure had raised $600,000. Of this, $500,000 came from the Church. Ads were aired on television describing the downfall of the Roman Empire and placing blame on Rome's tolerance of homosexuality. Its message was that a similar fate would occur to those who supported equality for gay Americans. Not only was this historical analysis completely fallacious, but this was a prejudicial ad designed to invoke a visceral reaction of fear and hate among the Alaskan citizens.

Apparently, the Church has raised $1 million in support of this [California] initiative. This is so disheartening because I feel that my own peers are attacking me. . . . In July, I realized that I was going to have to endure viewing millions of dollars of television ads designed with one intention in mind: raise fear against gay and lesbian Californians. What's worse is that this fear campaign has been orchestrated by my own friends.

My mom is completely distraught over the issue. She told me that she is scared to read the papers or watch TV. When her bishop read another pro-Knight letter last Sunday, she wanted to cry. . . . I have met with my bishop to discuss the matter. He too disagrees with the Church's involvement in anti-gay politics. It's very disheartening for him as well, but his concurrence still does nothing to ease my pain. . . .

When anti-gay advocates use the term "traditional," I always wonder what tradition and what time. Do we support early 19th-century traditional marriages when married women had no legal standing, could not own property, sign contracts, or legally control any earned wages? . . . I also find it somewhat hypocritical for the Church to appeal to people's emotions and use the "tradition" argument when it was on the receiving end of such abuse during its polygamy era. The Church more than anyone in this country should know how persecution feels. . . .

The false dilemma is that one is either pro-homosexuality or pro-family. This, of course, is false. I am gay. I hate to sound redundant, but whether I remain celibate or find a partner, the net effect on families is zero. . . .

Straight members have absolutely no idea what it is like to grow up gay in this church. It is a life of constant torment, self-hatred, and internalized homophobia. . . . The Church has no idea that as I type this letter, there are surely boys and girls on their calloused knees imploring God to free them from this pain. They hate themselves. They retire to bed with their finger pointed to their head in the form of a gun. . . . They are afraid of their parents. They are afraid of their bishop. They are afraid of their friends. They have nowhere to go but to lie on their floors curled in a ball and weep themselves to sleep. . . . On the night of March 7th, many California couples will retire to their beds thrilled that they helped pass the . . . initiative. What they don't realize is that in the next room, their son or daughter is lying in bed crying and could very well one day be a victim of society's homophobia. . . .

Most of my gay friends (and I) were suicidal at one time in their lives. I have friends who have swallowed pills, cut their wrists, burned their arms, placed bags over their heads. I have friends who have taken anti-depressant pills as if they were candy. Years of internalized homophobia have deeply scarred my friends and me. It is only after we began to accept our identity that we have been able to heal our minds. . . .

In the end, remember, Clay, that we gay people are your family. We are your brothers and sisters. We are your sons and daughters. In your case, I am your cousin. . . . I wish that I could shout this message from the rooftops, but alas, I sit alone in my room typing, wondering what will happen next.

Well, Clay, my fingers are blistered. . . . I apologize if my words were a bit strong. . . . On a more upbeat note, good luck preparing for your mission. I'll see you in the spring. Take care.

Warmly,
Stuart

⁓

There is a tragic addendum that must be added here. Stuart had become close friends with Clay Whitmer, not the cousin Clay to whom he wrote the letter, but a man he met as both served Mormon missions in Italy. They later confessed to each other their homosexuality, remained best friends, and tried to be a support to one another. *Newsweek* reported, "A few weeks [after Stuart's suicide], anguished at his friend's death and tormented by his own long-term depression, Whitmer put a gun to his own head." Clay was a brilliant young man with both an MBA degree and a JD.

Still another gay Mormon suicide made this a triple tragedy. Brian (DJ) Thompson ended his life two weeks after Stuart did. He had served as a missionary in Seattle, had been president of the Utah Log Cabin Republicans, and had once traveled to Paris as an artist's assistant. In his suicide note, DJ wrote, "It is unfortunate that the lives of good people such as Stuart Matis, Mathew Shephard [victim of a hate crime in Wyoming], and many others go unnoticed, unappreciated, and undervalued in this country. Therefore, I believe that the end of my life will simply be the same. . . . I see Proposition 22 as a last straw in my life-long battle to see peace in the world I live in."

⁓

It is true that the consciousness of many has been raised by Stuart's act, by the sharing of his story by his parents, and by the suicides of those that followed him. But, ah, Stuart, how I wish you had chosen life and taught us in a different way, taught us by bravely insisting that you, too, are that you might have joy, showing us how brightly a gay man can shine.

Moving toward the Light

Carol Lynn about
"Ron"
Sandy, Utah

"Ron," a Mormon gay man who just recently emailed me his story, ended it with, "I intend to take my life within the next few weeks." He gave me a phone number and said to call him if I wanted to hear more. I called, and we talked for an hour. Ron had married, had four children, had occasionally acted on his ongoing homosexual impulses, had been thrown out of the house by his wife, who had begun divorce proceedings, had been told by his children not to contact them or show up at their school functions, and had been excommunicated from the Church. "I'm a monster," he said. "My children look at me, and they see a monster."

I got sympathetic, and then I got mad.

"You don't get to do this, Ron," I said. "You don't get to drop off the team and make me carry the load you're supposed to be carrying. I and plenty of others are working as hard as we can to help us understand all this sexuality stuff better, to make the world and the Church safer for people like you to work things out. You have an assignment from life—from God—from whatever—and you've got to take that assignment and do your homework and learn whatever you're supposed to learn and maybe even be able to help teach. Don't you *dare* drop off the team and make me carry your part of the load! And what about your family, Ron? What would your killing yourself accomplish for them?"

He thought a moment. "I guess it would show them that I'm accepting the worst possible punishment."

"You're crazy," I said. "It would just underline their belief that their dad's a loser. It would give each of your kids ten more years of therapy. You know what your family really needs from you, Ron?"

"What?"

"They need you to become a man who is healed and whole. They need to see you become someone who will surprise the heck out of them by becoming the guy you're supposed to be. Don't you dare drop out. Your therapist is on your team. Your brother's on your team. I'm on your team. God's on your team. Choose life, and you know what? Even if your children truly never want to see you again—and that's highly unlikely—they will know. They will feel it in the air. They will sense that something has changed about their dad. That's what your family needs from you, Ron."

He was silent. "And in conclusion, Ron, you don't get to 'move toward the light'—not over there, like people who've been there come back to tell us about it. Not now. You get to 'move toward the light' right here."

I happened to be planning a trip to Utah for the following week, and I asked Ron if he would go for a walk with me. So on a chill March day when the sun was out between snowstorms, we walked for an hour and a half in suburban Sandy, where I was staying with my brother and his family.

Ron is a large man in his late forties, and I had to hustle to keep up with his pace. "So what have you been thinking about since our phone conversation?" I asked.

"Well," he said matter-of-factly, "I still think I'm going to do it. In fact, I've chosen a date. April first. But the thing you said that has stayed with me is about my dropping off the team and making you do my work. I never thought of that."

I learned more about Ron's history as we walked and talked. Like so many of us, he had not had the ideal home life. Misunderstandings and neglect had been passed down from generation to generation. And unfortunate teachings about things sexual had scared and scarred him. "I died at age twelve," he said. "That's when I died inside." He had masturbated, felt it to be a sin, but had not been able to stop doing it occasionally . He believed that God frowned and crossed him off the list. From then on, Ron felt he was deeply flawed. (It should not be necessary to mention that masturbation does not cause homosexuality; ask a few hundred million heterosexual people.)

As we approached my brother's house I said, "One more thing. I want you to listen carefully. You are positioned right now to do something remarkable. You stand between your unhealed ancestors and your posterity. You have the power to say, 'It stops with me.' You have the power to refuse to leave a legacy of failure to your children. Don't be the name on their genealogy chart they describe as 'gay suicide.' Don't give them that terrible gift. Give them a father that opted for healing and that came to terms with his homosexuality with self-respect. And you know what else, Ron?" I stopped walking and grabbed his arm. "You can heal your family not only in the future, but in the past. I don't know how this works, but I think about it a lot. Einstein proved that time is not what we think it is. Somehow you can do a work right now that will ripple forward and ripple backward and help to heal everyone who brought you here. A weird and awesome kind of work for the dead! I know you can!"

Tears were running down Ron's face. "Wow," he said. "Wow."

~

I speak now to those reading these pages who have contemplated or attempted suicide because of the torment they feel being both religious and gay. Especially to those who might be contemplating it now.

I cannot say I know just how you feel. None of us can who have not truly been in that hopeless, helpless darkness. I have never considered suicide. With three different events in my life, I have wished that all Being, including my own, would cease forever. In the dark night I have quoted to myself that awful, beautiful poem of Swinburne's that I memorized in college. I can write it here without even opening the book:

> From too much love of living,
> From hope and fear set free,
> We thank with brief thanksgiving
> Whatever gods may be
>
> That no life lives forever,
> That dead men rise up never,
> That even the weariest river
> Winds somewhere safe to sea—
>
> Then star nor sun shall waken
> Nor any change of light
> Nor sound of waters shaken
> Nor any sound or sight—
>
> Nor wintry leaves nor vernal
> Nor days nor things diurnal—
> Only the sleep eternal
> In an eternal night.

But I don't believe in eternal night. I believe in eternal light. The closest I ever came to acting on annihilation was the time I taped large posters over all the mirrors in the house so I would not have to see myself. But I find life irresistible. I find my own eyes irresistible.

If you are considering ending your life: walk with me. This I know. God loves you just as you are, and "abomination" is a word gone awry. We have been called to travel a hard frontier, but there is meaning in it and no one can play the part you or I came to play. Move toward the light *here*. Claim life. Claim love. *Be* love. Reach out. Trust. Trust tonight. Trust tomorrow. Trust yourself. Walk with me. Let's all walk together.

~

Today is April first. Yesterday I called Ron and left a message on his voice mail. "Hi, Ron, it's Carol Lynn. Just noticed that tomorrow is April first. It's going to be a good day for living. Still raining at my house, but that's okay. I'm going to do my best tomorrow to give and take a little love, and I'm counting on you to do the same. You're on my prayer list, Ron . . ."

This morning I got a call from Ron. His voice sounded good, sounded strong. He was calling from the California coast, where he was on a business trip. "I'm feeling pretty good. Looking out the hotel window at the ocean right now."

"Ah, the ocean. The movement of eternity right in front of us."

I made him promise to call me next week.

I'm counting on it, Ron.

All Our Sons

Recently I spent an evening re-reading a favorite play, *All My Sons*, one of Arthur Miller's best. It is a story about responsibility, and as I read I couldn't avoid thinking of the book you are now holding, which I had been working on during the day and would work on again tomorrow.

In *All My Sons*, we meet Joe Keller, a successful, middle-aged, self-made man who has done something terrible and is now forced to pay the price. During World War II, rushing to meet an order from the Army, he knowingly shipped from his plant defective airplane parts, which caused the planes to crash and caused the death of 22 men. In a strange twist of fate, Joe learns years later that his son Larry, whose plane went missing in the war, actually took the plane on a suicide mission after he learned that his own father was responsible for the deaths of some of his fellow pilots. Joe finally understands that the other pilots, in the mind of Larry, were "all my sons. And I guess they were, I guess they were."

Joe Keller cannot bear the guilt, disappears inside the house, and in a moment we hear the sound of a gunshot.

I can't get the title of Miller's play out of my mind. The pain of being homosexual, especially in a religious community like mine, can be ravaging. You can find a partial list of Mormon gay suicides on the Affirmation website (www.affirmation.org), the tip of the awful iceberg, all the faces male. Many were returned missionaries, BYU students or graduates (one BYU professor); some were Eagle Scouts. Their average age was 31. It is a numbing experience to look at the pictures, to read the names. They died from gunshots, by hanging, by poison, by pills. One bled to death cutting out his genitals.

Today I revisited the site, and I saw a new face there: handsome, young, smiling. He was a cello player. I had never met him, though my husband Gerald and I knew his parents long ago in Utah. The handsome new face at the website was their first child, their son.

He is the son of all of us. I see a shared responsibility. He held the gun. We failed to hold him.

We are as complicit in his death as Joe Keller was complicit in the deaths of the men whose planes went down and in the awful decision of his own pilot son. We too have allowed product with serious flaws to leave our plant. Over the years, our dear gay children have been given misinformation that has fueled the anguish and led to the deaths of far too many. They have been told that their feelings were simply an evil choice, a turning from God to Satan, that their problem was caused by selfishness, that they would be better off at the bottom of the Great Salt Lake with a millstone around their neck than to be in a gay relationship, that marriage to a good woman would straighten them out, that electric shock therapy would set them right, that fasting and prayer and righteous living would heal them, that reparative therapy would cure them.

Today was a hard day for me to see the new face on the suicide memorial site, for this week, writing the suicide section of this book, I have lived in grief and outrage. I have taken breaks to go for walks, even in the rain, then sat back down at my computer trying again to make sense of it.

There is no sense. There is the senseless appearance of the new face on the suicide memorial site, the sweet face of the cello player. And the other faces. All our sons.

At the end of Miller's play, Joe's other son, Chris, says to his mother, "It's not enough for him to be sorry. Larry didn't kill himself to make you and Dad sorry."

The mother asks, "What more can we be!"

Her son replies, "You can be better! Once and for all you can know there's a universe of people outside and you're responsible to it . . ."

We too can be better. We are better than we were twenty years ago at addressing the difficult subject of homosexuality, both as churches and as individuals. However, today brings an invitation for possible backsliding in our slow progress. The political and religious rhetoric around the "Protection of Marriage" concept provided the last layer of despair that drove Stuart Matis and others to take their lives. We must not allow this to happen again. Whatever our convictions about which unions are appropriate to legalize and which are inappropriate, we must recognize once and for all that in our universe of people there are many dear loved ones who happen to be homosexual and that we are responsible to them, responsible to see them as our own kind, to give them respect, Christlike love, to circle the wagons around them so that they too can be safe and warm.

I am hoping for that day soon.

3
STAR-CROSSED LOVES

*Should I smile because
we're friends, or cry because
that's all we'll ever be?*

—ANONYMOUS

I Speak for Romantic Love

I speak for romantic love
Like I speak for democracy.
It is revolutionary as America is.
It is the full flower of liberty
Opening of its own
All voluntary, hands freely raised
Because I, *I* will and *I* must
And I stand responsible for this great act
This wild frontier adventure. . . .

I salute the flag of lovers,
There is no going back.
The blessed, the free
Set foot on this land
Choice above all other lands,
Kiss the soil
And delirious, reckless
Dare the most magnificent
Pursuit of happiness.

Part of a poem I wrote. When I was in love. Having experienced all that I have, still I speak for romantic love. It is messy, inconvenient, individual, dangerous, and sometimes it counters the common good. But, ah, for two to find each other so deliciously bound, to bravely pledge allegiance to each other, to love by consent of the lovers!

We fail often. But we don't give up. Romantic love is, I think, no trivial thing. I reverence this kind of love like I reverence the weather, like I respect hurricanes and earthquakes and sweet showers, things we can report on but not very well control. They are all—all of them—acts of God. The mission of romantic love is huge. It is a call to heal the original separation, to remember heaven and Eden's garden before the fall. Certainly it is a most efficient teacher, a trap that snatches people two at a time and ties them so tightly together that they can't get away until they learn something, until they learn about love, real love—being in, working in, living in, rising in—all begun by falling in. Who does not yearn for this relationship, this intimacy, knowing and being known by another, past skin, through sex into soul.

My daughter Emily and I keep a short list of the best marriages we know, couples who not only endure to the end or seem to like each other pretty well, but those we suspect of being both lucky and vigilant, husband and wife, best friends, soul mates and lovers. We go over that list occasionally.

And then there is my list of favorite star-crossed lovers, Romeo and Juliet at the top.

> They are but beggars that can count their worth;
> But my true love is grown to such excess
> I cannot sum up sum of half my wealth.

Alas, they stem from incompatible families rooted in hate, she of the house of Capulet, he of the house of Montague. I grieve for their fate.

There is also my list, my long list, of other star-crossed lovers, those who did the best they could but came from equally incompatible families, she of the house of Heterosexual, he of the house of Gay. I grieve for them, too.

Gerald and I gave it our all. I remember once in Gerald's last months, we were on my couch holding each other and speaking things we didn't want to leave unsaid. He was very thin. "Gerald," I said, "what would have happened if you had just made yourself stay? If you had just made yourself put away that other part of you, just gritted it out, what would have happened?"

He thought only a moment. "You would have watched me die in a different way, that's all. Bit by bit, I would have gotten bitter and empty and ugly. That 'other part of me' isn't just a part, you know. It's the center. People don't understand that."

A plague on both our houses.

Democracy and romantic love are awesome revolutions. Most of us are past the place in history where marriage was an economic or political arrangement. Most Mormons today are past the odd place in our history where it was said of a polygamous match, "A man should like his wives, but not too much." Most of us yearn for that splendid pursuit of happiness, yearn to be in a marriage where no amount of love can be too much, where husband and wife adore each other, celebrate each other, are hungry for each other, body, mind, and soul.

Like Deepak Chopra, I believe that "falling in love is undeniably an act of the soul. . . . Romantic love is undeniably sexual; yet it contains the potential for great spiritual experiences. The beauty of sensuality has its own spiritual significance." And I love the statement of Thomas Moore, that "something eternally valid comes to us in the sensations of sex and romance. . . . Romantic love is as important to the soul as any other kind of love. . . . The soul of sex has the power to evoke relationship, to sustain it, and to make it worthwhile." I find deep meaning, too, in the statement of psychologist Nathaniel Branden:

Through the giving and receiving of sexual pleasure lovers

continually reaffirm that they are a source of joy to each other. Joy is a nutrient of love: it makes love grow. On the other hand, it is very difficult not to experience sexual neglect as rejection or abandonment, no matter what the partner's other protestations of devotion. No, sex is not all there is to romantic love; but can one imagine fulfilled romantic love without it? Perhaps under very unusual, very tragic circumstances; but never as a preferred way of life. Sex at its highest potential is the ultimate celebration of love.

Strange, Romeo and Juliet's society did all it possibly could to keep the lovers apart and, tragically, succeeded. My society goes to great lengths both to keep possible lovers apart and to put impossible lovers together. Mormon edict gives the threat of eternal loss to men and women who love and enter a relationship with someone of the same sex, as well as the promise of eternal exaltation to those who enter conventional marriage and are faithful to their vows. The results of this ultimatum can be tragic.

Sad Harvest

The seven-point scale devised by Dr. Alfred Kinsey some decades ago is generally accepted as a way to determine sexual orientation. At one end is 0 (decidedly heterosexual); at the other end, 6 (decidedly homosexual). The middle numbers are assigned to those who experience themselves, to varying degrees, as attracted to and able to have satisfactory sexual relations with members of both genders. A man I know who describes himself as definitely bisexual and has done significant study of sexuality, wrote to remind me that:

> When you talk about how our culture puts pressure on gay men to marry, and all the advice given by bishops and other leaders, consider the possibility that many of these gentle souls are, in fact, bisexual men. They, perhaps, are speaking from personal experience. They know they had attractions to men as teens or before their marriage. Perhaps many continue to have those attractions during their entire life. Consider the possibility that, like me, these bisexual men also have major sexual attractions to women. They know they have managed to ignore their same-sex feelings and marry and get along quite well in marriage, as I did. However if on the H-H scale they are a 3 or even a 4, they may think that is the answer for everyone, even those at 5 or 6. It is my hunch that this has happened a lot in our culture. But it is not the case that with enough willpower those on the far end of the scale (6) can ignore their homosexual feelings. And the young people trying to sort this out need

to understand that some of us are gay, some straight, and some are "in between." Actually, I believe there are more bisexual people than homosexual people.

Many married people who are the "in betweens" on the scale must certainly have their own challenges, among them falling in love with someone of their own gender while at the same time having a rather satisfactory relationship with their spouse, making this a "trickster" kind of orientation. This, however, is not the situation of the vast majority of people who have brought me their stories. The excerpts below are from or about people who seem to experience themselves as "decidedly homosexual."

∼

Dear Carol Lynn,

I closed the book, sat and cried—cried for Gerald, for you, for me. For all who have been fed false hopes, whose lives are wasted trying to live up to all of the dogmatic should-be's and ought-to's. How foolhardy, cowardly, to succumb to what others said was my responsibility in life— that at 26 I was shirking my responsibility by not marrying and bearing as many children as I could. I have reaped bitterness for the choice made 22 years ago to marry a man. There is within me an insatiable hunger, a loneliness that is indescribable. . . .

When I admitted to myself I had fallen in love with a woman, I talked with my bishop, who sent me to a psychiatrist. I visited social workers and psychologists. . . . They thought of me as a sinner, but said I could change—change to what? Change to them meant conformity. Can you force a fish to fly or a bird to swim? It would be easier to ask me to stop breathing than to try to deny the feelings I am told are evil. Carol Lynn, I am not evil. I am a hurting, lonely, fearful human being, angry at a God that has given me a burden I find intolerable.

∼

I have been a bishop twice here in Seattle. In a singles ward over which I presided, about one third of the men, both active and inactive, were gay. I held a support meeting for them in my home once a week. I sent six homosexual men off to the temple to live happily ever after with their wives. Later I learned that five of them had been excommunicated.

⁓

Then it happened, the confession, the crying and begging forgiveness . . . what I had feared and tried desperately to put out of my mind for 16 years was a reality. We have three great kids and he's a great dad . . . The pain set in . . . going deeper and deeper, crying is a way of life. . . . Suicide still creeps into my thoughts, but not as often. . . . I don't know any answers, I only have questions . . . I find myself with a great deal of compassion for my husband and feel for his years of silent suffering.

⁓

I, too, married a man who "shone" with the joy of living. Three years later he told me he was homosexual. . . . We loved each other and our children, and kept our marriage together for seven more years, until he committed suicide.

⁓

After my marriage, my homosexual feelings became stronger. It was like I had finally opened a door that I had kept closed for so long, but now that it was open, I could tell is wasn't the "right" door, and something in me insisted that I continue the quest.

⁓

My former husband's first marriage ended because of his homosexual activity. When we became engaged, his bishop counseled him not to tell me about that as he had "repented and was now clean." I would never had married him if I had known.

⁓

From an old friend of Gerald's and mine during our college days.
October, 1986. But it could have been any October or Novem-

ber or December or any other month. I have been wanting to write to you for years. Ever since the day K. told me about Gerald and that you and I were suffering the same pain, the same aloneness in a world filled with people. . . .

I had thought I had coped and adjusted when we finally decided on divorce. The pain wasn't going away, and I realized I couldn't stay out in the rain forever. I wasn't strong enough not to drown. We honestly tried—three years of counseling, two children, 16 years of each of us living in our own private pain. President Kimball [then on the Mormon Church's Council of the Twelve] had promised me that if I would remain true and faithful and be as feminine as possible, I could change K.

~

He goes through the motions and does a fine job of it—but it feels so weird to me. He cuddles, he hugs, he kisses, but it's so . . . sexless. He is forever telling me how much he loves me. And I love him. But there are different kinds of love, as we all know. . . . There is no sex because he feels more comfortable without it. I miss that aspect of our relationship . . . what we could have had or should have had. He has told me that sex is more of a hassle than it's worth.

~

He tried all the therapies available. He was written up as a "cure." He searched for a lifetime lover and was often disappointed. He died Sept. 19, 1983, Utah's first AIDS victim. I was holding his left hand and his lover holding his right. His father stood by.

~

From Connell O'Donovan, a gay Mormon historian.

One bishop told me that the cause of homosexuality was masturbation, so the cure was not to touch myself. For four years, I never once touched myself, but I was no more "cured" than I had been before. Another bishop said that the cure was for me to expend large amounts of energy whenever I felt sexually aroused. I spent the next year jogging sometimes 15 times a day, with the result that

I had an incredibly low heart rate, but I still felt homosexual tendencies. A stake president went so far as to suggest "induced vomiting" aversion therapy. I refused. I then had a general authority [an LDS ecclesiastical leader at the highest level] tell me that I would be better dead than to participate in the gay lifestyle. His counsel to me was that the "cure" was fasting, prayer, a mission, and a wife. "Experiencing healthy normal sex," he said, "will soon relieve you of your attraction for men."

I did as he advised. I fasted. I prayed. I went on a mission, a very successful one. And then I began dating in earnest, and about a year later found a wonderful, kind, sincere, compassionate woman who loved me deeply. I informed her that I was struggling with homosexual tendencies, but that I had never acted on my feelings and was planning to not do so in the future. . . . June came, and the temple was filled with our love.

Then came the Big Night. And I could not do it. And the next day and night and I still could not make love to my wife. Two weeks went by. My wife was a wreck. I was worse. I tried and tried and failed and failed. Finally, a moonlit walk together in the mountains and some serious conversation and a lot of soul searching and prayer. We descended back into the valley and made love. But I felt dirty. The whole thing felt pornographic and forced and, yes, ugly. The simple act of sex became a horror for me. Finally we ended the marriage.

I have finally forgiven the Church, my family, and my friends for what they implied and did and failed to do. That came with the realization that most people are doing their best. But, oh, the needless suffering!

~

You would be amazed at how many married gay men there are in the Church, in Utah especially, who lead double lives. They have secret same-sex partners or anonymous sexual encounters on their business trips. Their spouses are unaware, or suspect and live in denial. These spouses are at risk for many reasons. There are plenty of stories like "The Smith Family," who were featured in a documentary. The wife got HIV from her homosexual husband, who served in a bishopric. The Church's anti-gay attitude creates a destructive subculture of lies and deceit.

⁓

I could never go to Evergreen [a Mormon Church-endorsed organization devoted to transitioning out of homosexuality]. I know myself. I could never put myself in room with all those gay men. I know what I have to do. I have to be constantly vigilant about being with other men.

⁓

The 911 call I made to protect my husband from killing himself was the hardest, or maybe it was when he was disfellowshipped from the Church, or maybe it has been the day-after-day loneliness of facing one of the greatest "Goliath's" of life for the first time without the cultural support of the Church and extended family.

⁓

In ten years of marriage I had gone from believing that I could overcome my homosexuality to believing I could manage it to wanting out of life altogether because of it. I wasn't yet suicidal, but I had an active death wish. I wanted to die—I wanted to get sick, die in a plane crash, get pushed in front of a subway. I had a perfect life, and I cursed the God who made me in such a way that it wasn't good enough for me.

Within days of coming out to my wife, I told her I couldn't go to church anymore. I had just been released from serving five years as bishop, a calling I cherished. My wife said she understood. . . . Within a few weeks, she decided that she didn't want our girls to learn about homosexuality from the Mormons. Out of solidarity with me, she stopped attending.

We spent a couple of months searching for a new faith community, and this spring we became members, as a family, of Union

Congregational Church, affiliated with the United Church of Christ. We joined with our pastor's full knowledge of our situation, and we are now largely "out" to the congregation. My wife and I feel confident that even as we move into new phases of life without each other as spouses, we can continue to worship together with our children. The church is gay-affirming and provides outlets for service that were so important to us as active Latter-day Saints.

~

Wanting to know the experiences of gay members of a variety of religions in terms of marriage, I sent out a request for stories to several Internet networks. This one reminds me of the statement of Matthew Arnold, which Gerald quoted often: "The same heart beats in every human breast."

I am a Muslim woman in my twenties living in Egypt. Since my teenage [years] I knew I am a lesbian, and since then I have lived in a fight between what I want (to be with a woman) and what Allah wants (to be with a man). I had to fight every single desire I had. I denied everything, even greeting my friends with kisses. I asked Allah every night for mercy and to take away these feelings towards women from my heart. I asked clerics by mail about what to do, and they replied that I had to get married to taste men and I would be changed after my marriage. I didn't have any kind of relation with women, and then at age 24 my family proposed a man for marriage and [put] some pressure on me. I accepted that in hope that I would be changed after marriage. So I did it for Allah and my family. I got married to a man, but then my nightmare began. I tried to react, but I couldn't. I was suffering, and nothing changed. I began taking pills. My husband knew I hated being in bed, but he didn't care as I was his wife, and he was raping me every night. I was crying from the pain in my body and my heart. I was praying and asking Allah for mercy even by death. After a time of hopelessness, I stood up for my divorce to stop this crime I did to myself. It was hard to gain my freedom, but Allah helped me. I believe that Allah is merciful and fair and knows how much I was suffering. Now I am in love with another woman trying to find our way in Islam as Muslims and lesbians.

～

Mel White served the Christian church as a prize-winning television producer and filmmaker, a best-selling author, a pastor, seminary professor, and ghost writer to religious leaders including Billy Graham, Pat Robertson, and Jerry Falwell. After struggling to overcome his homosexual orientation through prayer, fasting, exorcism, various aversion therapies, and electric shock, Mel decided the path of integrity for him was to acknowledge and claim what he felt to be his essential self. His book, Stranger at the Gate, *contains a foreword written by the woman who for 25 years had been his wife, Lyla White. This is an excerpt from her words:*

Mel had no choice about being a homosexual. Believe me, if he had a choice, I know he would have chosen his marriage, his family, and his unique ministry; for Mel's values, like most of the gays and lesbians I know, are the same as mine and my heterosexual friends: love, respect, commitment, nurture, responsibility, honesty, and integrity. . . . Mel and I remain friends . . . and I wish [him] great success in his new life and ministry. . . . I think you . . . will be convinced by the case Mel makes against the current homophobic rhetoric of the religious right. . . . We are all on this journey together, and we must ensure that the road is safe for everyone, including our homosexual brothers and sisters who for far too long have been unfairly condemned and rejected. Isn't it past time that we opened our hearts and our arms to welcome them home instead of seeing them as strangers still waiting at the gate?

When It's Your Daughter

Of the various stories I would rather not have in my history, this is certainly one of them. My daughter Emily married a gay man. Psychologists might not find this surprising; we often seek in a mate the occasion to deal with unfinished business relating to a parent. But there was more to it than that. Emily is writing her own remarkable story of losing and finding her power. Her former husband Steven has already told his story. In fact, in a one-man play that details his personal journey, *Confessions of a Mormon Boy*, he does a good impersonation of me asking, as we discussed his response to *Goodbye, I Love You*, "Well, Steven, if there's anything on this subject we need to talk about, now would be a good time to do it."

"Oh, no, not me," he replied. "I wouldn't do that to you!"

Like her mother and father, Emily and Steven had discussed the same issues and had felt that their faith and devotion were strong enough to overcome them. Emily has written, in her soon-to-be-published memoir:

> Maybe God's plan was far bigger than our just getting married. Maybe together we had a "greater-than-us" work to do. Maybe we could marry and actually be successful at it. We could write a book together—a far different book than the one my mother wrote. Our book would show how we conquered successfully what the previous generation had failed miserably to do. Steven and I would be the poster children for reparative therapy.

Their temple wedding was lovely. Their "time and all eternity" was just under seven years and produced, along with a great deal of pain, two remarkable children and a lot of learning.

Those who know me well understand that I am a true Libra, walking around with my hands out like the scales, saying, well, on the one hand there's this and on the other hand there's that. On the one hand, I am a philosopher who says, there are no victims, each one of us brings into our experience exactly what we need for our growth. On the other hand, I am an activist who says, *that should never have happened! And I am going to see to it that it never happens again!* That's one of the reasons I wrote *Goodbye, I Love You.*

Blame? Let us say responsibility. In order that these ill-fated marriages do not continue to happen, we must assign responsibility. I hold myself responsible. I was too trusting. In unrealistic ways, I trusted God, Life, Emily, Steven. I hold Emily and Steven both responsible. It is my belief that Emily allowed what she had been taught at church to speak louder than her inner wisdom and that Steven allowed his desire to lead a conventional life, along with his admiration and love for Emily, to fuel an impossible hope.

And, to a significant degree, I hold our church responsible. The current statement from the leadership that marriage is not recommended as a therapy for homosexual attraction is a very different stance from that of many decades and is still not entirely followed. A stronger statement recently appeared on the Church's official website in the words of Elder Dallin H. Oaks: "We are not going to stand still to put at risk daughters of God who would enter into such marriages under false pretenses or under a cloud unknown to them. Persons who have this kind of challenge that they cannot control could not enter marriage in good faith." This is the first official statement I have ever seen that shows significant concern for the women who have routinely been sacrificed on the altar of attempting to cure our young men of homosexuality. I hope it will be taken very seriously.

Even so, I expect large numbers of unfortunate marriages to continue. The statement of Elder Oaks, strong as it is, pales in comparison to the teachings that permeate the entire fabric of Mormonism and give false hope to eager young women of great faith who knowingly enter such marriages and to men who are certain they can "control" their challenge. When my daughter's marriage was clearly falling apart and all the cards were finally on the table, past my anger and my grief I found myself able to muster sympathy for her husband. Men exactly like him had come to me so often, weeping in their distress.

The territory that Mormon children travel is well marked. From our first day in Sunday School, we begin to learn what we have to do to make it back into our Heavenly Father's presence. One of the things, heard hundreds and hundreds of times, is that we must marry in the temple and raise a righteous family. Songs imprint on our minds words like these:

While I am in my early years, I'll prepare most carefully,
So I can marry in God's temple for eternity.
Families can be together forever
Through Heavenly Father's plan . . .

These may be beautiful, inspiring words for most children to hear, but if there are forty in the room, two or three are likely on a collision course with those beautiful words. Especially the boys, who not only represent a greater percentage of those with homosexual orientation, but who receive more pressure to initiate marriage than the girls do. As they mature and feel those first twinges of sexual attraction for other males, they suppress the feelings because they know it is absolutely forbidden to grow up to be a homosexual. Homosexuals are the people who do not love God and whose evil is so huge that God cannot bear the sight of them. These sweet young men love God; therefore it simply is not *possible* that they really are gay. It is hard for me to find fault with any of the many gay men I have talked to who chose to do what they believed beyond question God expected of them, which was to marry and procreate.

The ironies seem never to end. My culture places a higher value on family than any other culture I know of. And yet we continue to create family after family that is virtually doomed to failure. Collateral damage, perhaps some say, in the war we are fighting against disintegrating values. But when it is *your* family, *your* daughter, *your* son, your *self*, the collateral damage is unacceptable.

~

A few years ago I was unloading some groceries from the car when Brother Sutton walked up my driveway, wearing a suit that suited his positions both in the church and in the law office.

"Good evening, Sister Pearson," he smiled.

"Hiya," I replied.

Brother Sutton was my neighbor and former bishop and never dropped by just for the fun of it. He, like my other local ecclesiastical leaders, had always been very good to me, indulging and even appreciating Sister Pearson's sometimes radical ideas.

"I'm, uh, canvassing the neighborhood on behalf of the Protection of Marriage Proposition . . ."

For months California had been embroiled in the politics of

Proposition 22, ensuring that marriage was to remain legally an arrangement only between men and women. As you read in the incisive letter written by Stuart Matis shortly before his suicide, our church had joined forces with other conservative organizations in a deadly serious campaign to insure that homosexual couples would never be granted the privilege of marriage. Thousands of faithful Mormons had been assigned to canvass voters in the state, inquiring about their intentions and, if they were unsure, giving them information on the correct way to vote. I was aware of a number of bishops and stake presidents who had significant reservations about what appeared to be the heavy-handed orchestration our church was contributing to this effort. But the members were given their marching orders, and out they went.

"So, uh . . ." Brother Sutton smiled nervously and adjusted his glasses. Clearly my house was not the one he most looked forward to canvassing. "What are your feelings on this proposition?"

"Well." I put down my two gallons of low-fat milk on the pavement. "My feelings." I took a moment to breathe a time or two and watch a squirrel dart by. "This is the deal, Brother Sutton." I looked at him evenly. "Marriage. It's not that the Brethren don't want gay men to get married. It's just that they want them to marry *me*. And they want them to marry *my daughter*. And that's not okay with me. It should not be okay with any of us. I know you're just doing your job here, but tonight as you go to bed I would like you to lie there for a while and think—would you like one of your daughters to marry one of our sweet, young, gay men, fresh off his mission and anxious to do the 'right' thing?"

"Well . . ." He smiled in embarrassment. "You always manage to give me something to think about, don't you, Sister Pearson."

~

I did not vote for Proposition 22. The "Protection of Marriage" concept did not protect my marriage, nor did it protect the marriage of my daughter or that of a significant number of other women and men. On the contrary, it created the ground on which a marriage was built that could have been predicted to fail. Our insistence that gay men must not be together, but instead must be either entirely alone or with a woman, carries within it the possibility of disaster.

It's not entirely correct that the leadership of my church want gay men to marry women. And now, years after that conversation in my driveway, there are statements discouraging such marriages. Our leaders are good and caring men. They want the most happiness possible for every member of the Church. I believe they pray for that daily. They hope for all of us to enjoy a happy marriage. And where that might not be possible, I believe they hope for us to enjoy the *appearance* of a happy marriage. We Mormons are very big on appearances. We avoid the very appearance of evil. And sometimes we make do with the very appearance of joy. The too-frequent marriages of one from the house of Heterosexual to one from the house of Gay are among those "appearances."

As you go to sleep tonight, whatever religion you subscribe to, consider: Today in your congregation there are many fine young men eager to do the "correct" and expected thing and enter a conventional marriage. Roughly five percent of them are gay. If one of them is your son, do you really want him to marry a woman at all costs? And if one of them is scouting the community for a suitable bride, would you like to invite him over to meet your daughter?

There Are So Many Kinds of Love

Carol Lynn and
Trevor Southey
Oakland, California

I just carried up the stairs (one at a time) the two heavy, beautiful bronze figures that together form "Resurrection." I wanted this fine piece of art on my desk while I was writing about my dear friend Trevor, the sculptor.

Anchored by thin metal posts, both figures are floating, each about fifteen inches from crown to toe. Naked as the soul is, a male and a female. His raised arm forms a hollow of protection for her head. Her face is lifted in powerful ascent. The light of the three candles I have burning on my desk to remind me why I write flickers gently across the sheen of their dark metal skin. I watch them rise, male and female, together.

Gerald bought the male figure from our artist friend Trevor Southey and presented it to me for our first wedding anniversary. When funds allowed, the female figure appeared. I used to sit and stare at the sculpture when Gerald and I were going through our most distressing times. The figures were so right. Trevor created male and female to be together, just like God did. Why couldn't Gerald see that, know that, feel that? The response I'd heard from him so often: "Of course. Male and female together. Only some of us find that wedding within ourselves instead of with another of the opposite sex." It never made sense to me, but it did to Gerald. And to Trevor.

In the sixties, when we were young and in Utah and zealously devoted, with other like-minded artists, to creating Mormon art, Gerald and I met Trevor, a convert to the Mormon faith, born in Rhodesia and very British. I had been hoarding a file of poems I'd written, and Gerald, in his mad enthusiasm, was determined they should be published. He arranged with Trevor to do some illustrations for the book, and put me and the poems and the drawings in the car and headed to the big city, Salt Lake, to see who'd be first in line to publish this work. Astutely noticing that the line was empty, Gerald decided to become a publisher, and we borrowed two thousand dollars from the BYU credit union. Before long, two thousand copies of a slim white volume titled *Beginnings* were housed under our bed and in my father's garage. I believed I had a lifetime of wedding presents. But by fluke or by fate, this book of simple verses sold, eventually over 150,000 copies, and put me on the Mormon map. It put Trevor there too. The book is here on my desk today along with the bronze sculptures, the cover featuring a brilliant drawing in blue ink, an adult male figure curled in the womb of eternal progression: "God in Embryo."

In the sixties, so young, so devoted, so in Utah, we knew little of sexuality. Our feelings were interpreted only through the pronouncements of our religion, and we were determined to do the right thing. That's why Gerald married. And that's why Trevor, also a homosexual, married. Our stories are remarkably similar. Four children and a divorce. Today Trevor lives in nearby Oakland and is an internationally acclaimed and much sought after artist and sculptor.

I love it when Trevor invites me over to his studio to see Jesus. I get to look up at the face of a life-sized Christ, arms out in blessing or stretched onto a cross, created with such care by Trevor's devotion to both his art and his subject. He emails me to come over and see a new Christus

> before he goes to the foundry in a couple of weeks. I have all kinds of insecurities, of course, but also a deep love. It has recreated a whole new and deeper feeling for Jesus.

And later:

> Jesus begins to crumble before my eyes as the foundry finished a long week's work and carted off the various sections of the mold yesterday. I feel a strange combination of bereavement and relief. A little like a death or maybe, for a woman, a birth. . . . Delivered the crown of thorns . . .

That's Trevor the artist. But I want you to meet Trevor the dear homosexual man who has walked the path of pain so many of my loved brothers and sisters have walked. Very much aware of his own orientation, Trevor discussed it with various counselors, including then-apostle Spencer W. Kimball. Repeatedly, he was advised to marry, assured that this step would be the answer to his problem. Trevor writes in his autobiographical art collection, *Reconciliation*, of his reluctance.

> Then one day I met Elaine. . . . She was earnest and learned and beautiful. . . . We immediately related in a most vital and extraordinary way, sharing ideals and hopes. . . . Our courtship was short. We slipped quickly into the decision to marry. . . . I blamed my fear on evil, even though I wept at times in panic. I told her of my fears and the reason why. We both concluded that faith and commitment would conquer all. She embraced

me wonderfully and wonderfully became part of my dreams and the mother of my children. I loved her so. There are so many kinds of love.

Trevor and Elaine and their growing family created what Trevor fondly calls his "Eden" in Alpine, Utah, where they bought a farm home, converted the garage into a studio, milked cows, and raised ducks and chickens, sheep and pigs.

We trudged through an endless sea of mud and manure in winter. Then we harvested all kinds of things grown by love and sweat in summer, apricots from an ancient tree, a tree which became a fortress, a haven, a dream machine, a classic setting for a tree house roughly fabricated by the children.

Sadly, by the time our last child was born, my capacity to suppress my nature was so diminished that our life together was already threatened. Doubts about the religion were now coupled with resentment at its condemnation of what I perceived to be my natural way. . . .

We had planted and pruned, had husbanded and nursed all kinds of animals, had built and renovated and cherished and loved. We had wept together and we wept alone. . . . I had to proceed with the newborn me while fiercely creating an entirely new way of family, she to rebuild from shattered dreams.

But . . . even after our divorce . . . and in spite of Elaine's suffering, she was blessed with a peculiar strength which made it possible for us to perpetuate a kind of family life. . . .

The Church was a priceless gift to me, freeing me to grow in a way which might otherwise have taken decades. Now though, the structure which had freed me was, with sad irony, becoming a prison. Is it perhaps the nature of structure, that it must evolve with the souls it houses. . . ? I suppose the delicate interplay between the status quo and revolu-

tion/evolution is one that should command constant attention in personal life, in family, in church, or in nation.

Trevor has never found a home for his homosexuality. For
him it has been something of a lone and dreary world, and he
sometimes wishes things might have been otherwise. "I really
do not regret being gay," he tells me, "as much as I regret that
the world is so inhospitable to the strange creatures that we
are." A constant and special regret is that his wife experienced
so much pain on the path they chose together. The conflict between his "natural hunger to be a family man" and his "natural
need for a same-sex companion" was irreconcilable. Trevor's
large "family of gay friends" has been an enormous blessing to
him. Still, he looks back on his Eden in Alpine, Utah, with fond-
ness and yearning, working beside his loved companion, raising
the children and the crops, creating art that sprang from that
rich soil. I see heartbreak in his eyes as he speaks of it, perhaps a
bit like the heartbreak we might have seen in the eyes of Adam
and Eve as they left the first Eden, giving up peace and simplic-
ity, responding to the harsh call of learning and experience.

Music Up: Cello, Sad

Carol Lynn and
Brent
Missouri

May 27, 2003

When I said hello into the telephone, the voice on the other end was a man crying, and I knew at once it was one of my Mormon gay men who had just finished reading *Goodbye, I Love You*. It was. Brent in Missouri. "I don't want to take much of your time, but I just need to thank you . . ." Same story, same heart-breaking story. . . . Brent is a professional cellist, teaches and also plays freelance in orchestras. He just moved out of his home two weeks ago. He kept saying he was taking too much of my time, and I said this is what I'm here on earth to do . . .

December 10, 2004

Yesterday I received in the mail a CD sent as a thank-you from Brent, the gay man who called me last year and is a professional cellist. Beautiful cello music he recorded. He wrote, "This lovely piece in three-quarter time reminds me so much of my mom and dad, dancing around the house together when I was a kid."

I sometimes listened to Brent's lovely cello pieces while I was developing a stage play, *Facing East*, the story of a Mormon couple dealing with the suicide of their gay son, Andrew, and soon it occurred to me, "Of course! Andrew was a cellist!" (This was a year before I received news of the suicide of the young cellist you read about some pages back.) During my many hours writing the play, I listened to Brent's deeply moving music, and often I shed tears, tears for the Andrew in my imagination and tears for Brent. I wrote Brent asking permission to use his CD in a production of the play planned for Salt Lake City in November 2006. He wrote back:

> What a sweetie you are! (Uncalled for tears making it hard to type.) Please use my music! In any way you like!!! You bet I'll be there for the play!

I also asked if he would share his personal story in his own words for this book. Here it is.

~

I keep putting this letter to you at the top of my things-to-do list. One reason I haven't written is because I'm a little dizzy from looking around in circles for the "my family lived happily ever after" part, and I can't find it yet. I can write this letter to you today as long as I remind myself that my story is not over. Oh, how I ache and long for the day when I can report to you that my family is healed! I hope that your book will help other gay-fathered families like mine.

Most guys dream about fast cars, sports, and women when they are nineteen years old. I dreamed of serving a two-year mission for the Lord. I got appointment after appointment with my college and home ward bishops, and my bishop in my college town—begging to be sent. In the finest oblique phrases of Mormonese I was told that I was effeminate (that was as close to the "g" word as could be spoken in a nice Mormon bishop's office), and that I would be a liability to the Church if I represented the LDS faith out in the mission field. I was told that I needed to get married as soon as possible, even though this was the era when every worthy male member of the Church served a mission, and those who didn't were presumed to have sexually sinned. I did not keep track of how many nights I fell asleep in tears, but it took decades to overcome the silent shame of being "one of those boys" who didn't go on a mission. I was pure, and I delighted in obedience to the gospel. I was the best little Mormon boy in the ward.

I knew I was gay long before I knew what gay meant. And I believed what I was taught in the bishop's office: I would be healed of homosexuality if I followed the Church's counsel, and I should keep my sexual orientation a secret from the membership of the Church. So with faith in the Lord's anointed, I did just what I was told. With absolutely no interest in women, I promptly married a wonderful BYU coed.

I worked hard at fitting into the Mormon mold and did all I could to hide my secret sorrow and protect my family from shame. I was a caring, thoughtful husband. I fathered children, hoping that by living my temple covenants I would be healed of my unspeakable attraction to men. I read to my children every night. We had our weekly family home evening. I taught my children to cook, clean, garden, and love their mother. (I even made my daughter's prom dress!)

I love the hymns of Zion. In a priesthood meeting, we were encouraged to sing a hymn when faced with temptation. I believed my church leaders, and the result is that I can now repeat every verse of nearly every hymn in the hymnal. I also attended my meetings, paid a full tithe, and attended the temple often, all with hope for the day of healing. My angst was bottled up so tight that finally my life exploded from within. While asleep next to my wife, I accidentally told her all of my hidden homosexual feelings.

My wife outed me to the Church, believing that it was her job as a faithful Mormon to report my homosexual feelings to the bishop, just as if I were a wife-beater or had robbed a convenience store. The bishop called me in. I was so ashamed! It did not matter to the bishop or my wife that I had not had sex with a man.

I was given the edict to attend Evergreen meetings. The closest meeting place was one thousand miles from home. I was a really good Mormon boy; in addition to tithes and offerings, I worked a third job to keep up with paying for regular flights into Salt Lake City for my Evergreen meetings. My bishop insisted that this all remain confidential. I didn't want to embarrass my children or my family, so it was a pretty lonely experience to fly into Salt Lake alone to go to the meetings. I had to keep a low profile and stay in the cheapest motels I could find rather than stay with my family. How could I stay with my sisters in Utah and tell them that I was going to Evergreen meetings?

My first Evergreen experience was an awakening. The chapel in the Joseph Smith Memorial Building was packed with clones of myself! Nearly everyone there was within five years of my age, and their stories revealed that we all had the same sort of experiences growing up as gay Mormon boys and men. Told to remain invisible in order to cover up our shame. Told to put on that white shirt and tie and blend into Mormon culture as quiet, whole men. I attended Evergreen meetings as often as I could.

I also went to LDS reparative therapy during this time, driving three hours a week for about two years to see my Mormon therapist. I did everything I could in therapy to heal from being gay, knowing that I had signed a mandatory therapy agreement stating that the therapist could tell all of my confidences to my bishop. My wife attended some therapy sessions with me. The therapist assured both of us that I could change and become heterosexual if I really wanted to, if I really tried. I was the best little Mormon boy in the ward. I knew how to work hard, to fast and pray fervently, and I am still working out the intense guilt that remains from not trying hard enough. I did not get healed from an orientation that I had never acted upon. From my experience, I suspect that the men who claim success in reparative therapy make these claims because they fear being excommunicated from the Church.

The burdens of dealing with my homosexuality proved too much for both my wife and me. After we separated, the stake president suggested another therapist who also serves as a stake president in a neighboring stake. And here the truth was finally told. This therapist-stake president told me that sexual orientation is not something that can be changed or healed. When I brought this new information to my own stake president—that I am truly gay and nothing is going to change that—my stake president was alarmed and indicated what a danger I was to the rest of the stake. He did not want other church members to believe that change is not possible. They would be better protected from that idea if I were not allowed to remain a member of the Church. And he was right. Since my excommunication, other members know not to believe me. They know to avoid me.

I believe the church court action led my wife, and later my children, to presume serious transgression and lifestyle choices had been made by me, justifying divorce. My ex-wife continues to believe that I could be straight if only I tried harder. I am also the convenient scapegoat for any problems she or my children have; their problems are my fault because, in their church culture, I am an untouchable. A latter-day leper.

My stake president told me that he would do everything he could to get me rebaptized into the Church. He also told me that the first thing I needed to do to qualify for rebaptism was to find another worthy LDS woman and to marry her.

Some may consider my ex-wife sinister because she fought in court for me to never see my children again. But I know that she is only demonstrating the homophobic culture that she worships in. I know that she is supported by her ward leaders and friends in fighting the unspeakable "crime against nature" by turning my children against me. But my tears turned to tears of gratitude when I heard the judge proclaim in the courtroom that there was no reason why I could not participate in raising my own children! I was awarded regular visitation and dual parenting rights. However, because of the homophobia my children learned at church, they will have nothing to do with me. My mailed gifts are sent back unacknowledged.

I do not know exactly how many grandchildren I have. It has been my lifetime dream to tour Europe, but if I were given the choice of spending the summer either traveling Europe or seeing my grandchildren, I would promptly hold my unknown grandkids close. I would put them up on my shoulders. I'd push them so high in the swing that they'd squeal with delight! I'd take them to the Dairy Queen for a chocolate-dipped cone, and read to them the same bedtime stories that I read to their parents. And, like I did for their mom and dad, I'd play the cello for them until they fell asleep.

One of my brothers knows. He called to tell me that even though I am "that way," I am still his brother. For a while, all communication between us was initiated by me, and invitations to stay at his home or to visit ceased. Recently, though, he has offered his friendship and caring, brotherly advice to me.

My elderly parents would suffer to find out their son is a son of Satan, so I hope my ex-wife does not further out me to my family. My parents worry about me not going to the celestial kingdom unless I find another woman to be sealed to. ["Sealing" is an LDS ordinance that creates an eternal bond between a husband and wife or within a family.] That alone has them fretting. I hope they live long enough that I can retire and help care for them. And eternity? It would be a wonderful thing, I think, to find a special guy and be ministering angels together.

I have come to believe that the words of tolerance spoken by current LDS authorities are aimed at the media, not at really healing families, and that the Church is still very homophobic, oppressive, and exclusive. If the Church was really seeking tolerance, my bishop would call my ex-wife into his office and ask her what she is doing to bring my children back into my life. If the Church was really seeking tolerance, my married children would be called into their bishops' offices and asked where their children's grandfather is and why is he excluded from the family. I often wish that I had raised my children in some other church. I believe that then our family of divorce, inclusive of their gay father, could work together in love.

I have heard stories of that kind of tolerant love working in Mormon divorced families where one parent is gay. And I am experiencing it here in the Congregational United Church of Christ. The UCC service reminds me so much of an LDS sacrament meeting. Young couples, elderly couples, extended families visiting this week. Children grinning at me from the pew ahead.

Some folks worship with an arm around their partner, and a good number of the couples happen to be same-sex couples. The first time I attended, I thought, Whoa! where are all the perverts, drug dealers, and child molesters? These same-sex couples worshiping God are friendly and kind, benevolent and virtuous. They go out of their way individually and as a church to do remarkable works of charitable service in the community. There are heterosexual couples with children. There are gay and lesbian couples with children. There are transgender people and elderly folks, and sexual orientation is not an issue of worship. This is most profound for me when, at the end of the service, everyone stands, hold hands around the chapel, and sings the first verse of "God Be with You Till We Meet Again." At the end of the song, hands are squeezed, all are smiling at each other and hugging. The spirit of God is as powerful there as I have felt in any meetinghouse or temple.

And I can still sing all the verses without the book.

⌒

I have been listening to Brent's beautiful cello music as I

wrote this section. I grieve for all who are denied the joy of dancing with the one they love. I have said a prayer that some-day Brent's wife will find herself in the arms of a man who can rejoice in her femaleness. And that Brent will be allowed to waltz with his grandchildren.

Recently, I received a terse email from Brent. It read, "I am doing well! In love (shhh!)!"

Planning the Wedding

Carol Lynn and
Russ Gorringe
Salt Lake City, Utah

Under a headline in Utah's *Deseret Morning News*, "Commitment Expo 2006 reaches out to gays," I read:

> Russ Gorringe is looking forward to the day when he can formally express his lifelong commitment to the man he's chosen as a life partner.
>
> The couple can't legally marry in Utah. But they're hoping a Commitment Expo 2006 this Friday will provide ideas as they shop for wedding bands, look for a caterer, and select invitations for their August commitment ceremony.
>
> "It's all the fun and excitement of a heterosexual couple as they plan their wedding," Gorringe said. . . . "We believe strongly in marriage, we believe in marriage values. . . . We believe in those values for everyone."

It was a short article, simple and happy, and it made me smile. But I knew that the story behind it was certainly not simple and not always happy. Russ became aware of his same-sex orientation as a boy, asked his mother to help him see a psychiatrist when he turned 12, and was in therapy until he went on a mission. He was terrified of that next step, marriage, but his church leaders assured him that his homosexual attractions would go away.

So Russ planned his wedding, not with excitement but with terror. His wife was a woman he still adores and admires, but his feelings didn't change, and his marriage had little physical intimacy. "I relied on the phrase, 'faith precedes miracles,'" he says. "I had complete faith I would be changed. When I wasn't, I felt I had been denied my miracle. I spent hundreds of thousands of dollars on reparative therapy, trying to heal an emptiness inside that was killing me. I spent years feeling suicidal. My years working with Evergreen were helpful at first, giving me for the first time others like me to talk to, and I became a leader there. But eventually the experience became counterproductive when I realized my feelings were not changing." Through all this, he served in a bishopric and a stake presidency.

After 25 years of marriage, Russ's wife requested a divorce, and he agreed; they remain good friends. He has close relationships with his four children as well, all of whom will attend his commitment ceremony.

Absent at the ceremony, however, will be Russ's parents. His father has not spoken to him since 1997 and will hang up the phone if he is the one who picks it up when Russ calls to talk to his mother. For years, Russ's father has said to family members when a recreational event is being planned, "Remember, if Russ comes, Grandpa and the four-wheelers stay at home."

"Still," Russ told me in a recent phone conversation, "what has surprised me in all this is that I have not been hurt by the hateful things my father has done. God has endowed me with peace and joy, and my father's actions have had no ill effect on me. I am at peace with my Savior, and I feel his acceptance of me as a gay man—his creation. Last Thanksgiving, as we talked around the family table about things we were grateful for, I told my children how thankful I was for this great peace that passeth understanding."

Recently one of Russ's sons brought over a gay friend who was planning his own wedding to a woman. Russ's son hoped his father could help his friend see what he was getting into. "We talked until four in the morning," Russ told me. "I assured him that it was highly unlikely that marriage was going to change his romantic and sexual feelings and that he was in for a very rough ride. The young man was certain he and his fiancée were going to be granted the miracle that I was denied. He said, 'Our generation is different from yours. We are a royal generation, a generation that has a special relationship with the Savior, and we are the ones who will beat this thing.'"

At this writing, the young man continues planning his temple wedding.

Russ continues planning his commitment ceremony.

Choosing and Keeping the Star-Crossed Love

If we are honest, we all want that brass ring of romantic love on the carousel ride, reasoning that a sweet, passionate, permanent relationship will follow. That's not always the way things turn out. Many create a very good life that does not include marriage. Many make do with a decent marriage and are grateful for the good things that are there. And, surprising though it seems, many from those incompatible houses of Heterosexual and Gay do maintain, for better or for worse, 'til death do they part—or possibly for time and all eternity.

These are not marriages that include a bisexual partner as capable of happily relating to one of the opposite sex as to one of the same sex. I am speaking of the marriage of the person who is completely homosexual in his or her spontaneous feelings. Two such marriages come to mind. One is a longtime Mormon friend who lives on the East Coast, and one a man not of my religion who lives on the West Coast. Both of them spent a number of years pursuing life in the gay world. Both were out of control. One was abusing drugs and alcohol. Each made a very rational and radical decision to change. My Mormon friend came back to the Church. Each found a woman who was a good friend; each confessed his gay history and proposed marriage. Each woman agreed.

The man on the West Coast told me, "I am a married man. I

am also one hundred percent homosexual, and I know that I always will be. I love my wife, and we have a lot of happiness together. This is a decision I'm glad I made." I have no reason to believe their marriage did not endure and provide satisfaction for both husband and wife. The man made the decision from a clear head. He was in his late thirties when he made it, and he knew the lay of the land, both out in the world and inside his soul.

My friend back East is also still in his marriage, but not so happily. He and his wife have four children and numerous grandchildren, who are the absolute best thing in his life. I asked him, "Are you glad you married?"

He smiled sadly. "I'd be dead by now if I hadn't. But I'll tell you one thing. When I get to heaven, if marriage to a woman is my reward for all eternity, and if God has not taken out his magic wand and changed me, I'll say no, thank you, I'd rather be down below with my friends."

Other gay men and their wives have made similar choices and have succeeded, with varying degrees of satisfaction, in building lasting marriages. Their comments follow:

∽

Sister Pearson: I just finished *Goodbye, I Love You.* Fortunately, I had an hour in which I could cry before seeing anyone. . . . I, too, am same-sex attracted and married to a marvelous woman. . . . I feel an extreme connection to your story, to the sweetness of your marriage to Gerald, to the bizarreness that percolates into the otherwise very normal LDS existences of those intimately touched by its difficulty.

I've been married for three years to "Janet," a girl I've known since childhood. Our marriage is wonderful. It's sweet. It's the most precious gift Heavenly Father has given me. Our story amazes me even still. . . . At any rate, as I'm sure you can imagine, as Janet and I have encountered the dumbfoundingly complicated difficulties of our situation, we have wondered if we were confronting this frontier entirely alone—if we were the first to have struggled in this way. There is a bleakness to this whole thing, even in today's society, even when our life is basically good. An isolation. A feeling of desperate solitude. . . .

Janet has many times asked me if my attractions to men are because she is not attractive, even though she knows that is not the case. I don't know what to tell her in those moments. It makes me feel so bad and so incredibly sad. I would truly love nothing on this planet more than to view my sweet wife as most men view women. It makes my heart ache that I can't give that to her. But I hope to make it up to her in keeping the promises that I have made to her and never breaking them.

~

It has been our religion that has held my wife and me together through very rough times. Our religion gives us hope for an eternal future where all things will be healed. Our love is a different kind of love, but it is a good love. I know we're not out of the woods yet, but we're taking it day by day.

~

I can't imagine not being married to my husband. We discussed his homosexuality for years when we were just friends. I knew what I was getting into. Well, sort of knew. Yes, I wish we had the physical relationship other couples do, but I would never give up what I have with him.

~

I was born seventy years ago when people didn't talk about such things. Although I am gay, I met the expectations of the Church in filling a mission, then came home and married a wonderful woman and with her raised four of the best kids in the world. I continue to live happily with my wife of thirty years, although not entirely without regret for a life that might have been.

～

I saw *Brokeback Mountain* twice. My wife did also. We did not see it together. It was simply too painful. We have been married 36 years and raised five children together. During all the years of struggle, reparative therapy, finally excommunication, not a day passed that I didn't think that death was my only alternative. Damn. I couldn't leave "Dawn" with the kids. I loved them all too much. Yes, I did love Dawn—I just found having sex with her something difficult, even unnatural. I couldn't leave the children. I wanted to be there for them, to help them, to protect them and watch them grow. Our kids are out on their own now. Four of them are happily married. I think they all love me, in spite of my sexual orientation. After Dawn saw *Brokeback Mountain* the second time, she cornered me in our living room and put her arms around me. She told me that she still loved me and was so sorry that I never had found the love of my life. I hugged her back and told her I wished she, too, could have found the love of her life. I also told her that I had chosen to stay with her and the children. It was my choice, and I was not blaming anyone. Dawn's understanding, love, and compassion are amazing.

～

Marriage is so hard, despite how I love my wife and kids. Your story gives me encouragement to stick to my decision to be here and *to be understood!*

～

I will keep going to Evergreen meetings. Not that I expect anything to change in the way that I experience my sexuality, I've tried for too long. But it helps to know there are others like me, and we give each other encouragement to just hang in there, to manage our feelings, and to control destructive behavior. Breaking up my family is not an option, for me anyway, and certainly not at my age. Is my glass half empty or half full? I try not to look at the empty half. The full half contains lots of blessings, and I keep my eye there. I love and appreciate my wife enormously, but I experience sex as obeying the letter of the law with no way of obeying the spirit of the law. Sex is like being a stranger in a strange land. Sex is like going through the motions of something that should be wonderful but isn't. Still, I'm here for the long haul. My wife deserves so much more, but every time we talk about it, she tells me our love is enough. I have no belief that, if I chose a different life, what I would be giving up would be worth what I might gain.

~

The wife of a Presbyterian minister wrote this to me:

When my husband acknowledged to himself and to me that he was gay, I was shaken, scared, angry—but, surprisingly, I was not so much angry at Bob as at our church for treating sexuality as something not to be discussed, for being so secretive that I had no idea to whom to turn for help throughout this upheaval, for having made Bob feel sick and evil, a Dr. Jekyll and Mr. Hyde for so many years. He was one who had learned such negative ideas about who homosexual persons were that he did not even recognize his own orientation until well after we married. How he was able to serve the church so well during all this time is still mystifying to me—and to be a caring husband and father, too! We did realize that our marriage was built on much more than sexual attraction, that family, our history, deep caring, shared friendships, and service to our church as a team in ministry were too important to end. And we have tried in various ways to help the church come to new understanding. I think of the bound feet of Chinese women in ancient times. Have not minds been bound in like manner, making it hard to open them to new thinking! Far too many have been ostracized from the fold. I feel this sin of inhospitality is most grievous in God's eyes.

~

There are many other stories like those reported above. To deliberately create and maintain a marriage in which the celebration of sexuality is not part of the bargain is likely something few of us would do. Most would consider such an arrangement tantamount to a "redefinition of marriage," never mind that over time many heterosexual couples lose interest in each other and still manage to make their marriages last, even adding new children from time to time. But there are valid reasons for creating a union between a person who is gay and a person who is straight, and there are valid reasons for maintaining that union. If there is love and kindness and mutual helpfulness there, if both parties are very open about what is important to them, if sexual infidelity does not mar either trust or health, if this is what they *choose* with no misapprehensions, these marriages deserve to be honored. Star-crossed they may be in terms of romantic love and sex, but perhaps there are other stars that bless them.

∿

That inner philosopher of mine insists on finishing this section. All day long my activist is out and about, doing what she thinks is her good work. But at the end of the day she gets tired and sometimes discouraged and she needs a little comfort, so I let my philosopher come out and sing her a lullaby and stroke her hair as we're going to sleep.

Just now as I sat down to write, I opened an email from my Catholic friend, Christin, a former nun, asking for prayers on behalf of her sister. After her signature was a quote from a great fourteenth century English mystic, Julian of Norwich:

All will be well, and all manner of things will be well.

It put me in mind of my own pioneer ancestors crossing the plains and singing the hymn we still sing in church: "All is well! All is well!" Their days were spent clearing a path to the West, firming up a new religion, stretching the flour and bacon as far as it would go, burying the dead. And at night, around the campfire, they allowed their active part to rest in the arms of their philosopher, singing the song penned by William Clayton: "Why should we mourn or think our lot is hard? 'Tis not so; all is right . . ."

All will be well, and all manner of things will be well.

I want to speak for a moment to the husbands and wives whose dreams of a joyful married life have been shattered by the reality of the homosexual condition. And to the children whose birthright ought to have included the security of a loving, intact marriage between their parents, except that one of them was gay.

What if . . . ? We storytellers use that phrase a lot. It can be the beginning of magical things. What if—things are not always as they appear? What if, in the grand design of things, none of us finally is a victim? What if our Large Eternal Self actually agreed to certain general challenges that our small mortal self would experience in the service of profoundly vital understanding and growth? What if we are each in the correct classroom being assigned the correct homework, and what if the answer to the question on every test is to love a little more? What if all pain can be labor pain? What if it's okay that there are so many mysteries? What if we are held in the arms of angels all the time? What if, strangely, all is well?

In *The Third Millennium*, Ken Carey speaks of the general history of the human race, but I read it as my personal history:

> Whenever there were deviations from the optimal patterns of development, they have always been used profitably. In the end there is not one moment that does not contribute in some way toward perfection. Even at those critical junctures where

the optimal path was not taken, if you follow the tale further down the path that was chosen you find that, though its course twists and winds, it turns eventually not merely to the original path but to a level of perfection one octave higher on the spiral of creative unfoldment.

The year I write this, 2006, is not only the twentieth anniversary of the publication of *Goodbye, I Love You*, but my fortieth wedding anniversary. Don't send congratulations. But don't send condolences either. Looking back at the path I chose, but from which there were forced deviations, I see the twists and turns, the momentous gains and the stupefying losses, and the ongoing gathering of wisdom and peace and new layers of love. I do not know resentment. Grief visits, but I don't make up a room for it.

I speak for romantic love.

I speak, too, for trusting the mystery, for forgiveness, and for believing that love in all its forms once created can never be undone. And that not only in eternity but *here*, hidden under the grey, all is well, and all manner of things shall be well.

I'll Walk with You

Some years ago, I was intrigued by an article about homosexuality that suggested nature frequently has a wisdom that we often don't understand, and presented the possibility that a small minority of the human family has been designed somehow to be freed from the usual domestic responsibilities in order to bless the culture by doing unusually creative work in other areas. History and my own experience tell me that gay people often are among the most brilliantly creative of us all.

I know, too, that some cultures have honored their gay members as shamans, revered healers, and those with special gifts. Eugene Tachinni, gay Mormon Navajo artist, whose story is told in the next section, would traditionally have been called a "Two-Spirit." The Navajo creation story, as told by Walter L. Williams, professor of anthropology and gender studies at the University of Southern California, suggests that:

> Humans are dependent for many good things on the inventiveness of the nadle [Navajo term for the Two-Spirit]. Such individuals were present from the earliest era of human existence, and they . . . were part of the natural order of the universe, with a special contribution to make.

In our schools we manage to create different tracks for different needs. We have a track for highly gifted students; those who are naturally talented in music, in science, in art or in other fields are often given scholarships and extraordinary encouragement. We also have a track for those with learning disabilities, frequently giving them opportunities designed around their special needs. At church we try to be very sensitive to those with special physical and mental needs. I have a bright memory of my first few years in my ward here in Walnut Creek. Every Sunday without fail, unless she was ill, Barbara would be in the foyer before and after church, smiling and shining and hugging, sweet mind of a child in a thirty-year-old body. Everyone knew her. Everyone loved her. She bathed in the love, and I knew that Sunday morning was possibly the highlight of her week. Often I thought: this is what the Church is for, precisely this, so Barbara can share her light and receive ours.

When I learned three years ago that a couple in our ward had a four-year-old autistic child, I asked the mother to go for a walk in the hills with me, as I wanted to learn about autism. Heather and I walked and talked and, as I quizzed her about how she felt in the ward regarding her situation, she said, "Well, it's really pretty frustrating. I know the members love us and all, but they don't know how to respond to Parker. They're embarrassed, and then I'm embarrassed, and nobody seems to want to try to understand all this."

Being one who can't quite manage to mind my own business, I spoke to the president of the Relief Society [women's organization], and the upshot was that I was asked to teach a special lesson on how we can better understand and support those among us who have unusual mental and emotional situations. Women participated who had experience with eating disorders, obsessive compulsive disorder, Tourette's syndrome, and, of course, the mother of our ward's autistic child.

Heather told me that day was very helpful in breaking down

some of the barriers she had been experiencing. Our ward now has a "Parker's Special Person" calling, someone who devotes full attention to Parker during class time at church. When we learned the family was raising money for a service dog, trained especially to assist autistic children, many of us held unofficial fund raisers, and a few weeks ago, when I spotted a woman with a dog in the church hallway, I said "Oh, yay!" Then I ran to stand in line to hug one and pet the other.

As a society, we have recently greatly improved our understanding of people with differing abilities, such as those with autism; we have learned that they are indeed "special," uniquely gifted perhaps, and have many precious insights to share with those of us who care to learn from them. I yearn for the day in our church and in the world when our sensitivity to those who are different from "the norm" will extend to those whose sexual orientation differs from that of most people. Recent studies estimate that autism affects approximately one in 175 children in the United States. If the estimated statistic of five percent of us being of homosexual orientation is correct, then there would be close to eight children in that same 175 who will experience themselves as homosexual people. This means that we are called to have that many more opportunities to create safe and nurturing places where our gay brothers and sisters can develop their unique gifts and talents to share with us, as well as that many more opportunities for us to see them as children of God just like everyone else.

I don't know what it will look like when we manage to develop a church, a society, that is sensitive to the needs of our young people who find themselves to be gay. I have some hopes. We will be aware of certain tendencies and go out of our way to make those who exhibit them feel comfortable and welcome.

No one will be made fun of for looking or behaving against gender stereotypes. When our children or adolescents feel that they need someone to talk to about sexual feelings they find alarming because they're different from those of their friends, parents at home and leaders at church will be more able to respond without shock, with more responsible information, more compassion, and more humane guidance.

Our rhetoric will find ways to allow for different goals. While marriage between a man and a woman will still be greatly honored as the state that most of us choose, there will be a sense that some of us may not be called to that relationship, an acknowledgment that will not carry shame. For those gay people who for their own good reasons do choose to marry a partner of the opposite sex, it will be with full disclosure, without unrealistic expectations of change, and at a stage in life where there is mature judgment.

Early in August 1987, one year after *Goodbye, I Love You* was published, I received a call from a member of the General Board of the Primary, the Church's organization for children. She said, "Sister Pearson, we have a problem, and we wondered if you could help us solve it. We're preparing a new songbook for the Primary and it's ready to go to press, but there's one more song we need and we don't have it. We're asking you to write it for us. There are so many children in the Church who have special needs, so many who are handicapped or are different in one way or another. We want so much to include them, to encourage the other children to be kind and loving to them. We need the song immediately. Can you do this for us?"

I said of course, I would try.

"I'll Walk with You" is found on page 140 of the *Children's Songbook*, music by Reid N. Nibley. It has an illustration of one girl in a wheelchair being pushed by another, both of them smiling. Sometimes when we sing it in Relief Society, I am asked to lead the singing. It pleases me so much to know it is sung in LDS congregations all over the world, by children and often by adults. As they sing, they have in mind children like Barbara and Parker and the girl in the illustration, but as I wrote it I also had in mind the little children who, as they grow up, will find themselves of a sexual orientation sure to present a challenge for them in our church and our society.

Writing this section, I recalled that a couple of years ago I received a sweet and moving email from a gay man to whom this song meant a great deal, telling me of an interesting experience he had with it. Having located the email, I find there is even another layer of interest to add. The email was from Brent, the cello player who told his story just a few pages back, writing to thank me for the phone conversation we'd had a couple of days before:

> Carol Lynn, I am so very grateful for the time you gave to me. I want to share a meaningful coincidence with you: I emailed my friend Larry Mann, to tell him the incredible effect that talking to you had on my well-being, and at the end of my post, I told him that I had a Primary song buzzing in my head that reminded me of how kind he had been to suggest that I call you. I wrote out all of the words of the song in my post. (I memorized lots and lots of hymns and Primary songs to try to cure the gay out of me.) The song was:
>
> > If you don't walk as most people do,
> > Some people walk away from you,
> > But I won't! I won't!
>
> Larry quickly emailed me back to tell me that *you wrote this song!* He heard you sing it at a [Gay Mormon Fathers] conven-

tion. . . . I grinned for the longest time, aglow with our phone conversation and with this simple but powerful coincidence. I played the piano in Primary for years and years until recently. I would put a jazz, rock, or boogie beat to the non-sacred songs, getting the kids into movin' and a-groovin'! But "I'll Walk with You" I would play with great reverence. I would quietly weep as the children sang it because of its very special meaning to me as a closeted gay man in the Church. This song has helped me these past four difficult years more than I can express in words . . .

Love,
Brent

~

I'll Walk with You

If you don't walk as most people do,
Some people walk away from you,
But I won't! I won't!

If you don't talk as most people do,
Some people talk and laugh at you,
But I won't! I won't!

I'll walk with you. I'll talk with you.
That's how I'll show my love for you.

Jesus walked away from none.
He gave his love to everyone.
So I will! I will!

Jesus blessed all he could see,
Then turned and said, "Come follow me."
And I will! I will! I will! I will!

I'll walk with you. I'll talk with you.
That's how I'll show my love for you.

4
CIRCLING THE WAGONS (ONE)

Civilization is the process in which
one gradually increases the number of
people included in the term "we" or "us"
and at the same time decreases those
labeled "you" or "them" until that
category has no one left in it.

—HOWARD WINTERS

When There's Love at Home

One of the hymns we sing often at church always moves me:

> There is beauty all around
> When there's love at home;
> There is joy in every sound
> When there's love at home.

About a month before my mother died, when I was fifteen, she quoted that song, and when she came to the line, "Oh, there's one who smiles on high, when there's love at home," she told us she would be the one smiling on high, watching to see how her children cared for one another. When I sing that hymn in church now, I know everyone else is thinking of God as the "one who smiles on high," but I think of my mother.

The words of that hymn sometimes float through my mind when I hear of a Mormon mother who, upon hearing from her daughter that she is a lesbian, locks herself in a room with a revolver, saying she would rather die than be the mother of a gay child. Or when I hear of a family planning a family reunion and managing to make sure the gay son is not informed of it.

Family is a gift. It's our safe place to fall, our primary system of support. My four siblings are a constant support to me, and, like my mother, I have no greater wish than that my children love one another and feel the love that I have for them.

Members of the LDS Church are taught that love between family members is to be prized and nurtured. We are urged never to turn our backs on our children, even when they appear to be "wayward." Frequently heard are statements such as this one from President Gordon B. Hinckley: "Keep your families close together and love and honor your children."

I love the statement from Rabbi Harold Kushner:

> When you have a child, you start to dream of how this kid will grow up and make you proud. The only thing you can predict with 100% certainty is that the reality will diverge somehow from that dream. Some of our children will disappoint us by not being the scholars we hoped they would be. Some children will disappoint us by not being the athletes we hoped they would be. Some will disappoint us by coming out and telling us they are gay and they won't give us grandchildren. . . . The real question is not, what book can I read, what technique can I use to raise a perfect child? The real question is how will you handle that gap between the child you dreamt of having and the real child growing up in your home. . . . What I have learned is that any religion, if you do it wrong, will leave people feeling condemned and dismissed and unworthy and any religion, if you do it right, will leave people feeling cleansed and affirmed.

And these words from "Always Our Children," a statement prepared in 1997 by the Committee on Marriage and Family of the National Conference of Catholic Bishops:

> How can you best express your love—itself a reflection of God's unconditional love—for your child? At least two things are necessary.
>
> First, don't break off contact; don't reject your child. A shocking number of homosexual youth end up on the streets

because of rejection by their families. This, and other external pressures, can place young people at greater risk of self-destructive behaviors like substance abuse and suicide.

Your child may need you and the family now more than ever. He or she is still the same person. This child, who has always been God's gift to you, may now be the cause of another gift: your family becoming more honest, respectful, and supportive. Yes, your love can be tested by this reality, but it can also grow stronger through your struggle to respond lovingly.

I love the charming story told by Jewish comedian Eddie Sarfaty in *When I Knew.* He tells of coming out to his grandmother and giving her a copy of *Now That You Know*, which he characterizes as *Everything You Always Wanted to Know About Homosexuality But Were Afraid to Hear.*

Two weeks later I am home for a visit and to do some laundry. I see the book lying on the nightstand; the wrinkled spine and folded corners tell me it has been read. I turn to Granny who is busily working on yet another afghan.

"Hey, Granny, did you read that book?"

The crochet hook stops, she looks up and says point blank, "Yes, and it's disgusting!"

My heart sinks and my guard goes up. "Disgusting?"

"Yes, it's disgusting! It says that some of the parents don't love their children anymore."

She makes me cry.

For Mormon families, and certainly for many other religious families, there is a great deal at stake in the call to get every child safely back to heaven. We sing:

Families can be together forever
Through Heavenly Father's plan . . .

But an unrepentant homosexual, we're told, cannot inherit the highest degree of heaven and will be forever cut off from the rest of the family who faithfully kept all the commandments. In the words of a lesbian quoted in the *Deseret Morning News*:

> You see a great deal of pain. It puts parents in an impossible position. They're enjoined to keep their families together at all costs, yet there's a family member who won't be able to join them in the celestial kingdom.

Many Mormon families find a way to trust that God will be more gracious than that, and manage simply to love their gay children. But there are many who live in fear, anger, resentment, and crushing defeat, believing that they have failed as a family and that their homosexual member has sabotaged their eternal hopes. Various organizations have sprung up to be of service to such families, notably Family Fellowship, formed in 1993 by a group of Mormon parents of gay children and others interested in bringing light and truth to what they saw as an "information vacuum." This group has given invaluable support to thousands of Mormon families, holding educational forums, conferences, retreats, and publishing a newsletter (www.ldsfamilyfellowship.org).

I appreciated the words in an opinion piece in the *Salt Lake Tribune* by a Mormon woman, Gayle Hayes Castleton:

> Every time I have seen families embrace and accept their homosexual family members, nothing bad has happened! The association has always been positive and the loving, caring "family" experience has only grown and flourished. They are available to each other for that family support that is so valued in our culture. Families are strengthened, not weakened.
>
> When families have rejected their homosexual family mem-

bers, it has not turned out well, even when that rejection was done "lovingly." You know, love the sinner...hate the sin? I've known homosexuals rejected by their families who looked for acceptance in all the wrong places. Bright, promising lives lost to drugs, disease and death. I've seen families who reject those they should love, depriving themselves of that valuable relationship.

In the spirit of that great Chinese proverb, "It is better to light one candle than to curse the darkness," let us light candles as we share the stories of families and church members, primarily in the Mormon community, who have circled the wagons around their gay loved ones. There will be an occasional spot of darkness, but the candles we light will create a bonfire whose light and warmth, I believe, will be seen and felt far into the distance.

I Drew a Circle That Took Him In

Sometimes, instead of or along with the family, it is the gay child who puts love away. So I speak here to them, the gay son and the lesbian daughter, reminding them that being rejected is not always sufficient grounds to reject.

In my church—I assume in all Christianity—we pray to become more like Jesus. "Oh," says the Great Bestower of Blessings, "then you will want the rejection experience, the Gethsemane experience. I can arrange that."

"No . . . no, that's not what I had in mind . . ."

"Perhaps—ah!—being a gay child in a very religious family, that will do it!"

Who knows how the harsh blessings are dispensed, the ones that give us the clearest opportunity to:

> Love your enemies, bless them that curse you, do good to them that hate you, and pray for them which despitefully use you, and persecute you; that ye may be the children of your Father which is in heaven.

A rejected homosexual has this daunting opportunity—to respond with love, toward family, friends, the larger community, both social and religious. I love a statement in a sermon by Martin Luther King, Jr.:

> Now there is a final reason I think that Jesus says, "Love your enemies." It is this: that love has within it a redemptive power.

And there is a power there that eventually transforms individuals. That's why Jesus says, "Love your enemies." Because if you hate your enemies, you have no way to redeem and to transform your enemies. But if you love your enemies, you will discover that at the very root of love is the power of redemption. You just keep loving people and keep loving them, even though they're mistreating you. Here's the person who is a neighbor, and this person is doing something wrong to you and all of that. Just keep being friendly to that person. Keep loving them. Don't do anything to embarrass them. Just keep loving them, and they can't stand it too long. Oh, they react in many ways in the beginning. They react with bitterness because they're mad because you love them like that. They react with guilt feelings, and sometimes they'll hate you a little more at that transition period, but just keep loving them. And by the power of your love they will break down under the load. That's love, you see. It is redemptive, and this is why Jesus says love. There's something about love that builds up and is creative. There is something about hate that tears down and is destructive. So love your enemies.

~

I want to tell you about Sikoki's "Arizona Orphan Boy." In a recent conversation with Sikoki, about whom you will read later, he told me about his "Orphan," and I asked him to write the following story for me.

I first met "Larry" over the phone, when his friend (who incidentally is the daughter of my high school music teacher) called from Arizona to tell me his story and to express her concern for his well-being. He had just come out to his very active Mormon family and needed someone to talk to because they had all turned their backs on him. His friend knew I was openly gay, Mormon, and in a happy, loving relationship and hoped I could guide Larry through this difficult period in his life. I spoke with him briefly and he agreed to meet when he came to Los Angeles a few weeks later. He arrived on our doorstep early in December without a place to stay, feeling totally unsure of his future, and wanting to get away from his family because of their attitude toward his homosexuality. His mother had handed him a booklet that prescribed the process of praying and fasting one's way out of homosexuality, and instructed him to follow it.

Richard and I took him in, calling him our "Arizona Orphan Boy," and spent the next couple of weeks counseling with him and trying to help him make sense of his life, which seemed turned upside down. We encouraged him to return home for the holidays and "let his light so shine" with his family that they would realize he was the same lovable son and younger brother he had always been and that his being gay hadn't changed who he really was on the inside. We tried to impress on him how crucial it is to *stay connected* to our loved ones and friends *after* they learn we are gay so they will see we haven't changed and become despicable monsters or depraved heathens, as some religions might teach, but are the same individuals they have always loved.

After struggling with his decision, Larry did return to his family in Arizona on Christmas Day and began rebuilding the bonds with his parents and siblings. He is living at home and going back to school to get a degree in nursing and his relationships with his family are growing stronger. A few weeks ago, he drove out here with his father to pick up all his earthly goods left in storage, and I got to meet his dad. (Would you believe, he was also a missionary to Samoa?) Needless to say, we hit it off very well, and they took me to dinner and we reminisced about our missions all night. He also asked me about how my good LDS parents accepted *my* being gay, which turned out to be a "missionary experience" of another kind for me!

~

Excellent advice on this subject was shared with me by John, a conservative Baptist man who obtained an MA from Liberty University, Jerry Falwell's school. He married, became a pastor, then at forty "ran out of energy to keep going with the inner struggle while trying to minister to others," resigned his church, went into unsuccessful "change therapy," divorced, is now in a committed relationship with another man, and is good friends with his ex-wife and her husband. His father calls John's partner "Son," and recently one of his daughters said, "Dad, I think that we have the best family!" John wrote:

> What have I learned? First of all, be patient. I struggled with my sexuality for years before accepting it. It would be unreasonable to expect others to accept it overnight. Too many gay men, when coming out, want immediate acceptance and understanding from family and friends. We need to give them time to deal with the issue just as we needed time to deal with it ourselves. I think so many men have cut themselves off from family because they did not get immediate acceptance.

I remember the words of the mother of a gay man: "My son rarely calls home. I send him cards over the Internet, and when I get the notice that the cards have been opened, I know he is alive." And a woman who said of her lesbian sister: "I asked her why she wouldn't bring her partner to our family dinners. More than once we invited her to, but she wouldn't. She said, 'Oh, I'd never put her in a position to be judged by my family.' I said, 'But we love *you*, and we would love the person you love.' 'I never knew that,' she said."

I recall the story told me by Carol as we drove in her car to a women's conference. She had a gay brother, "Jack," who had all their adult life been vicious to her. "I was broken hearted. I tried everything I could to be nice to him, but he was mean all the time, condescending, wanted nothing to do with me. I was the good child, the peacemaker. Jack got AIDS and was in Hawaii at the end. We knew he was going to die soon. I hadn't seen him in three years or even talked to him. I called and asked him please, please, could I come over and see him. He refused. I begged. Finally he said, 'Carol, I can't see you. There were two people in my life who never judged me, who only loved me. You and grandmother. And I wouldn't let you. I can't face you now.' He cried. I cried. We both said I love you. I realize now that some of the barriers gay people sometimes put up are so they won't be hurt."

Of the hundreds of responses I received to *Goodbye, I Love You*, none pleased me more than stories of family reconciliation, usually initiated by the family, but sometimes by the gay member, such as this recent email:

> I don't know if I can ever resolve the past with the Church, but the love that flowed from your words made it clear to me that, not only could I, I had to resolve with my family.

I found myself moved at the words another gay friend, Frank Matheson, sent me. As chair of Equality Utah, he presided during the most pitched political battle in the organization's history, during which it had mobilized in an unprecedented way in an attempt to defeat the anti-marriage amendment. Giving the closing comments at the annual dinner in 2004, shortly before that vote was to occur, he said in part:

> "They drew a circle that left me out. I drew a circle that kept them in." Like many of you, I learned this little saying as a

child in Sunday School, long before we knew how many circles would be drawn and redrawn to leave us out.

But the power of that saying resides in the second part. And it forms the foundation of our campaign: a deeply held conviction of the basic goodness of the people of Utah . . . Republican and Democrat, Mormon and non-Mormon . . .

As we live our lives with dignity, transparency, generosity, and forgiveness, we change the landscape . . . I ask this: Draw your circle. Make it as expansive and inclusive as you can. With hope and love, draw your circle to let them in.

Ah, isn't that what Jesus said? *Bless them that curse you. Circle the wagons around those who circle you out.*

Nothing Could Stop Me from Flying to His Side

Sydna Freeman
Salt Lake City, Utah

April 8, 2005. A date forever etched in our memories. Saying it aloud still sends a jolt of emotion through me.

My husband Mike had the day off of work and planned to pick me up early from my job to go to a matinee. It was a beautiful day, and my husband and I both had a feeling that everything was right in the world. Our youngest son had just left the Missionary Training Center and had arrived safely at his destination; our oldest son was entrenched in his studies back east, working on his PhD; both of our other children were busy with work and studies and doing well. I had a sense of peace about life and the future.

Mike called me at about 2:00 p.m. with that tone in his voice that is reserved for communication of a death or some other tragedy. It took him a few moments to speak, and his pain hung in the silent air between us. Finally, choking on his words, he asked, "Do you want me to read the letter to you?" I knew instinctively what the letter was and from whom. My oldest son and I have always had a soul-deep connection, and suspecting intuitively that he might be gay, I had lain awake in the dark many nights, bargaining with God, "Please . . . anything but that." It was a shapeless, formless fear that I wrestled with. I didn't allow myself to move beyond that vague emotion to consider the implications for Max, and for all of us, if my suspicions were correct.

"Yes, read me the letter," I said.

"Dear Mom and Dad," he began, "I love you so much. You always told me that I could tell you anything, I hope that is true. As I'm sure you must already know, I am gay." And then the words, "I have left the Church, there is no place in it for me."

There, finally, a name for my fears. The Church. In all of my nighttime vigils, I had never considered how this would impact our family and our faith. It had never occurred to me that my wonderful son could be faced with a choice between his religion, which had been such an essential part of him throughout his life, and his need to express himself as a man who is, through no choice of his own, homosexual.

Mike came to pick me up at work, and we immediately fell into one another's arms and stood crying until we were able to make our way home. We called our twenty-two-year-old daughter at her apartment and asked her to come home. She responded fearfully, as there was no masking the emotion in my voice. I was able to reassure her that everyone was all right, that she just needed to come home.

I thought that because I had known on some level that Max might be gay, surely the rest of the family must have known it as well. This was not the case, and as we read the letter to our daughter, she responded as if to news of a death. Her grief filled the room; her wails frightened and pained us to the depths of our hearts. For parents, there is no anguish so great as witnessing the anguish of their child. We shared the letter with Max's younger brother as he returned home from work, and he accepted the news in a much calmer way, becoming a steadying force for all of us in those first hours of our new lives.

As we sat together in numbed pain, my husband and I knew that we must be with our son. That he lived on the other side of the country was of no consequence. We needed to put our arms around Max and tell him how much we love him, have always loved him, and that nothing could ever change that.

Mike and I called our bishop, and he agreed to meet with us immediately; our bishop was kind and gentle, although we quickly surmised that we would be left to find answers and guidance from God, which, after all, is as it should be in a family.

When we came out of the bishop's office, our daughter was waiting and told us that she had spoken with Max. She informed us that he did not want us to come to see him yet; in fact, we were absolutely not to come.

We spoke with Max repeatedly on the phone that evening and into the night. He became increasingly adamant that we not come; he wanted us to wait a few weeks, to let things settle a little bit first. We were unable to get a flight out that evening, and after a tortuous night, my husband had decided to respect Max's wishes and delay our visit.

Part of the reason that Max and I are as close as we are is because we are much alike in many ways, including our stubbornness. I announced to my husband that morning that I was going to Max. He could come with me or stay behind, but I was going. I needed to hold my son and remind him that he had a family, and that his family would never forsake him; that whatever life presented us, we would face it together. I brought him into the world and held him close as a baby. We had loved and nurtured our son through the adventures of life thus far, and it seemed preposterous not to go immediately to him now. Nothing could stop me from flying to his side.

We secured a flight that day and arrived late that night in Boston, leaving a message for Max on his answering machine that we were coming and asking that he meet us in the lobby of our hotel the next morning. We rose early and sat at a table overlooking the bay, long before the scheduled arrival time of our son. I never doubted that he would come. Despite Max's protestations, he is and ever has been a loving and gentle son.

The cab pulled up to the curb, and out stepped our beautiful son, his usually confident gait somewhat trepid. He looked around and took a seat next to the front desk. Unseen, we watched him for a few moments. To his parents, he looked like a child once again, full of apprehension but trying to look steely and brave.

Then we stepped forward, and the moment we embraced is forever imprinted in my mind. There is a love that can only be expressed in such a way. No email, no phone call, no letter can convey the love and emotion of an embrace. In that moment, I knew that whatever lay ahead, we would be all right. He is our son. He was the same that day as he had been the week previous. All that had changed was our level of honesty.

We stayed with Max for only a day or two, and they were very difficult days. Those first trembling steps toward under- standing often felt as though the ground underneath us had given way; but we were able to express our feelings and fears to one another in a way that we could never have done without be- ing together. We said things to one another that weekend that were painful, some of which I regret, many of which stemmed from a lack of understanding and information on our part. I have come to better understand the reasons that Max felt we should wait for emotions to calm before coming to be with him. Much of Max's resistance to our visit grew out of the difficulty he'd had in making the most critical decisions in his life, which he knew we would initially disagree with. We can only imagine how painful the years had been for him, trying to reconcile his faith, familial expectations, and his recognition that he is gay.

Despite the pain of that weekend, I believe it was the right thing to do, the only thing to do. Somehow the groundwork was laid in those first hours for the honest and open expression that leads to healing. In my mother's heart, I know that I would have regretted forever not having gone immediately to our son, to hold him and tell him that he is loved deeply, unconditionally, and always.

As we stayed in our son's apartment and slept in his bed, my husband and I felt his very being in everything around us. His bulletin board was covered completely with pictures of his family. The walls on every side were neatly stacked to the ceiling with books. His scriptures lay, well-worn and marked, at his headboard. We cried together when we found his bookmark in a heavily annotated Book of Job. We turned out the light and lay beneath the neon moon and stars on Max's ceiling, talking about our love for our beautiful son, for all of our beautiful children.

I wish I could say that we have since figured everything out, that we have found a clearly marked path for our family, but I now see the nobility of putting one foot decidedly in front of the other, day by day, and with God's help, making our way.

Your Tear in My Eye

Carol Lynn and
Ladd McClurg
Wheaton, Illinois

My diary tells me it was Monday, November 17, 1986. "Sister Pearson?" The voice was hesitant, apologetic. "I—I just got your book. I'm really sorry to bother you . . ."

"But you're the reason I wrote it! I'm so glad you called."

Soon the whole story poured out. Ladd was gay, in his early twenties, the son of a prominent Mormon family. "They can hardly speak to me anymore, and when they do it's mostly to call me again to repentance. They tell me I'm proud, I'm unwilling to sacrifice for Christ. I've heard that so often I begin to wonder if it's true. I want to be humble. I've been suicidal. Maybe that's the answer."

"No, Ladd. No, that is never the answer."

"My father told me, 'You're dead to me. I know we won't have a relationship in the next world. You're lost for eternity.'"

"And your mother?"

"She says 'Homosexuality is an abomination in God's sight and in my sight.' That's all she will say on it. They're certain if I just made up my mind to be normal, I could be."

"I'm so sorry, Ladd."

"All I want to do is to make a positive contribution. I want to be seen as a human being with dignity. I have thought, if only

I could talk to somebody and just tell them how much I am hurting." He started to cry.

"Listen to me, Ladd. I can tell that you are a beautiful person and that you have a lot to contribute. Oh, Ladd. I wish I could hug you. What are you doing for Thanksgiving? Why don't you drive up and spend the weekend here with me and my children. You should not be alone."

"You want me to come—for Thanksgiving? Really?"

"Please. We would love to have you."

"It's hard for me to be around people. I don't know . . . I'd better go now."

"Think about it, Ladd. Please call me again. Promise me that you'll call again."

He drove in Wednesday evening. I had told him I would position two lovely blond girls out front as a welcoming committee, one eighteen and one eleven. Sure enough, just before dark, Emily and Katy hauled in a slight, smiling, embarrassed young man. "Here he is, Mom," Katy giggled.

"Ah, my friend Ladd!" I hugged him and he would hardly let go.

The kids were great to him, made him play Scrabble, made him eat more pie because he was too thin, made him laugh at stupid kid jokes. And we talked, Ladd and I, for hours. Would I ever get used to the pain of these stories?

Ladd grew up in Provo, Utah. He was aware of his homosexual feelings from a very early age, but they were very carefully hidden. His father was a bishop, and when Ladd was about twelve he read some of the literature in his father's office about homosexuals and how they were to be referred for shock therapy. He was certain that if he mentioned his feelings he would be "sent to the shocks," so he spoke to no one. And his body created a very interesting adaptation. Every time he had any sexual feelings, his body turned them into a seizure. His parents were alarmed and sent him to doctor after doctor. Serious depression set in, and no one could understand or help.

"One doctor thought I might just stop breathing. He told my parents to come in and check on me several times during the night to make certain I was still breathing. I started college, but I was suspended for failing all my classes. I was absolutely nonfunctional. Went on a mission, though, and it was some bad and some good. I came to love the Book of Mormon, and I try to live my life by it. After I got home, I knew if I tried to stay in the Church I would die, so I had my name taken off the records. When I told my parents what I had done and why—told them finally what I had never been able to say before, that their son was a homosexual—they were heartbroken. They disinherited me."

His sister had asked him to come for Christmas, but two weeks ago she had called and revoked her invitation. She had two little boys and said, "We don't know yet how people become homosexuals, and I just can't risk my boys being around one."

The last day Ladd was here, a strange and wonderful thing happened. I had taken him with me to pick up Katy at the horse stable. After we came back, I was fixing supper and he was sitting on a stool across the kitchen bar from me, drawing in his sketch pad for his art class, drawing my face from the picture on the back of *Goodbye, I Love You.*

"It was not easy for me to be with the horses today, Carol Lynn," he said.

"How's that?"

"They're so *alive*. There's this pull that goes on in me all the time. Part of me wants to go with the living, lively things, to just be, allow myself to live. Another part of me says I cannot live, am not worthy to live, must die. It was hard to get that close to the horses. I'm envious of horses. They're just allowed to be. People have more respect for the sexuality of horses than they have for my sexuality."

Sobs stopped his words, and he dropped his head onto his drawing pad. I walked over behind him and put my arms around him. For minutes I just held him while he cried. Then he raised his head and said, "Look!"

I glanced at the picture of me he had been drawing.

"Look! My tear—is in your eye!"

One of Ladd's tears had dropped on the paper directly onto my eye and was running down my cheek.

The next morning he left very early. We had said our goodbyes the night before. I found the picture on the kitchen counter, with this note: "There is only a smudge of a tear left there. Maybe with more love, tears can be wiped from the eyes of others also. How can I ever repay your love? God bless you all. L."

The thank-you that I treasured most was written on the Christmas card we received from him a few weeks later: "Thank you for living according to the covenant you made at baptism, found in Mosiah 18:8-10 [in the Book of Mormon], "To bear one another's burdens, that they may be light . . . to mourn with those that mourn . . . and comfort those that stand in need of comfort."

⁓

Ladd's journey continued to be a difficult one. In a letter the following March, he wrote:

When you have no one to love, life doesn't seem to have much meaning. I have one good friend now, but I still need a buddy, a mate, a companion. I'll tell you, it's not easy meeting people. I have yet to find a place where appropriate and good friends can be met. . . . Promiscuity is not where it's at, nor is compromising one's standards in the hope that something might work out.

The following September, a letter from Ladd came from a hospital, where he was being treated for severe depression after a complete breakdown and where he had made an attempt to commit suicide by electrocution. But it also held some good news.

I think things are going better with my parents. I'm realizing what I've always suspected: that is, once I change my attitude and approach to the relationship, things will get better. It is all too easy to project the homophobia I still hold onto my parents. I need not make them responsible for my homophobia as well as theirs. . . . I honestly believe there is something godly to be born out of this suffering as I see it through.

The following Thanksgiving Ladd was with us again, and again we had a warm and happy time together. In his thank-you letter, Ladd wrote:

I made a Christmas wish this year, a quiet prayer to God, that I would be granted the capacity to go one day without bitterness and angry feelings. Two days before Christmas, I was driving home along the Pacific Coast Highway when suddenly I realized it had been granted. I had gone through the day quietly singing within my heart, "Let there be peace on earth, and let it begin with me." I realized I had been able to forgive. The bitterness I felt toward my family is gone. Tears were flowing freely down my face, and I sang aloud in perfect peace the words of the song. Oh, the joy that I felt and feel.

And a few months later:

I think things are on the mend with my parents. . . . I wrote them a nice letter shortly after Christmas, and I think I may have found the words and the timing to touch their hearts in a positive way. I told them I felt their situation was much like Tevye's in *Fiddler on the Roof*, in that because of their tradition they had no "other hand." It seemed to have made a difference. They asked me to be patient with them. I will be.

I find myself deeply moved as I copy Ladd's words today. What a wise and good young man. In so many ways his parents had taught him well. Still, he was Tevye's youngest daughter Chava, whose choice in a partner was one who was forbidden, and he had brought into his parents' life a crisis bigger than they had ever known. Truly, from all they had been taught—on the one hand, homosexuality is a very grave sin; on the other hand . . . There is no other hand!

In the original story, Tevye never again speaks to his beloved Chava. In the musical version, however, Tevye ultimately shows a quiet good wish to his daughter. The audience needs to see at least that much softening. We want so much in our stories for love to conquer prejudice. And as we watch the story of Ladd and his parents played out on the stage of our mind, we want to see a joyful embrace before the curtain comes down. For we have come to love him. And we have come to understand the heartbreak of parents whose faith and tradition divide them from a dearest child.

I cannot tell you exactly how Ladd's story ends. I lost track of him years ago. The last couple of letters I sent came back "unknown at this address." And so I write my own good ending to his story. In his final letter, he seemed tentatively hopeful:

> I'm going to Utah for Memorial Day. I am going to stay with my parents a couple of nights. I am somewhat anxious about it. . . .
> My dad and I plan to go horseback riding. He bought a horse

this last year and has access to another one I can use, so we are
going to go riding in the hills together.

The horses that Ladd had envied so. I like to think of him
on that horse, riding that "living, lively thing," riding beside his
father. Both of them choosing life.

～

The end, I thought. But then, a few weeks after finishing
Ladd's story, it occurred to me: Google! Why hadn't I thought to
do an Internet search? Wait, what if the next chapters were not
happy ones? I typed his name into the browser—Ladd McClurg
—and there he was!

Ladd insists that I use his real name in the rest of his story,
braided together from emails and phone calls:

> Thank you so much for keeping that accurate record when I
> could not! Carol Lynn, my story is many years more struggle
> to find compassion and love for myself. I still endure long-term
> clinical depression, but now my heart is at peace.
>
> Quick update. We're celebrating the 11th anniversary of our
> wedding with the Quakers on March 25. Brad and I have been
> together 16 years now. He is doing marvelous HIV work and
> has been recognized by the UN as a world leader in the preven-
> tion of AIDS. I sell professional liability insurance to attorneys
> (a perverse joy in my life). It is actually kind of fun.
>
> Things with my parents have become remarkably warm and
> friendly. That early story still needs to be told. However, my
> parents and I are *not* the same people now that we were then.
> That was a snapshot in time, and I know they did the best they
> could with an impossibly huge challenge, as did I. We have
> had years together to learn and love and progress. I asked my
> dad not long ago why he has become so warm toward me, and
> he quickly said, "Well, it's because of my religion, especially

the Article of Faith that says, 'We claim the privilege of worshiping Almighty God according to the dictates of our own conscience, and allow all men the same privilege.' You have the right to act from your own conscience, and I respect that."

Brad and I visit them in their home in California, and they stay in our home here in Illinois. We took them on a trip to Nauvoo not long before the new temple opened. They've even entertained Brad when he had to make a trip to California without me. When my mother asked me, "Ladd, who does most of the cooking in your family?"—I thought, *bless her*, she sees that we are a family, albeit not the family she would still like me to have; yet I know that she loves us. My sister, who disinvited me long ago, now invites me frequently and is very good to Brad and me. My brothers are friendly, too. When I speak now to gay people whose families still don't talk to them, I say, *"Never give up.* Good things can happen. Be patient."

And yes, Dad and I went horseback riding. We still may on occasion. "Tevye" and his "Chava" are family again. Peace, love, compassion, and integrity prevail. Though worlds fall away, I know we can rest in our divine nature. All is well.

You Don't Know Him

Carol Lynn about
Lowell Bennion

Lowell Bennion, one of the best known and most loved teachers and humanitarians in Mormondom, said:

> I'm willing to walk by faith in darkness . . . but the problem comes . . . when I'm called upon to do something that goes against . . . the spirit that I am accustomed to hearkening unto, when it's also against what I think is the very heart and soul of the gospel of Jesus Christ and of theology.

That sentiment was spoken during the time his church withheld priesthood privileges from black men, but it emerged again in his life when his son Howard told him he was a homosexual man. Howard had made two previous efforts to follow the traditional path of young Mormon men in missionary service but couldn't do it. Finally, on the third try, after his mother had purchased missionary clothing and scriptures for him, he told the bishop he just couldn't go, that he finally had accepted the fact that he was a homosexual. At the urging of his bishop, Howard then told his father. Lowell's biographer, Mary Bradford, says that the news "caused Lowell to burst into tears. 'I've never seen him cry like that,' said Howard. 'Not before, not since. It just crushed him.'"

This was an issue that very few families in the 1960s and 1970s were prepared to deal with, but Lowell and his wife Merle, orthodox Mormons though they were, refused to let this come between them and their son. They learned all they could about homosexuality, concluding that it was an inborn trait. They stayed close to their son through long depression and through a suicide attempt, urged him to work toward an RN degree, and invited him and his partner to build a home on their property.

After Howard had been "living quietly with a partner for several years, not attending church, not calling attention to himself in ward or community," the bishop and stake president in his area convened a church court to review his worthiness to remain a member of the Church.

Howard recalled that he was "profoundly touched when his father called with the words, 'I want to testify. Will you pick me up?'" During the court proceedings at which Howard was excommunicated, he found himself moved to tears when he heard his father speak in his defense, saying, "How can you judge this young man? You don't know him."

At the end of Lowell Bennion's life, his relationship with his son was still loving and strong. Howard nursed his father in his last days and was present at his death.

The Story She Couldn't Tell

"Melissa Johnson"

Our youngest daughter, Diane, had come home for the summer. She had been attending school at Ricks College in Idaho after serving a successful mission in South America. In our neighborhood, she was best known for the stories she could tell and the smiles she could bring to the faces of children and adults alike. Diane gathered awards and won countless competitions in speech and drama. But more importantly, she loved to share her stories at family gatherings or at parties for friends or neighbors. When she taught Primary, her class loved to sit in a circle, long after the time to go, and beg to hear another story. It was her gift, I think, one that helped her cope through many years of isolation and pain and, ironically, one that kept much of her inner beauty hidden from everyone, including her family.

There was one story that Diane couldn't tell, not for many years. It was a true story. One about a frightened girl with feelings that she couldn't understand and, for much of her life, couldn't accept. It was a story about shame and wanting to shrink from the rest of the world because she was a lesbian. But rather than tell this story, Diane escaped into the make-believe lands where everything would always have a happy ending.

In looking back now, it all made sense. The struggles with depression, all the emotional highs and lows, and the ultimate silence. Diane used to leave an audience crying with laughter,

143

then quietly shut herself in her room to do a different type of crying. I've listened to her sob in an almost silent manner so that no one would know. And when I would ask what the matter was, she would simply breathe in and place a practiced smile on her face just like it was a Band-Aid. And she would say, "Oh Mom, it's nothing . . ." I asked her once if she was having boy problems, and without looking at me she whispered, "I guess that's what it is."

Before she left for college, Diane had been dating Nathan, a fellow who lived in our ward and was the son of our current bishop. He continued to try to work something out with Diane even after several displays of disinterest on her part.

When Nathan learned that Diane was coming back for the summer, he was knocking on our door the day she returned. That weekend they had a date, and when Diane returned I could tell that something was terribly wrong.

"How was your date?" I asked, already knowing the answer.

Diane walked past me, head down, as if she didn't even hear me. Then suddenly she turned, and the tears started flowing. My little girl seemed to crumble right in front of me, and all I could do was hold her. We sat on the floor, and she wept. It must have taken every ounce of effort for Diane to finally start talking. With a heartbroken laugh, she said she had a story to tell me. And she wanted me to just hear it all until the end without saying anything. And so I listened. It was a story I never expected to hear. This one was real. This one was filled with raw emotion and told with real pain. I tried not to let my own judgments cloud my capacity to love and just listen as Diane explained her struggles to accept herself as a lesbian. She had tried to explain the situation to Nathan, but he turned a deaf ear before she could say the words. Telling me must have helped because she seemed to be comforted in explaining it all. She asked me not to tell Wayne, her father, because she was afraid he would react like Nathan had and become cold and silent. I promised to say nothing.

After seeing Diane to her room, I stepped outside and went for a long walk, and there did my own crying. I had never before had to face even the possibility that one of my children might be gay. Even after Diane's explanation, I was still so unsure as to what it all meant. But I was sure of one thing: that regardless of how much time it took to understand my daughter, it should take no time at all to show her that I still loved her. That was certain.

That Sunday, I invited Diane to attend church with her father and me. Many of the young men and women Diane had taught knew that she was home and were so hoping that she would be at church so they could say hello. A lot of people would be happy to see her, and I felt like she would be comforted by their fellowship. She seemed reluctant but agreed. She was concerned that Nathan would be there and seeing him would be awkward. Unfortunately, her concerns were more than realized.

After the meetings, Wayne, Diane, and I were standing near the front entrance. Diane started to stiffen up, and the color faded from her face. Some young men were approaching us from one of the connecting halls just around the corner. They were speaking in Spanish. I couldn't understand the language, but Diane could, and one of the voices was Nathan's. And then I heard it, a single word, spoken from his mouth, in English and punctuated with prejudice. The word "dyke" echoed in my ears as laughter followed. Diane bolted from the church, almost as if she had been slapped from where she was standing and thrown outside by the force. She was reeling as she raced for the car.

Wayne turned with lightning speed and hurried after her.

Just then Nathan and his friends turned the corner. He surmised what had happened, and his face reddened. Our eyes connected and communicated volumes.

"I'm so sorry," he said.

I fought back a burst of anger. "Diane needs to know that."

Nathan began to venture outside, but I stopped him. "It might be best if you waited a bit," I said. As I looked through the church doors, I could see Wayne and Diane sitting together in the car. Nathan nodded and, with great embarrassment, walked away; his friends followed.

I meant to join my family right then, but I believe the Spirit kept me still. Instead of leaving the chapel, I stood inside and, through tear-filled eyes, watched a miracle unfold.

Wayne had his arm around Diane. He was listening to her. Between sobs, she was telling him something, and I knew that she was telling him the same story she told me. It was like watching a silent movie. I was already familiar with the plot. They hugged and held each other for a long time. It seemed like eternities. Warm and wonderful eternities.

That day was a turning point for our family. After years of seeing our daughter withdraw, that day we came closer together than we had ever been. Wayne had witnessed the harsh effects of careless and even mean-spirited words. He also saw how honesty and compassion could soften his own heart.

Neither Wayne nor I have formed a satisfactory opinion concerning homosexuality at this point. We still struggle to simply talk about it. But with Diane's help, we are able to let the story unfold and tackle one chapter at a time. We're not sure how this story will end, but the Spirit seems to tell me that somehow the ending will be a happy one.

Healing at Christmas

Joe Dallin
Honolulu, Hawaii

It was December 22, 3:00 a.m., in Utah. I wondered what time it was here, hovering over the Pacific Ocean, hundreds of miles away from anything. I was on route from my home in Honolulu to be with my family at Christmas. Years had passed since I'd spent the holiday with them, and 3,000 miles of geographical distance wasn't the only reason why.

I shifted in my seat again, trying to get some sleep over the drone of the plane's engines and the constant shuffling of the passenger next to me. A million thoughts agitated my restless mind. Any time I returned home, I faced some anxiety, but anticipating the additional religious fervor that comes with the Christmas season increased that apprehension to a slightly higher level. Still, I hoped that somehow this visit would help dispel some of the awkwardness that had tainted our relationship since I left the fold six years earlier. Heading east at 600 miles per hour, I was on my way to again face the challenge of negotiating the fine line of authenticity to myself while maintaining courtesy towards my family's religious sensitivities.

Somehow I managed a couple hours of sleep. "Would you like a splash more?" the flight attendant asked, holding up a coffee pot. I nodded, thanked her, and sipped the brew, feeling the subtle gravitational shift as the plane began to descend towards Salt Lake City.

I willed the caffeine into my bloodstream to combat the lethargy of sleep deprivation. Self-conscious, I worried that my zombie-like state would jeopardize the appearance of happiness that I legitimately felt and hoped to exhibit to my family. I wanted my cheerful countenance to both soothe their concerns about me and show them that I was succeeding at finding happiness on my own two feet.

I disembarked and walked to the bathroom to splash cold water on my bleary-eyed face. Blinking the sleep out of my eyes, I smoothed my hair down with wetted palms. I continued to baggage claim, where I knew they'd be waiting. *Maybe they're as nervous as I am*, I thought to myself.

Despite my complicated anxieties, I felt a spontaneous thrill in my heart when I spotted my parents and younger brother standing next to the carousel labeled with my flight number.

"Joseph!" my mom sang, taking her turn first to welcome me with a hug. Actually, I was surprised at how comfortable they seemed when greeting me. After all, my dad and I had hardly had any exchange in years. A few months before, I had revealed the hot-button issue to my brother in a letter—a letter that he had destroyed in a paper shredder after a fit of tears. My mom had been upset that I'd written it. She thought I had overstepped my bounds, that she and my dad should have determined the best time for the 16-year-old to find out about the family's skeleton in the closet.

But now, as they helped me with my luggage, it almost felt as if none of that had happened. My mom wrapped a heavy parka around my shoulders as we walked out of the airport doors into temperatures hovering in the teens. They all teased me with joking sympathies as my body, accustomed to tropical balminess, shivered in the Rocky Mountain winter weather. Yes, I was cold, but my heart was warmed by the welcome.

Still, a pesky trained response in me held cautious reservation between us.

Christmas was enchanting. As with each holiday season, family and friends seemed extra cordial and content. Smiles appeared more sincere, and I felt even more welcomed home than normal. The sounds of kids playing—my young nieces and nephews—brought a magic back into the home that only children can generate. We watched movies, cheated at board games, and laughed hysterically at the table. We drank way too much hot chocolate and ate extra helpings of Mom's apple pie. Though things had changed in the household, it was like I was living some kind of modern reminiscence of holiday memories I'd cherished from years past. The awkwardness that had thickly prevailed over the last few years seemed to have faded under a renewed sense of family. I was very happy I had come. Some tension still lingered, some subjects remained unspoken, but the love in the home was generous and endearing.

The day after Christmas, the festive energy wound down as the holiday commotion softly died into the winter and the new year looming just days away. I also felt my departure approaching—I'd be leaving for Hawaii again the next day.

In the family room, I settled into an armchair to watch the ten o'clock news. When my dad came in and took a seat on the other sofa, I smiled at him, feeling contented that we had spent more cordial time together. There was no mistaking it, I thought, things were softening between us.

Still, a part of me desperately wanted to turn off the TV, pull up a chair right in front of his knees, and insist, "We need to talk!" Such confronting tactics had failed miserably in the past, however. Instead, I took a breath, just reminding myself to give him time—to give our healing relationship time—to move ahead at its own pace. As the Fates would have it, we were about to take a big step forward anyway.

It just so happened that Larry King had interviewed Gordon B. Hinckley, the current Mormon prophet, on his talk show that day. Naturally, in Utah, this was a newsworthy event and clips from the dialogue were shown.

I watched the segment apathetically, knowing that my dad, in contrast, was hanging on every word spoken by his prophet. Probably, I thought, he was also silently praying that the inspired words being broadcast were stirring in me some dormant Mormon sentiments.

I can't say that I remember anything of the interview until Larry King began asking President Hinckley, almost in passing, about gay marriage. My interest sharply rose. Expectedly, the Mormon leader reemphasized the established church position opposing same-sex unions, while insisting that the Church wasn't actually anti-gay. Normally I would have just rolled my eyes. But watching this next to my dad made my heart race. My gaze was on the TV, but my focus was on him. I began to wonder what he would do or say, if anything. In any case, one could have heard a pin drop on the green carpet of that room.

Larry King went on to ask if Hinckley thought that people were born gay. His answer probably surprised my dad as much as me. "I don't know," he admitted, "I'm not an expert on these things . . ."

My mind went spinning. Part of me actually felt excited by Hinckley's confession of uncertainty on the issue. Maybe this could be a small step forward? An implicit token of understanding? A softening of what had been such a rigidly insensitive position? On the other hand, I couldn't dismiss the contradiction in the statement. After all, past church leaders had declared, unequivocally, that nobody is born gay, that it is simply a wicked choice, end of story. Now, according to "God's mouthpiece," it didn't sound so clear-cut. My mind reeled a bit from the inconsistency of church dogma. But what dominated my thoughts was *what could my dad be thinking of all of this?*

When the news clip was over, my dad hit the mute button and began to speak. A true devotee, he expressed his undying respect for his leader and noted the prophet's spryness at such an advanced age. "He's a great man, isn't he?" I did my best to accommodate his respect. I wanted to talk about what had been said about *my* situation—*our* situation, really. It was the elephant in the room, but after such a history of discord with my dad on the issue, I didn't feel entitled to bring it up. Luckily, he did.

"It was interesting what he said, too, you know, about the gay thing." My eyes must have widened to the diameter of teacups. I sat full up. He continued, "I don't think we really know much about it, and President Hinckley just said that." This was the first time in six years my dad had discussed *The Issue*. I was definitely ready to talk. As if by instinct, however, my mind couldn't help jumping back six years, reflecting on a very different discussion we'd had on the subject.

～

"I don't want you in my home, and I don't want you around my children," he says in a moment of fury, after finding out that I've begun a relationship with another man. The way he sees it, the phase of homosexual temptation is over; the lifestyle of a gay man has begun. Bucking at defeat, my dad is shaken by the irrevocability of that step.

I wonder how, through pursed lips and gritted teeth, he can even speak. "You selfish little shit. I would never do this to my parents." There is no attempt made to hide the revulsion in his voice. Face reddened in utter frustration, he goes on, "Everything I've done for you has been a waste. I baptized you, confirmed you, ordained you to the priesthood, and you're just throwing that all away." He reels. "We've done a terrible job as parents."

Tempers are flaring, that is obvious. Assessing the seriousness of his resolve, I ask if I'm fired from my job, in which he is the employer. His angry, icy blue eyes answer before his voice does. "Absolutely."

I am stunned.

"So, what," I prod, "do you want me to just move to some other state so you'll never have to see me again?"

His terse response once more is, "Absolutely."

That *really* jars me. I sit down, shaking my head in complete disbelief. My dad, the man with whom I'd been so wonderfully close all my life; my hero who had taught me to hunt and fish and live my life with integrity, is now disavowing me for acknowledging my very nature. It was the nightmarish family disaster scenario that I thought could never happen to me.

I look up from the floor and into his eyes, feeling hurt and angry, yet sober and empowered. Something inside me calms down. Somehow, I know I'll be all right. A hidden force finds its way to my lips: "I honestly hope that you and your family have a good life. I'll always love you."

There is nothing more to say. We feel crushed by what has already been said. Breaking his hardliner position, my dad hugs me with tears burning his eyes. "Oh, Joseph . . ." He weeps. He turns around and walks away. I am completely bewildered by what has just happened, almost as though it had been an obscure movie I'd seen somewhere. It feels like my heart has completely shattered, but a thousand miles away. One last thing steals my breath and turns my world just a bit more upside down—I see that man of so much strength walk away with a vanquished, feeble gait. His tenuous steps betray his despair. My eyes are glued to his back as he climbs in his car and slowly drives away. I literally have no idea if I'll ever see him again.

~

Now here we were, addressing the six-year-old wound that had never healed. "I know that you never chose to be gay," my dad said, in the familiar, compassionate tone under which I had been reared. "And I want to apologize for calling you selfish, Joseph. You're not selfish." Somehow, I let this monumental statement sink in. Never had I imagined or even dared hope that I would hear what I was now hearing. I'd thought that maybe time would gradually heal these old wounds, but this—this was miraculous. My thinking mind whirred with disbelief, but my heart seemed to settle into what the Fates had lined up as gracious destiny.

He stopped talking, and it felt like my turn to say something. Stammering, I apologized for how I had acted when I had come out. "I'm sorry I forced everything on you all at once, Dad. I know I was insensitive and impatient . . ." He responded to my apology with a deferential shrug, as though it were unnecessary.

He continued, "I've come to realize that, above all, my religion teaches charity. I know the most important thing we can do is love." I could hardly do anything but grin and nod my head. The goose bumps on my arms confirmed that I felt exactly the same way. He went on, "I was talking to my brother the other day, and I told him that you'll probably do more good in the world than I ever will."

"Oh, but Dad, you've done so much with the youth, you've changed the lives of so many people." (My dad seemed perennially appointed to leadership with the young men of the congregation, an assignment he was good at and clearly enjoyed.) "When I was in Scouts, you were the leader the other kids looked up to the most." He smiled, surely knowing that it was true, but too modest to acknowledge it. It felt good to verbalize our respect for each other.

"I'm just glad that all of this hasn't destroyed our relationship," he said. "I'm thankful that our family has gotten through it." With satisfaction, I nodded in agreement. All of the negativity that had festered and made our relationship so awkward over the last few years was now being replaced with respect and love.

With that love enlivening our hearts and snow falling softly outside in celebration, we hugged and then retired for the night. I rested soundly, knowing that things were getting better. The single largest source of discontent in my life was now healing. It was funny—a week before I wouldn't have thought we'd ever get this far. That Christmas we leapt over a chasm of misunderstanding and began working, anew, on a relationship already bonded by blood.

Family turmoil is so painful because it hits us at the root. Our relations are, quite literally, who we are, and family conflict feels remarkably like inner conflict. Sometimes we simply have to live the best we can with the discord we've been dealt, but healing is a sweet blessing when it comes. The catch: true healing can only be born of authenticity, and honesty can be scalding. Though diplomacy is important in sharing one's truth, it can't serve as a substitute. Such was the case with my parents and me. I certainly fell short on tactfulness with them; after all, as their child, I had naturally wanted them to understand me completely and immediately. But I felt, and I feel, no regret for revealing to them the fundamental facts of my life.

In a recent letter, my mom told me: "We've come a long way over a rough road, but I know I'm a better person for having traveled it." Just yesterday my dad said: "I'm a better person because of you!" How grateful I am to be returning the favor.

Importance of "The One"

A Grateful Mother
Utah

It's been a year since our deeply loved son revealed to us that he is homosexual and consequently leaving the LDS Church. He had not been inside a Mormon chapel since his disclosure to us, continuing to have feelings of anger and hurt regarding the Church. We pray that in time he will be able to make peace with the church he once loved, which he always served more than faithfully and for which he served a praiseworthy mission. The year has been difficult for us, full of questions and fear, but ultimately it comes back to love, the kind that binds families together through life's journey and beyond.

Our beautiful daughter left on an eighteen-month mission for the Church last week, and we were deeply touched by the love our son showed for his sister by returning home to spend that special time with her and our family. As parents, we were moved by his willingness to attend the sacrament meeting at which his sister would speak and say her farewells to loved ones.

How difficult it must have been for him to return to the ward he had grown up in, to return to the people he loves and who have always loved him, wondering who among them knew, and who remained unaware of his life changes. Certainly he anticipated the usual innocently offered questions to an unmarried LDS man in his mid-twenties, such as the standard "Found a girl yet?" But he could not possibly have anticipated the challenge that emerged.

The Saturday evening before our daughter's talk at church, we were enjoying time with extended family when someone mentioned "the letter" which was to be read at every LDS sacrament meeting the following day, the letter reaffirming the Church's opposition to same-sex marriage and asking members to contact their senators regarding a proposed amendment to the Constitution on this issue.

My son looked ashen, then said to me, "Mom, I don't know if I can do it. I don't know if I can sit there and listen to that."

I am sure that he would have attended despite the letter, out of devotion to his sister and family, but the day would be marred, not just for him, but for his family as well.

Any mother understands the feelings that this mother had at that time, the fierce instinct to protect my child. What could I do? I saw only one option: calling our bishop and asking for his help. I sent the family off to rent movies so that I would have time alone to pray and to steel myself to make that phone call. I love our bishop. He has been a kind and understanding support to us throughout this year.

After pleading with the Lord to help me, I found myself sobbing as I dialed our bishop's number and told him the distressing situation our family found itself in. I was amazed and moved as he responded without the slightest pause or hesitation, "I don't want you to worry about this one more moment. I will take care of it. The letter will not be read." I told him that I realized that this was a huge thing to do in deference to just one person, just one family. "The One," he said, "is always important." I continued to cry, but now out of gratitude.

The following day and the time we spent together that week were wonderful days, filled with joy and laughter. Nothing marred our family unity, at home or at church. I will always remember the beautiful lesson our bishop taught us by example, that genuine love and charity are always the answer—indeed the very message and mission of our Savior's life.

This Story Has Taken a Wrong Turn

Carol Lynn and
Darl Mangelson
Chicago, Illinois

When I was still Miss Wright and not yet Sister Pearson, during my one year of teaching at Snow College in Ephraim, Utah, I offered children's "creative dramatics" classes after school. No script. Give the kids a character and a situation and a goal, and let them have at it. I would step in if the action took a wrong turn and narrate a new direction.

Darl Mangelson was my favorite, eleven years old, gangly, smart, eager. I chose him to play the part of Petruchio in a short, improvised version of Shakespeare's *The Taming of the Shrew*, which we gave as a sort of performance for the parents at the end of the session. Standing there in a crazy costume from our box of odd pieces of fabric, with a pudgy, nine year-old Katherine in an armlock, Petruchio would have said something like: "So there, Kate my love, you wench you, I guess I showed you who's boss, huh?" Such fun we had.

As with many Mormon gay men of my acquaintance, Darl has popped up in my life now and then, and I tracked him down recently to see how he's doing. During a wonderful hour-and-a-half conversation, Darl told me he had written something of a "second coming out" piece that brought an "almost shocking new sense of identity." I asked him to send it to me.

~

December 1, 2004

Last week, here in Chicago, I went out for breakfast with a friend who teaches piano to gifted children. In the restaurant, we waited for a table in a big crowd. Like everyone else, we were visiting and enjoying the morning. A man came to pay at the register and suddenly called out, "For this cause shall a man leave father and mother, and shall cleave to his wife: and they twain shall be one flesh . . ." Everything got quiet. The crowd looked at him. I realized he was looking at us—that we were being singled out for public humiliation by someone who felt empowered to rebuke us for the way he judged we conducted our lives. I started shaking and reacted from pure instinct. I told him I was sorry, I hadn't heard him, and could he please repeat what he'd said. He spit the scripture out again. I said, "Are you all right, sir? It seems like you need to talk. Are you ill? Can we help you?" He said he was just fine, and he left. He wore a photo ID from the national Moody Bible Institute across the street.

I had to work the whole day to overcome the kind of hurt and anger that can poison the spirit. I wasn't being socially inappropriate or criminal. But sometimes I'm exuberant in ways that our society considers feminine. For my own survival, I've learned to guard my public demeanor. And I'm lucky to live in Chicago. People like me know that metropolitan areas are where mutual respect can be highest. In many rural parts of America, our lives could be in jeopardy. But we are seeing things change even in cities. On the street here, a stranger called me "faggot." That hasn't happened in years. A couple of months ago, a man with a microphone and portable amp-speaker was preaching gospel on the street. When I walked by, he said: "There's no gays in heaven . . . there's no homosexuals in heaven . . ."

I remember being a child standing by a white fridge in an Ephraim kitchen. My mother stood by—I was no taller than her waist—she was coaching me on pronouncing my problematic "S." Later I learned it was called a lisp. She was helping me to survive in the world. A little boy with a lisp is funny. When he gets older, it isn't funny anymore.

When Ray and I were in the first of our 23 years together, we were walking one afternoon to the grocery store. Maybe we weren't walking far enough apart. Was there an air of domesticity between us? I'm not sure. But two big guys came at us. One of them smashed my face with his fist and knocked me to the ground unconscious, then ran off. I didn't suffer much—my mind blocked it out. But Ray bore the brunt of it. He had to witness it and then carry the memory of someone he loved being attacked. One night we woke to horrible screams in the street. Police came, but a soft-spoken fellow had been beaten with a steel pipe. We saw him sometimes in the neighborhood—lots of scars and permanent physical damage. It was a gay hate crime.

I spent the years of my childhood living with physical and verbal abuse at school and being the constant butt of jokes. I was always called the most terrible names a boy can be called. I was a girl, a sissy. When the bell rang to end an English class in 10th grade, a kid stood up and yelled, "Darl is a homosexual!" That raw, clinical slur traumatized me beyond words. Years later he made an oblique attempt to apologize, but such things began in my earliest years and continued when puberty brought me into religious battery.

In junior high, a couple of bullies found out the Mangelson "girl" could pin them to the ground. But a fairy is really no match for the whole school, year after year. In high school a fight could mean broken noses or knocked out teeth. I couldn't do it. But I had my weapons. Queers survive with their wits and intelligence.

My memories begin at three years old. There was never a time when I did not perceive the world around me in wonderful ways that were at once both male and female. During the years of innocence, children can only be purely who they are. But I remember those very specific moments (long before the proverbial age of eight) when it was made clear that my being was not good. It was passed to me that it was bad to play "dress-up," bad to want a doll for Christmas, bad to be bored with sports. It's a terrible thing for a child to grow up with such burdens and then, as an adolescent in church, to be made to think that blossoming feelings are filthy.

Spiritual and mental health means forgiving these things and letting them go. Most often my forgiveness feels complete. But sometimes it seems only ragged. The hardest part of forgiving is knowing how many children and young people, at this very moment, are being taught that their cores are dirty and weak. Luckily, most of them survive with the mental health to find their way in the world. Like anyone else, they can learn the lessons that the selfish use of their bodies doesn't equate with happiness. Adversity can make them unusually sensitive to others' feelings. Gay people are and always have been peacemakers. Right living can bring them inner strength.

But we millions of gay citizens are living again in an atmosphere of hatred we haven't felt since our schoolyard days. September 11 traumatized the country and outraged Christian fundamentalists who, in the absence of seeing justice for other fundamentalists who attacked them, are blaming their nation's immorality on their easiest target: gay people. That means me. Jerry Falwell said that September 11 was punishment for our nation's homosexuality.

Large numbers of Christian churches clustered this year in an unloving political campaign against me and my community. It's hard for me to imagine the face of Jesus on the shoulders of Falwell and others who preach hate. Would their words flow from Jesus' lips? I'm the target of such bigotry. These words are fuel for those who call me "faggot." These words are the kind of life-long poison that brought me once within two breaths of suicide.

When a gay person comes out, they've been through a time of deep suffering and soul-searching that few can understand. At this point they are usually cast from their churches. Often their families disown them. In the mid-1970s I came out to my family as a gay person. I decided I wouldn't give up on them, and I wouldn't give them a chance to reject me. I made the sincere effort and hoped my integrity would speak for itself. They made their sincere efforts, too.

But in the restaurant last week, words of scripture were abused to humiliate me. It turned out to be a life's moment of critical mass. I spent the next few days waking up as a changed person with a new consciousness and different priorities. This person has nothing to prove. He knows the campaign against him is not driven by a gentle Christian spirit. He knows that the ills of nation and family are shared equally by *all* citizens. He's grateful for those around him who know his soul is whole and good.

Last month, however, many of his American brothers and sisters made the choice to vote for legislation that would legally shut him out from the rights that any good human being deserves. Some of them chose their national government based on its promise to enact specific discrimination against him by changing the United States Constitution. Their actions empower those who would hate him for hate's sake. Their actions give strength to those who claim his life is evil. Their actions give confidence to the one who would smash his face again.

∼

Darl had sent that essay with an apology that it did not have a proper ending. But I see it as the exact place for a break. For now the teacher is stepping in and saying to the class, "Hold it, hold it!—the action in this story has taken a wrong turn."

We are all kids inventing the story as we go along, heavily made up, costumed, some rich, some poor, some black, some white, some straight, some gay, some Christian, some Jewish, some Muslim, all of us little pieces of divinity, well disguised. We're plopped down into a situation, given a character and a goal and a bit of the story, and left to improvise. Sometimes the kids get out of control.

I am the teacher, and I am stepping in now and saying, "No. We have lost the goal of the story, class. We will back up now and try it again." You are the teacher, too. Everyone is the teacher who chooses to be the teacher. We can say together, "In this story we do not call Darl names, and we do not smash his face in. The goal of the story as God outlined it is that we all end up Home, together, in love. Keep in mind the golden rule of acting that we learned the first day: Treat Darl the way you would like Darl to treat you."

~

An email from my sweet friend Darl gave me another fascinating theatre image to ponder:

> I went to the Mormon Miracle Pageant a couple of years ago. In its early homespun formation, I played the Joseph Smith role for five years, and they were still using the same soundtrack we recorded at KSL 36 years ago. Strange to hear my 17-year-old voice (as boy Joseph) echoing through the Sanpete Valley. More than four million people have heard the voice of that earnest little gay "prophet" almost pleading, "Why persecute me for telling the truth? And who am I that I can withstand God?" It's occurred to me since that this kid knew a thing or two about being misunderstood.

Pieces of Eugene: Navajo, Mormon, and Gay

Carol Lynn and
Eugene Tachinni
Salt Lake City, Utah

Most Mormon gay men do not choose to come out publicly for the first time in the *Salt Lake Tribune*, but Eugene Tachinni did. When I read Peggy Fletcher Stack's excellent article of February 25, 2006, I was more than intrigued. She was writing about his art show, which was part of his master's degree in fine art at the University of Utah. His early interest in "enlarging and taping segments of a photo onto rolls of paper to create a giant image" he thought would be a temporary one. Writes Stack:

> Before long, though, the cutting and pasting emerged as his primary artistic medium—metaphor for a fractured life. Tachinni is Navajo, gay and Mormon, and those identities don't adhere easily. . . . [N]either the Church of Jesus Christ of Latter-day Saints nor the Navajo Nation has been welcoming to gays. . . . Yet Tachinni prefers to tape his contradictions together.

Eugene grew up in New Mexico on the edge of a Navajo reservation, the fifth of nine children, his father a member of the area's stake presidency. He learned to sew and to crochet from his mother, a gifted seamstress, though he had to put these interests out of sight when his dad came home because "That's what pansies do." One day in junior high school, mystified by the giggles and laughter around him, he finally discovered that a classmate had written on the back of his "brand new, creamy, cotton puff jacket," the words, "I'm a fag." He remembers:

> You know that feeling of falling in blackness during dreams? That feeling of your four limbs being cut off and the blood disappearing instantly from your entire body? . . . I didn't know how to respond. . . . What could I have said those 25 years ago?

Later, confiding in bishops, mission presidents, LDS therapists, Eugene was counseled just to be faithful and the problem would soon go away. But it didn't go away.

> It wasn't enough. I wasn't enough. I wasn't strong enough to make the change, or at least those were my thoughts—"not enough," "weak," "uncommitted," "feeble." But at the same time knowing that I was a child of God, knowing that I was "saved to be born in the last days," knowing that Christ had come for me, specifically for me and my weakness. And if I committed myself, then he would set me free and make me no longer defective. But I couldn't do it. I just couldn't make those necessary things happen which, according to all the counselors, mission presidents and bishops, would allow Christ into my life and remove the thing wrong with me.
>
> I wasn't able to hold any longer the identities that were living in my body. I didn't know how to reconcile the cultures that weren't mixing, Mormon and gay. I was finding it impossible to hold to one and rid myself of the other. Do I be Mormon and deny any sort of sexuality? Do I leave behind Mormon and assume my gay identity?

I had read in the *Tribune* article that Eugene's anguish became such that he "couldn't find any reason to live anymore and thought about ways to not. I was sure I would do something terrible if I didn't speak it." Finally, in 1995, he told his sister, Sasha. "I owe her my life," he says. "That night she saved mine." Wanting to know more about both Eugene and his sister Sasha, I contacted them and found each willing to share with me more of their story. Sasha wrote:

I remember my dearest, most loving, understanding, handsome brother coming into my room one evening, and I could feel something stirring in the air. I was unsure what was going to come of it, but I knew it was sensitive. Eugene cried and cried. I remember thinking, "*Nothing* could honestly be that bad." I tried to comfort him with hugs. Time for us that night stopped, because to me at that moment nothing else mattered, nothing could be more important.

I cried with him. He told me that he was attracted to men and he didn't know how to deal with these feelings that he had locked up for years. I vowed at that moment that I would never let anyone hurt my brother. I wanted to protect him. It scared me that he may be persecuted for his homosexuality. I loved him more than I thought anyone could love someone. I wanted more than anything to have him feel this from me. That night in the dark we sat together, our arms around each other, and cried in fear, in love. He asked for full confidence, and I never spoke a word to anyone except to my Father in Heaven. We knew this was against church teachings. To this day I still don't understand, but that doesn't change my love for my brother.

Eugene wrote to me:

I am forever grateful for what Sasha did for me that night. I don't know how much longer I would have survived if she hadn't been there to listen.

So now, I don't try anymore to separate the two cultures,

Mormon and gay. I hold them both. Up until just recently I was in a relationship with a wonderful man. One morning I found myself thanking God for allowing this man to enter my life. I immediately stopped myself! I couldn't believe that I was thanking God for this homosexual relationship. It seemed blasphemous. I stood there for a moment and thought about it. When I said it again, that I was thankful for this man, I waited to see what I would feel. What I felt was peace and calm.

Another important blessing is that in the last few years I've had a warm reconciliation with my father and my older brother. We have spoken about the issues I face, and we have connected on very deep levels. I'm so grateful for that.

I go to the university family ward here in Salt Lake City. When the article came out in the *Tribune* about my art, about the struggle of being Navajo, Mormon, and gay, it was a Saturday. Of course, the next day being Sunday, I couldn't miss church. Of all days to even think about sleeping in, this was not the day! I was so afraid but felt strongly about what I said and what was written. So I put on my pink shirt and marched right up to priesthood meeting.

I didn't know what to expect, but the reaction was more than what I was prepared for. I guess I thought there might be those who would look and stare, possibly whisper to each other. But what I got was fellowship, more than what I had received prior to the article. I had several people come up and ask questions, truly interested in my experience.

I don't take the sacrament. That is my own choice. I don't volunteer to pray. I have wanted to bear my testimony, and once felt incredibly strongly to do so but talked myself out of it. Standing where I do now is peaceful. I haven't felt this sort of peace in a long time. I don't pretend to think that I am fully accepted by the Church, but I can't deny the peace and calm I reside in.

Snapshots for the Family Album

My oldest sister was throwing a big party, and when the photographer was assembling people for the family photo, I knew there would be awkwardness. My mom, who has had the toughest time of all with my being gay, had always found a way to make sure we got shots without my partner in them. I knew she needed a photo she could show in her Utah home, where wives of the General Authorities would come for Relief Society parties. My mom just couldn't—and still can't—put a picture of the two of us in her home. So, at this family party, there was unspoken awkwardness about my partner and the photo. Then my oldest sister suddenly called out to my partner, "Hey, David! Get in here. I'm paying for these photos, and I want you in them!" David stepped into the scene, and the record finally shows him—ten years later—as part of our family.

～

"Gayle" and I have attended the same women's club for years, but for eight months she didn't show up. Finally I went to see Gayle at the shop where she was working. I cornered her and said I knew something was going on and I really wanted to know so I could help. Gayle burst into tears and told me that when she'd learned that her son was gay, she just could not face anyone. I said, "Gayle, that's not okay. You need to be with people, you have to face your life. There are so many people who love you and want to be with you in this." Finally Gayle allowed me to create a kind of "party" for a large number of her friends from club and from church so she could tell them all at the same time. We had a wonderful evening, and with everyone's eyes on her, Gayle finally said the words, "I love my son to pieces, and he is gay." Everyone was so kind and supportive, and things were much better for her after that.

~

My parents and I had been alienated for ten years, but when *Goodbye, I Love You* came out and they read half of it, they got in the car and started driving five hundred miles to where I live. My mom read the rest of the book out loud to my dad as they drove. When they arrived, they told me they love me and accept me just as I am. I hadn't felt that since I broke off my engagement at BYU after a mission to Italy. My parents left the book for me, and after I finished it, the held-back tears of ten years of being out of touch with my family, missing the fellowship of the Church, and dealing with the frustrations of being gay left me sobbing half the night.

~

A Muslim family came to our local PFLAG meeting. The father related that for ten years their son had been terribly depressed, becoming more and more disconnected from the family, staying in his room day after day. The parents could get nothing out of their boy to help them understand. Was he on drugs? Would they find him dead in his room one day? Finally the son confessed to them that he was gay. "Oh my gosh," said the father. "We can handle this!" Yes, it was a disappointment, but he wanted his son alive and not depressed more than he wanted him in line with the religion.

~

When at age 50 I told my sister that I was gay (which she

said she had always known but just hoped I would never act on it), she told me I was no longer welcome in her home, as she couldn't have her children thinking this was an acceptable choice. I had always been very close to her children, and this was deeply wounding to me. One of her sons wrote me a letter from his mission, calling me to repentance and quoting scripture. Recently, a number of years later, that same nephew contacted me and told me that he'd learned a lot about homosexuality and he was sorry for his severe judgment. "Uncle," he said, "I need you in my life."

~

When my son told me he was gay, he said, "Please, please Mama, don't stop loving me." I said, "Oh, my boy, I can never stop loving you." Years later when he said, "Mama, I have AIDS," I sobbed so that he disappeared for months and would not answer the phone. After my emergency surgery, he called and said, "Mama, I'm so sorry. I love you so much!" I said, "Oh, and I love you too, I love you too!" When he moved home and asked, "Mama, am I going to die?" I said, "No! No! We're going to bicycle through Europe together," and then I went to the garage, where only the washer and dryer would see me weep. When, in the hospital, his 205 pounds had melted to 76, he said, "Mama, I want to go home," and against the doctor's order I took him. I rubbed his feet until I thought he was asleep, and then he would say, "Oh, please, Mama, just for a little while longer." On Christmas Eve I carried him to the balcony overlooking the living room, where he could see the fireplace and the big, flocked Christmas tree with a star on top. He put his head on my shoulder, and he said, "Mama, am I going to die now? Am I really going to die now?" The tears were falling on our cheeks, and I said, "Yes, darling you are! Did you know the lions really do lie down with the lambs? There will be no more pain. You can go home to our Heavenly Father now." He looked up at my face and said, "I sure do love you, Mama." After he was gone, I went back to the hospital many times to see those dear, sweet other boys, many alone, with no family to care for them in their last days. I ran around to all the beds and gave hugs and kisses. They beamed, and I thought I could hear my own son say again, "Mama, Mama, I sure do love you, Mama."

~

I came from a very strict evangelical family, and when I joined the Mormon Church they were very upset with me. After I came back from my mission and realized my homosexuality was never going to change, I entered a relationship with a man and was excommunicated from the Church. I went back to visit my family and told them two things on the same day—that I was gay and that I had been excommunicated from the Mormon Church. My grandmother said, "It's great that you're no longer a member of that church! But I'm sorry that you're still going to go to hell because you're gay!" However, my great-grandmother said to me in private, "Never mind about that. I've had a lot more experience on that subject in this family than you know about. Just don't ever lose faith in yourself. And when you find someone special, bring him home to meet me."

~

I was in the bishopric here in Germany when I realized I could not longer deny who I was, though I was still chaste. I talked to my bishop and asked him to take my name off the records of the Church. He cried when he listened to my story and offered to help me in any way he could. Later, I met a wonderful man and we lived in a monogamous relationship. He wanted to know more about the church I had belonged to, so for the first time since I left, I went to a sacrament meeting, taking my partner with me. I was hurting a lot, as most members avoided talking with me. Only my bishop did something I never will forget. Directly after the service, before the congregation stood up to leave, he came to us, welcomed us and talked to us so that everybody could hear. He said, "It's a pleasure to have you with us, and please know that you and your partner will always be welcome to attend any service or activity of the Church." There is so much pain. I am praying for the day I can return to the Lord's church.

~

My college sophomore son came out to us just before traveling to the Amsterdam Gay Olympics with his club's water polo team. It was very hard for us, and we never talked about the "elephant in the room." Finally my husband and I accepted our son's invitation to attend the team's award banquet and dance about five years ago. The evening went pretty well, but we simply could not stomach the same-sex dancing and prepared to leave. One of the hosts went out of his way to thank us profusely for our support, for raising such an intelligent, giving, talented son, and just for being there, since most of the team members seemed not to have any family support. That one experience reaffirmed in me the mother-son bond that cannot be broken. Now my only prayer is that my children, whether gay or straight, will be decent, loving, intelligent members of society.

~

The stake president in the Salt Lake City area where we used to live sent a message that it was urgent that he see me. We had moved to a different town, but I arranged to come to his office, wondering what he wanted to see me about. When I entered his office and we shook hands, he embraced me and became very emotional. We then sat down and he said, "I am about to be released from my calling as stake president, and I came to realize that there is just one more thing I need to do while I am still in this office. I cannot leave this position until I apologize to you. While you were in this stake and your family was having such struggles around the issues of your gay son, we failed you. We did not know what to do, and I see now that not only did we not help you, we made things worse. We failed you and your family, and we failed your son, and for that I am so sorry."

～

From Robert Steffensen, a leader of Family Fellowship, mentioned before, whose full story can be found on that organization's website.

When our 22-year-old son Erik told us he was gay, with tears streaming down his cheeks, he said, "I don't think I am an evil person." These words broke our hearts because he was and is one of the finest persons we have ever known. One of the things Kathryn and I did, along with hosting the first meeting of Family Fellowship in 1993, was to compile a thick packet of good information on homosexuality, material which fought the myths accepted as true by society and church, material from science and psychology, as well as reports on the questionable results of "change therapy." We mailed a large number of these packets to everyone who was important to us, most members of the ward, the bishopric, and the stake presidency. The following Sunday as I went to priesthood meeting, I saw that all three of the stake presidency were there, and I thought, "Oh-oh." They came directly to me, shook my hand, and each said things like, "Thanks so much for sending us that information. We need to learn a lot more about this subject, so keep us informed and keep up the good work." We intend to continue our activity in the Church, and we absolutely intend to embrace and love our children. We hope that all LDS parents of gay children will do the same.

~

"Paul" and I are divorced now. I refuse to have a bitter and contentious relationship with my children's father. The world has enough of that already. Our conversations on the phone are frequent and loving. We support each other in our lives. We rejoice together in the children's accomplishments. We consult each other about their challenges, and even buy their birthday presents together and say they are from Mom and Dad. When Paul visits, he still attends church with us even though he no longer considers himself LDS. He supports me in teaching the children the gospel and joins us for family prayer and scripture study. Last week on the phone, Paul told me that he really did want to see me in a new relationship and that he didn't want me to be worried about him being in a relationship. His words were, "It's okay with me if our children have three dads." I responded, "I can see it now, three dads with the three boys at the father-and-sons outing. Won't the bishop love that!" Laughter and love seem to build the bridges for our future.

~

My brother Karry was Mormon, good humored, freckled, gay, born almost entirely deaf, and was a respected employee working with the severely mentally retarded. When he came home to die of AIDS in 1991, our entire family gathered around him with great love. But would our church community? I am so thankful that my parents lived in a ward with an understanding, kind bishop, who from the very first was so supportive and loving to my brother. The bishop felt especially impressed to work with Karry in preparation for going to the temple before he died. On that special day, my brother was accompanied by an abundance of family, friends, and ward members.

On one occasion, as I stayed at my parents' home so they could have some time away, I retired to their bedroom and heard Karry's voice. He had knelt down at his bed in the next room and was saying his prayers out loud. Since he was deaf, I'm not sure if he could hear himself praying, but I could hear every word he said. And it was so simple, so sincere, and so beautiful. He prayed about his love of family and friends, for God's will to help him. He prayed for strength for my parents, and expressed his love and appreciation for them. I will always cherish those few moments when I listened to those sweet, simple words as my brother prayed.

I hope with all my heart that one day the Church will accept gay individuals with love and understanding, rather than with shame and despair. I hope that I will continue to live my life so that I am not ashamed of the gay community, my gay friends, and my wonderful brother, Karry, who died too young.

~

During Utah's campaign that resulted in amending the state constitution to prohibit gay marriage, I found myself deeply hurt every time I drove through the streets near my house. Having a gay brother and a lesbian sister, both of whom I dearly love, all those signs in support of the initiative that were planted in the lawns of the members of my ward felt like knives in my own heart. I decided to speak to the bishop (who, incidentally, along with the stake president, did not vote for the state initiative) and told him my feelings. Subsequently he spoke to the ward members and told them there were those in the ward who had gay family members and who were feeling very hurt by the strong political statement being made by all those signs. The next day, as I traveled down a certain street where before there had been at least 15 signs, there were now only three.

~

An unusual spiritual experience from Alone in the Trenches, *written by Christian gay NFL football player Esera Tuaolo:*

Three days after our first date, Mitchell wanted me to meet his mom. Driving over to her house, he said, "You have to help me. I've heard your name pronounced so many ways. What's the correct way?"

"'A-sarah,' like the girl's name with an A in front," I said.

He was quiet the rest of the drive. . . .

We parked in the driveway. Rang the doorbell. His mom, Shelly, answered. "Mom, I'd like to introduce you to A-sarah," Mitchell said.

"Nice to meet you," she said politely.

"No, Mom," Mitchell said. . . . "This is *A-Sarah*."

Shelly suddenly became very emotional, almost hysterical. She hugged me and nearly tackled me.

I was dumbfounded. "Okay, let me in on this," I said. "Why are you so happy?"

We went inside, and Shelly told me the story.

Mitchell had come out to her when he was eighteen (he was 31 when I met him). She was in shock, trying to be understanding but afraid of the unknown. She sent Mitchell to therapy.

One day, as she was trying to sort through what it means to have a son that was gay, she was driving home from work and looked in the rearview mirror. She saw her parents, who had died ten years earlier. . . .

"Why are you here?" she asked. "Are you here to tell me that Mitchell is sick? That he is going to die of AIDS? What?"

Her mom talked to her, consoled her. The last thing she told Shelly was, "Don't worry. He's going to be all right once he meets a Sarah."

All along, for thirteen years, Shelly thought Mitchell was going to meet a woman named Sarah who would straighten him out. She had told this story to Mitchell . . . to everyone she knew. . . . So when I showed up, it was as though a prophecy had come true. For me to find someone with whom I seemed to fit so perfectly in a supernatural way was amazing—especially after my prayers to find a lifetime partner.

⁓

A Southern Baptist mother sent me this from Florida:
Once my son told me he was gay, there was never a time I wanted to deny him. Instead, I found it was my religion I had to question. I prayed that God would show me in no uncertain terms what I was supposed to do. I got the answer that I needed. There are other things in the Bible that our religion has changed its mind about over the years. It may take a while, but I think that changes will come on this one, too. The reason I have decided to stay and not leave the church is to show that our gay members are just like everyone else and that God wants us to love them and love one another.

⁓

A Presbyterian woman told me this story:
When my brother told the family he was gay, we were horrified. He invited me and my aunt to come with him to a PFLAG Sunday afternoon in the park, but we said no, we couldn't go, we just could not support that part of him. My aunt and I went to church instead. At the service, the minister told of his 30-year struggle with his homosexuality, his coming to terms with it, and in a very moving way urged us all to love our gay family members. Well, my aunt and I could not get out of the church fast enough. We hurried to the park, hugged my brother, and spent the rest of the afternoon with him.

Religion, Politics, Sex, and Chocolate

Cheryl Bruno
Vernal, Utah

I am a 46-year-old woman; my best friend is lesbian and I am not.

Lynne and I first met in our early 20s at La Leche League, and we nursed our many babies together, sharing the difficult time of early Mormon motherhood. We took our young children on picnics and to the park and discussed religion, politics, sex, nutrition, and herbs.

After a few years, my family moved across the country. Some years we didn't talk at all, but we continued to stay in touch. Our paths diverged. Lynne went through the process of discovering she was lesbian, leaving her husband and her childhood religion. I became a teacher in many church capacities, payer of tithing, and temple attender. Through it all, we wrote letters and talked on the phone about religion, politics, sex, food, and preparing quick meals.

My husband had a real problem with our friendship after Lynne "came out." He forbade me to have any contact with her. He reported me to the bishop. He threatened divorce. He delivered ultimatum after ultimatum. For all these 20 plus years, I have resisted choosing between my husband and my friend. I love them both in different ways, and I will give up neither.

When email came along, Lynne and I began using the computer to discuss religion, politics, sex, and chocolate.

Now we are just two middle-aged ladies who have gone through many disappointments, sorrows, and joys, with gray hairs and wrinkles and a few weekend retreats in the mountains. Lynne knows me better than anyone else in the world. She remembers what I was like as an idealistic young person and knows how I became what I am today. Whatever kind of existence there is after this one, I know that her spirit and my spirit will still be friends.

I will never say goodbye.

My Voice Will Not Be Silenced

Lanette Graves
Clifton, Virginia

I am an accidental activist. At least this is what I used to think. But as I see the pattern of my life, I begin to think that God has held me by the hand all along, showing me what I am to do in my life. Who could have imagined that a Mormon woman with church roots stretching all the way back to Newel Knight (close friend of church founder Joseph Smith), would sing with the Mormon Tabernacle Choir as a young woman and thirty years later find herself marching in the Salt Lake City and Washington D.C. Gay Pride parades?

It has been a long and difficult journey, rooted always in a love for truth and compassion, which I learned beginning in childhood from my parents and church teachers. And what teaches love and compassion more completely than becoming a mother?

On October 15, 1971, a boy was born. "Just one more time, one more push," the doctor encouraged me, and then . . . *he was born.* The sweat and the blood and the pain were instantly forgotten in the wonder of this miraculous child. As I caressed Kerry's tiny fingers and toes, how could I know that one day I would experience a second "labor and delivery" of this same child?

~

"Mom, have you ever wondered if I might be gay?" A moment frozen in time. He had planned it so differently, I would come to find out, even thinking that he would brave coming out to my dear friend first so she could be a support to me. But there it was, the words hanging in the air—unplanned, but *needing to be uttered*—revealing the secret his tender, anguished heart could no longer bear to keep.

"Dear God," I silently prayed, "give me the right words to say." The answer came quickly: "It's *his* words that need to be spoken. Don't talk, just *listen*." Breaking the silence, I said, "Have *you* ever wondered if you might be gay?"

He no longer wondered. He *knew*. The words and tears came gushing out. He told the story of his pleas and promises to God that he would live the gospel and be the best son and brother possible, serving family and friends selflessly, if only he could be 'normal'; the lurid tales of homosexuality he heard at church, the assertion that "gays are filth and scum, lower than animals" and should be reported to the bishop if suspected; the story of being attacked in his dorm room and held on the ground while a hatemonger used a black marker to write 'queer,' 'faggot,' 'homo' on his bare skin; the story of his mighty struggle against feelings that refused to go away; the story of his survival, of his coming to accept that he was, indeed, gay.

I listened from a faraway place, knowing with inchoate awareness that life had just changed radically and irrevocably. "You're not crying, Mom," my son said. I would need to cry, I told him, but not yet. I told him how much I loved him. That, at least, would never change.

We went home, and I continued with preparations for a weekend trip with my husband, Robert, astonished to see that my hands could remember how to do normal things such as cook dinner and pack a suitcase.

As we drove away from the house, I finally cried; not just with my eyes and face, but with my entire body—a keening cry from a broken heart. I grieved over what my son had already suffered and grieved still more about the hard life he was facing. I grieved over the loss of the wife and children he would never have. I wrapped my arms around myself and rocked in pain—contractions of the soul. And there was no one to deliver me.

Watching me cry in a way he had never before seen, Robert was confused and even a little afraid. I could not speak to answer his questions. Finally I had to make myself say the words: "I have something to tell you that is so hard and that will hurt you. Kerry told me that he is gay." Almost immediately Robert turned off the highway and into a shopping center.

"What are you doing?" I asked.

"I need to find a phone," he said. "I will not have Kerry worry a minute longer about what his father's reaction will be." I listened as he spoke loving words of comfort and reassurance to our son. (As a result of AT&T's employee diversity education program, Robert already understood that homosexuality was an inherent, fixed trait.) I will always love and admire Robert for that telephone call and for his unconditional love for our son.

In the ensuing weeks, I barely ate or slept and cried all the time, or at least when my beloved Kerry was not at home. I avoided close friends who would instantly sense there was something wrong. I also avoided church, correctly surmising that it would not be able to help me. This state of affairs continued for several weeks, and my health began to suffer. I felt a continual anguish of soul that crossed over the mind/body boundary, causing physical pain.

Finally, in the middle of one night, as I sat on my bathroom floor grieving, I looked up at the night light shining in the darkness, and suddenly my sorrow was gone as I thought of the words of Christ: "I am the Light of the World . . . he that believeth in me, though he were dead, yet shall he live." A rush of blessed peace replaced the anguish I had carried for so long, and my mind was filled with thoughts that were intensely pristine and clear: "This is your son; this is who he is. Love him fiercely. His homosexuality does not shut him out from God or moral goodness. Get up off the floor, and work to make the world a better place for him and for others like him."

Just as I marveled over him in the moment of his physical birth twenty years before, as this "second labor" came to an end I was "delivered" to a new understanding of my son— that he is not only a gay man but a man of courage who loved me enough to be honest, who risked losing everything by telling the truth. In doing this, he has blessed my life.

And yes, I became an activist, an informed one. I read countless fine books written from both Christian and secular perspectives, attended numerous conferences and seminars, took university classes and listened carefully to many, many gay people who trusted me with their stories and experiences. The book *Peculiar People: Mormons and Same-Sex Orientation* was particularly helpful. Through all of this, I became convinced that homosexuality does not describe something one "has" but something one "is." I learned that it is an inherent, fixed trait that is morally neutral.

As I grappled with my questions and learned about homosexuality, Kerry came out to his brothers and sister, who have all been wonderfully loving, affirming, and supportive. In time, he also confided in his aunts, uncles, and grandparents. Because we were an extremely close-knit family, I assumed they all would react much the same way I had, that they would follow a similar pathway through shock and sadness followed by education, understanding, and ultimately acceptance, undergirded by a strong, unconditional love. I was wrong.

~

I had an idyllic childhood, with a mother who stayed at home to care for the children and a father who so loved being with us that he swept the floor long after it was clean just so he could be in the kitchen with us and engage his children in conversation. Ours was a simple, abundant home; there were books, home-baked bread and chocolate-chip cookies; quilts, games, and family vacations with grandparents; home-grown vegetables and eggs from our hens; there was music; there was conversation; there was laughter, and most of all we had love.

In addition to teaching us to care for each other, my parents taught us the importance of service to others, both in private acts and church responsibilities. After we children were mostly grown, my father served as counselor to the stake president for nine years and as bishop of our ward for seven years. My mother loved to teach Gospel Doctrine class and served in the stake Relief Society presidency for ten years. They were members of the Mormon Tabernacle Choir for more than twenty-five years. I became the second youngest member of the choir at the age of seventeen. During my years in the Choir, I enjoyed not only the opportunity to perform in many countries, representing the Church, but also the chance to share these experiences with my wonderful parents. I learned, however, that where there is great love, there is also the potential for deep hurt and disappointment.

My parents' initial response to having a gay grandson was to continue loving him, as always, but also to try to persuade him that he was not really gay. I tried to describe to them some of the things Kerry had confided in me—that he had known from the time he was seven or eight he was different—but they refused to listen to this, insisting that homosexuality is a sinful choice. Over time they explored every potential cause they could think of, particularly those propounded by certain conservative political organizations—molestation, impure thoughts, poor parenting, etc. They were immovable in their belief that God simply would not "create" a homosexual orientation and adamant in their defense of the teachings of the Church.

Over time our conversations grew more difficult. Lines were drawn. Some family members were not willing to share Thanksgiving dinner together if Kerry were to bring a partner (children should not be exposed to "addictions"); they were uneasy about leaving their children alone in the same room with Kerry, one even suggesting that he could be a pedophile. The fact that we were not actively seeking "reparative therapy" for Kerry and felt that the Church was simply wrong on this issue meant that we, too, were on the wrong road. On one occasion we invited my parents and my sister out to dinner to celebrate my mother's birthday, but they declined the invitation, saying that we no longer shared their values. Our precious relationships began to unravel. The expectations we had of one another—for me, that they would learn what I had learned and gradually come to be accepting; for them, that we would repent and follow the teachings of the Church—began to fail, and hearts were broken. Nothing I tried could change hearts or minds that were set on obedience to the Mormon Church and, therefore, its teachings on homosexuality.

My heart breaks to tell the story of how our deeply loving

family was torn asunder; it can be summed up in the single sentence my very hurt, very angry, *very beloved* mother spoke to me the last time I saw her. "I cannot go where you're going," she said; "I cannot be your mother anymore."

~

In darkest moments, I discover God anew—an ineffable, calming presence that illuminates the path just ahead that I must walk. One such moment involved a good friend of my daughter Bonnie, Arthur Lewis. He was short, slight, and perhaps a bit effeminate. He was also handsome, witty, enormously intelligent, and deeply spiritual. In addition to all of this, he baked the most fabulous "marble brownies." I remember the last time Art stood in our kitchen, each of us with a brownie in hand, talking animatedly about the approach of graduation and college acceptance letters. He and Bonnie engaged in some good-natured rivalry about their choice of schools; she was headed to Harvard and Art to Princeton. He was valedictorian of their class, and that was the last time we saw him—standing there at the podium so full of promise for the future.

In the summer before Art's senior year at Princeton, we learned that he had died by suicide. Apparently he could no longer bear the pain of trying to reconcile his homosexual orientation with the homophobic rhetoric of society in general and his Presbyterian Church in particular.

Art's funeral changed my life. As I sat in a pew with Bonnie's head on my shoulder, her tears falling onto our clasped hands and silent sobs shaking her body, I looked around at the grief-stricken faces of the congregation and realized that many of them had unknowingly contributed to his despair. Above the picture of Art in the apse of the church was a beautiful stained-glass window depicting Jesus holding a lamb with the scriptural injunction, "Feed my lambs." With startling clarity, I knew Art was a lamb we had failed to feed. And in that moment I decided two things. I would feed the forgotten lambs of God, and I would never be silent on this issue again.

We feed these dear ones literally at a special Thanksgiving dinner at our house every year in what has become an annual tradition for the Washington D.C. chapter of Affirmation, an organization for gay and lesbian Mormons. Last year, with Robert as chief potato-peeler, Bonnie and I cooked up a whole lot of turkey, mashed potatoes and gravy, stuffing, rolls, etc., for the nearly fifty gay Mormons (most of whom are returned missionaries) who were gathered there. As they arrived one by one with a vegetable dish or dessert in hand, the house began to fill with love and laughter and goodness until it was almost palpable. The dinner is followed by a kind of "testimony meeting" in which we go around the room and each person shares whatever is on his or her mind and heart. Their sometimes whispered, halting voices tell stories that are too often heartbreaking—the holy and the haunting present at once. I wonder again how some of these good, deeply loving, spiritual people can be rejected by their families.

And yes, I am fulfilling my vow not to be silent on this issue. Often, if an opportunity arises and I speak my own experience from my heart, I can touch the heart of another. Sometimes, however, people don't want to hear what I have to say. This was certainly the case at Brigham Young University in the spring of 2006, when I participated in a rally sponsored by Soulforce, a national gay and lesbian organization that seeks to end religious and political oppression through nonviolent resistance. BYU was one of the religious and military colleges targeted because of the anti-gay atmosphere prevalent there. I happened to be in the area because of a family funeral and was asked to give a speech at the rally at Pioneer Park in Provo in support of the students from the perspective of a mother of a gay son. The courage of these students was an inspiration to me, as are the words of St. Thomas Aquinas: "To bear with patience wrongs done to oneself is a mark of perfection, but to bear with patience wrongs done to someone else is a mark of imperfection, and even of actual sin."

As people before me took their turns at the microphone, some people drove by blaring their horns, trying to drown out the speakers. Others put up a banner accusing Soulforce and the gay students of "religious intolerance" and played Tabernacle Choir recordings also intended to drown out the speakers. As I stood and took the microphone, I said, "I have a voice that will not be silenced. My voice is loud and my voice is strong. My voice used to be a part of the very choir whose music is at this moment being used as an instrument of bigotry. I speak today as I sang then, in defense of truth and of love!"

From the back of the crowd, several detractors began to chant, "Shame on you! Leave BYU! Shame on you! Leave BYU!" Even as I spoke, I was struck by the thought that these BYU students think I am a dangerous "foreigner" come to do them harm, when in fact *I am one of them*—I am their neighbor, their Relief Society president, their friend, their aunt, their mother. But in their fear and blind obedience, they cannot see who I am nor hear what I have to say. They had circled their wagons, leaving truth and honesty on the outside—and on this day, respect and courtesy as well. Perhaps one day we'll be done with enemies, real and imagined, and the circles will become one.

~

I will continue to raise my voice as I feel prompted by the

spirit of truth. And I will continue also to listen. For as I have sung so often:

> . . . if by a still, small voice he calls
> To paths that I do not know,
> I'll answer, dear Lord, with my hand in thine:
> I'll go where you want me to go.

(Postscript to Kerry: *Thank you* for taking a chance on me. I'll love you forever . . . Mom)

I Am So Blessed

Carol Lynn and
Robert
Utah

During a recent phone conversation with my friend Larry in Utah, he said, "Last week at the grocery store, I overheard a little group of people in the next aisle saying the name of my gay friend, Robert. They were talking about how much they admired him and his partner for dealing so well with their unusual situation. Everything they said was positive."

The unusual situation of these two men is one, I think, that can inspire all of us. I contacted Robert, and he graciously shared his story with me.

It follows the same path as that of so many Mormon gay men—trying hard to be "normal," feeling unloved of God for feelings that won't go away, serving a mission, marrying, serving as a bishop, collapsing emotionally, being excommunicated for confessing to a homosexual encounter. But then Robert's story takes a unique path. He became a widower and single caregiver to Matthew, the last of his four sons, the child who came into the world with Down syndrome.

As Robert was establishing a relationship with David, also a former Mormon, "a man so wonderful I believe God led me to him," he was suddenly deployed to serve in Iraq as a member of the Utah National Guard. "My original plan," Robert said, "was to send Matthew to stay with his brother's family while I was gone, even though it would be very disruptive for him to change locations, schools, and everything he was used to."

Realizing this, David made a remarkable offer. "I'll take care of Matthew while you're gone," he said. "I want to do that—for you, and for him." This selfless act of service cemented their relationship, and Robert, David, and Matthew became a family.

During the fifteen months Robert was in Iraq, David, who had never been a father, became parent to a nineteen-year-old boy with special needs. Many times he took Matthew with him to his teaching job, and while David was instructing his classes, Matthew did his school assignments at the back of the room. Even though David did not make a big show of it, his co-workers took notice of his courage and devotion and admired him greatly for it. In fact, David's commitment in this unusual situation was noted in a promotion that he received.

As would be expected, not everything always went well. Robert reports, "There were some days that David was ready to pack Matthew's bags and send him to me in Baghdad, but then Matthew would say something sweet and give David a hug and melt his heart, and everything would be all right again." In fact, something happened during that year that actually turned the tables and made Matthew the one giving needed emotional support. David's mother suddenly passed away, a very traumatic event for him. Matthew became especially sensitive to David's needs and "gave him a great deal of love and kindness, which was extremely helpful."

Robert is home now, and the family of three continue their journey together. They worship at a very welcoming Presbyterian church, where Robert now leads a special service intended to "reach out across all denominations and creeds to build bridges in an attempt to bring people together to worship Christ."

"I truly am one of the lucky ones," he writes. "My parents, who are still with us, accept me and David. My other three sons are close to me. My siblings are very supportive. And I know, through an extremely powerful witness of the Spirit, that my Heavenly Father accepts me as I am without any need to conform to an external standard not of my nature. I am so blessed."

Hatred Saddens Mom of Gay Son

Carol Lynn and
Christine
Utah

That was the headline of Cathy Free's column, which my Utah brother had emailed to me from the *Deseret Morning News*. I read it with interest.

The conversation started pleasantly enough. First, everybody around the luncheon table talked about the weather, then there were the usual questions about children and grandchildren.

But then the subject somehow switched to gay rights and voices started rising in disgust and anger.

"I'll tell you what," one immaculately dressed woman said. "All of the gays ought to be strung up, sent out to the middle of the ocean and drowned."

Christine felt a rage rise inside her. Several relatives and casual acquaintances were sitting at the table, but she could no longer be silent.

"That's a horrendous thing to say—how can you speak so hatefully?" she said. "The truth is, you're judging people who have a lifestyle they didn't choose. (I believe) that it chose them."

Nobody at the table knew it, but her son was one of the people the ridiculous woman in the elegant attire wanted "elimi-

194

nated." He'd recently come to Christine in confidence to tell her that he was gay.

"I sobbed for weeks when he told me—not because he was gay but because of the pain he'd endured all these years, repressing who he is," she says of her 34-year-old son. "My heart ached for him."

Christine says this over a Free Lunch of fruit salad and muffins at the Little America coffee shop. The 60-year-old mother of four wanted to meet because she is saddened by the hatred directed by some people toward Salt Lake City's gay community, especially since the movie "Brokeback Mountain" came out.

"I'm tired of listening to people downgrade things they know nothing about," says Christine, who did not want to reveal her last name because her son hasn't yet made other family members aware of his sexual orientation. "Somehow, we need to facilitate some understanding."

Imagine, she says, if somebody were to criticize you because you are tall or because you have brown eyes—things that you can do nothing about.

"My son has suffered at the hands of misinformed people who have labeled him as sinful, weak and less than his 'straight' male counterparts," she says. "I know this is controversial—that there are many in our community who believe a gay person can change. But my son didn't ask for this identity. Why would someone choose to hurt so profoundly?" . . .

Christine knows there are other young men who may be experiencing the same torment, hoping to talk to somebody without being put down or shut out.

"To those parents, siblings and friends of young gay men and women, I'd like to tell them they're not alone," she says. "Have the courage to speak out. With understanding and compassion, we can dissipate this hate."

~

This morning I went for a walk in the hills with Christine. I had sent a message to her through the *Deseret Morning News* columnist, told her of the book I was writing, and said that I would love to know more of her story. Now, a few weeks later, she had found herself in my area, and we planned a visit. We sat on the low branch of my favorite tree in the hills and talked about life, talked about having a gay loved one, as I have talked with so many. And then, back at my house, we sat on the couch, and she read to me the pages she had written at my request. "Todd's Story," she began. Emotion occasionally stopped the flow of her reading.

My youngest child whom I will call "Todd," was the child who could magically read my mind. "Are you all right, Mommy? You look tired. Are you sad?" I was constantly amazed at his uncanny ability to feel what my heart was saying. He would rather spend time with me than almost anyone else. I took him with me to visit elderly patients in nursing homes. I was amazed at his delight upon seeing these often very frail members of our society. He would climb on their beds, snuggle next to them, often patting their faces. One woman in her nineties would save cookies and brownies for him. With great joy she would hand Todd a bag of often stale crumbs. He would throw his arms around her neck, kissing her leathery cheek. Needless to say, the nursing home staff, as well as the patients, loved to see him come! Much like an unconditionally loving puppy dog, he lighted up their lives and gave them hope.

He was the young teen who loved to accompany me to the mall, library, grocery store, etc., while other boys were playing sports and otherwise engaged with their friends. We had wonderful soulful conversations about many things. I knew he didn't like contact sports although he was a member of a Little

League team. He also did not enjoy Scouts, although he did his best to conform to expectations to be like other boys his age. I had no idea there was anything "different" about my son. I cherished him as a unique, intuitive, and deeply caring young man. I never knew of his profound suffering. I didn't know that he, in order to survive, was forced to retreat and take upon himself the mantle of conformity until he "became" that persona. It was much easier to be thrown into the pot of "alikeness" where he would somehow be "okay." He just melted and merged into this "sameness," using his humor, gentleness, and compassion to receive much needed positive feedback and acceptance from his peers. I didn't know that other boys teased him mercilessly, taunting him, calling him "fag," "sissy" or "faggot." He never defended himself, thinking, "What would it accomplish anyway?"

I didn't know he had a strong attraction to boys when he was eight years old. When most young kids were having "crushes" on members of the opposite sex, he was having "crushes" on other boys. He liked girls but didn't think of them as anything but friends. As he began maturing, his desires became even stronger. When other guys were "checking out chicks," he was checking out guys. At the time, he thought that he was just more evolved spiritually than the other guys and just didn't let himself feel anything for girls.

I didn't know that he was once in a home alone with a very attractive cheerleader when he was in high school. She literally "came onto him" in a very sexual way. He was actually disgusted, frightened, and "turned off." He made a beeline for the door! He thought it was odd that he didn't feel anything but fear, but once again felt that he was just so spiritual that he was above that "carnal" feeling. At the same time, however, he did look at boys and think they were really "hot." He could remember the names of every single boy or man he had been attracted to, but not one woman. He never talked about these feelings because he had convinced himself it was nothing extraordinary. Because of his religious upbringing, it was incomprehensible to think otherwise. These "parts" receded, changed, shifted, and took their place in a secret room with a padlocked door that was heavily guarded by an impenetrable force. Occasionally a crack allowed an uncomfortable thought to ooze out, but it was quickly overpowered and pushed back into the room of rectitude and repression.

I didn't know how hard it was for him to be alone and quiet, studying, writing, formulating ideas, resting, reading. As long as the "guard" was in place and he was busy, he could keep up appearances. Solitude was often his enemy instead of a dear friend. How lonely, sad, rejected, and overwhelmed he must have been. To express, admit, and address this struggle would make it *real*, tangible, formidable! The dangerous bubble would burst, spilling its contents all over the emotional landscape.

Todd began drinking to keep these "evil" forces (for that is what he had been taught) at bay. Then he would not have to feel anything. He could numb himself and develop a false sense of power and assurance. He could kiss girls without feeling unnatural, because that was what he was "supposed to do." He made himself do it over and over again. He had sent those other "parts" faraway, hopefully never to resurface again.

Going on a mission seemed like a very appropriate decision. He worked hard to give up his drinking, believing the experience of a mission would solve his problems for good, awaken his spiritual "sleeping giant," bring solace and comfort to his soul, and magically bring his emotional chemistry into alignment.

He was called to serve in Finland, a cold and austere country. He went into a severe depression, left his companion, and walked the streets of Helsinki alone and dejected. Once again, I did not know. We were not told this was occurring until after the fact. When my dear son begged the mission president to send him to another mission, he was coldly told that he was a "disgrace to his family, church, and God." Todd was soon on a plane, with a drink in his shaking hands, on his way back to the States. He eventually, after many false starts, counseling, etc., went on another mission, feeling that he had to "make it right." He came home early from that mission also. By this time his sense of failure and despair were complete, and he went into a deep downward spiral of drinking and despondency. I held him in my arms on numerous occasions, trying so hard to comfort and console him. He was not a failure. He was a fabulous person in every sense of the word!

With the loving help of a young woman who had been his dear friend for many years, he was able to get into a good alcohol rehabilitation program and ever so slowly bring himself up from desperation and oblivion. She stood by his side, supporting, validating, and loving him completely and unabashedly.

Several months before marrying his "very best friend," Todd asked me, "Mom, shouldn't I be feeling some chemistry, some desire for my bride-to-be? I love her so very much, she is truly my soul mate—we think alike, enjoy the same things, have the same philosophy on life, but I don't feel attracted to her physically. Is that normal?"

Still not knowing, I responded, "Maybe you should wait until you feel that. It seems to me that desire is very important in a marriage." He did choose to marry this choice young woman, feeling again that somehow it would all work out. He soon became the proud father of two darling boys.

Seven years into their marriage, Todd's hidden "parts" gathered together and burst out of their prison. He found himself being drawn to things that symbolized male sexuality, clothing, pictures. On one occasion he was in a gift store and was casually looking at cards. Here he found himself drawn to cards that featured males, some of the cards very explicit. He had to get out of the store immediately. He was literally ill and felt he could throw up at any moment. It was like a huge wave completely engulfing him. Nothing he did or could do would push it away from shore this time. He had previously made the decision, with the help he had received, to never drink again to bury his feelings. For the next few weeks, he did throw up, over and over again. He knew, in his heart, for the very first time, that he was homosexual. There was no denying or suppressing it any longer.

Soon thereafter, he tearfully told his wife (who also had no idea) and several days later told his mother. Upon hearing this, after getting over the initial shock and disbelief, I found the past thirty years of his life flooding back into my memory. The things that had endeared me the most to this lovely man were the attributes that defined his very being and were deeply connected to the hated "parts" he had kept hidden for so long.

At this moment in time, he is living with his loving family. He and his wife are doing the best they can day by day, unsure of the future.

You may ask, "How as a mother, did you not know?"

I reply, "I did not know, because he did not know. How could we? Our culture insisted that homosexuality is not 'real,' and we were true believers."

∼

Christine finished reading, put the paper down, and began to sob. "Why did he have to suffer so? He came so close to suicide, several times. Why do we treat these dear people so badly?"

5
CIRCLING THE WAGONS (TWO)

The future belongs to those who
believe in the beauty of their dreams.

—ELEANOR ROOSEVELT

I Never Would Have Dreamed

Carol Lynn and
Bruce Bastian
Orem, Utah

When I first met Bruce Bastian, I didn't know he was anybody extraordinary. It was October 1986, and *Goodbye, I Love You* had just come out. At a book signing at Deseret Book in Orem, Utah, a very tall, thin, melancholy man approached and said softly, "I'm gay, and I'm married, and I'm really having a tough time. Could I fly to your home sometime and talk with you?" I said of course he could and gave him my phone number. A couple of weeks later, Bruce appeared at my home in Walnut Creek, and we spent the day together.

As we ended our visit, Bruce asked me, "Do you have a computer?"

"No," I said. "Hopefully soon I can get one."

"Well," he said, "I'm in computers, and I would like to give you one."

"Wow! Well . . . well, okay!"

A few weeks later, Bruce flew in with seven boxes and set me up with a fine Dell computer, laser printer, and lots of software, including something called "WordPerfect," of which, he told me, he happened to be co-inventor. I later learned that this word processing application was a big part of the personal computer revolution in the 80s and 90s.

Bruce and I have kept in touch over the years, and I consider him to be a very valued friend. As he has shared his story with me, in personal conversations and in emails, I find that in many ways it follows the well-traveled path of so many gay Mormon men. Few, however, gay or straight, find themselves on the Forbes list of the 400 richest Americans. And while money never buys happiness, it certainly puts one in a position to do remarkable things, even more remarkable than gifting a needy writer with her first computer. His journey to a place of self-acceptance and personal power was not an easy one, but one I'm glad he wants me to share with you now.

~

I came from a very loving Mormon home in Idaho. Though I always knew I was loved, I was always lonely, always felt strange. I knew from age 14 or so that I had no attraction to girls but did to guys. It shamed me and scared me because I believed everything I had been taught about it being wrong.

I was an honor student in seminary, went on a mission to Italy, did everything I could to be righteous, but the feelings inside didn't change. Finally, at age 28, I asked my "best friend" to marry me. I knew she loved me, and I knew she would be a great mother. But I also knew I did not love her the way my friends loved their wives. When I had my interview with my stake president so that I could get married in the temple, he asked me all the regular questions, which I had no problem answering. Then he asked if I had anything to ask him. I told him that I was worried because I knew I was not in love. He looked at me sort of funny and then told me if I would get married and follow the Lord's commandments, I would learn to love my wife as fully as anyone. How could I doubt the word of a stake president? I did marry. I am the proud father of four wonderful young men. I did everything the Church told me to do and was even "worthy" enough to be in a bishopric. But I was not really happy. I loved my wife as much as I can love a woman—and I still do.

Years later, I did fall in love—with a man I met on a business trip. For the first time in my life I did not feel suicidal, I saw some good in myself, I felt some of the darkness lift. When I got home, I was an emotional mess. I was scared. I couldn't eat or sleep. My wife knew something was really wrong. We stayed up nearly all night talking until I finally broke down and told her what had happened. She sat quietly for a very long time, then she just said that many things now made sense to her.

Although I stayed with my wife for several more years, struggled with my feelings, went to counseling, our marriage would never survive. We separated in 1988 and divorced a few years later. It was really the only honest way I could proceed, yet it was still extremely painful for all of us. It was made worse for my wife and kids because they were being told that I could "change" if I wanted to. It was hard to begin telling people about my sexuality. When you grow up being told that being gay will bring you nothing but pain and misery, and that every decent person will turn you away, you believe it. Luckily for me, I discovered that those were mostly lies. True, some people did treat me harshly. My parents and my brothers and sisters did not.

Even as "the boss" at work, I did get "hate mail" from employees, always anonymously. Some employees claimed that God would not bless the company because I had decided to be gay. I would have loved to sit with those employees and explain how the real success of the company came *after* I had admitted to being gay. I do not blame those employees alone for their misguided hatred. They learned to hate gays in their churches and their homes.

While my children were growing up, they sometimes experienced very hateful treatment from schoolmates. Yes, their father was a rich, successful man who was more and more open about being gay, but that was not their fault. Children were being told in their homes how evil and sick this rich man was. Some children were forbidden to play with my children because I was gay. To protect my kids when they were younger, I tried as much as I could to keep a low profile.

During that time, I had continued to take my children to church although it became more and more difficult for me personally. I knew people talked about me. When I heard that one zealous member of my ward was verbally petitioning my bishop to have me excommunicated, I decided I would not allow the Church to control my destiny and asked to have my name removed from its membership records.

Now that my boys are older, I feel I can be more active, more visible in doing the work I feel called to do. I don't want any more gay farm boys in Idaho growing up hating themselves like I did. Most of my energy and money now go to causes to help gay people receive the respect and the rights they deserve.

～

I have kept a file of correspondence with Bruce. Here's a note from him that makes me smile: "About the 'true love' bit, I will just say that if you end up loving yourself, then life is a success. Everything else is a bonus!"

When I was going through a difficult time, he wrote:

Life is strange, and hard, and wonderful all at the same time. Our paths cross for happiness and sadness, but always for growth. We made the decisions to get into these difficult times before we came here, and now the show must go on. And . . . we will survive. I wish I could hug you right now. Try to stay strong. Let your love lead the way, as you always do. I send you love and light and whatever there is good in me. Always!

Bruce's Christmas letters always carry pride in the accomplishments of his sons, gratitude for his family and friends, and hopes for a better world.

"Peace on Earth"—I have thought about this phrase a lot recently. Most people, I believe, associate this with physical peace, or the opposite of fighting or even war. I, however, feel that the peace spoken of in scriptures of nearly every faith may actually refer to the inner peace and tranquility that comes from unconditional love and respect. Every great spiritual leader has taught that if we learn how to truly love ourselves and others, we will find the peace we all seek. If we could actually get to that point, then it would be almost automatic for the next step of loving our fellow man and treating all with respect and kindness. That would mean real "Peace on Earth." It may seem like only a dream, but I believe it has to start sometime, and there is no better time than now.

~

I have watched in admiration as Bruce has used his great heart and financial fortune to make the world a place of peace, love, and respect, and especially to create a very strong circle of safety for his gay brothers and sisters. The *Deseret Morning News* covered a wonderful recent event. The headline was, "Religion called important in lives of gays, lesbians." The line under that said, "Gay bishop says only churches can undo oppression."

My daughter Emily and I were there. At Bruce's large and gorgeous estate in Orem, 850 people had gathered on a summer evening. It was the annual fundraiser for the Human Rights Campaign, the largest gay advocacy organization in the country, on whose board of directors Bruce serves. Under a large white canopy complete with colorful chandeliers, we were served an elegant dinner, enjoyed entertainment, short speeches and awards. The keynote speaker was the Reverend Gene Robinson, the first openly gay bishop in the Episcopal Church. The *Deseret Morning News* quoted him as saying in an interview:

"I think the Holy Spirit is leading us to think differently about gay and lesbian people." He said he views gay activism as being a "godly and holy work. I think it is so important for religious voices to speak out because we are responsible for most of the oppression that gay and lesbian people have experienced. . . . I think it's only religious voices that can undo that oppression."

Robinson said many religious institutions have taught their gay and lesbian members that they are an "abomination" in the eyes of God.

He concluded his speech by affirming an opposite view.

"If you don't remember anything else, I want you to remember that you are loved beyond your wildest imaginations," Robinson said. "The God that we know—his love is so boundless that we can all be God's favorite."

Bruce's smile lasted all evening, and his comment to the *Deseret Morning News* tells it all: "When I was a kid, I never would have dreamed about what's happening here. . . . To realize that it's actually happening at my home is beyond belief."

Is She Still My Daughter?

Anne Marie Nielson
Sandy, Utah

I received this moving story through my brother, Don Wright. In his words: "After one of our monthly visits to our assigned families, my home teaching companion told me he had just returned from New York where he visited his daughter and had attended a commitment ceremony for her and her gay partner. I listened and appreciated the struggle, but mostly I appreciated the love and acceptance of a daughter who was still a daughter and a father who was still a father. Later, when I was in church meetings with this good man, several times I felt a distinct unease when the speaker made uninformed, disparaging remarks about gays." I asked Don to find out if the family would be willing to speak to me about their story. Here is what I received from Anne Marie, who is happy to have me use her name and is thrilled to be of value to other parents.

I am the mother of a lesbian. I love her. I am proud of her. Am I embarrassed? *No!* Am I ashamed? *No!* Do I make a great announcement of her sexual orientation? *No!* There are many in the world who do not share my view of this. I choose to live in the real world. This is the story of how I learned to be at peace with a situation I never dreamed would be mine.

We had been on a cruise with our two children and my husband's extended family. Our daughter, Keli, lives back East and was able to come out and be with us. We had a wonderful and relaxing time. A few weeks after we returned home, my husband and I received a letter in the mail from our daughter. My husband read it and handed it to me, not saying anything. I sat down, read it, and hit a brick wall at full speed. Keli was telling us that she was gay, that she had a partner, Elizabeth, whom she would be living with, and that they were planning a commitment ceremony for the following summer.

My heart sank. I wanted to shake her and say, "*No, you're not! No, you're not gay!* I made frilly dresses for you when you were little! You took ballet and danced in point shoes! I made prom dresses for you! I was going to make your wedding dress! *No, you're not!*"

Instead, I had an overwhelming feeling that I should tell her that I loved her, and so I did. What had really changed? Is she still my daughter? *Yes!* Is she still beautiful? *Yes!* Does she still have a wonderful personality? *Yes!* Does she still have her great sense of humor? *Yes!* Do I still want to spend time with her? *Yes!* Do I still want to be in her life and have her in mine? *Yes!* Do I still love her? *Yes!* I love her with all my heart. What I learned in addition to all of this is—she is gay.

Keli told me once that she thought after she told us she was gay she would no longer be welcome in the family and would be on her own the rest of her life. She knew that Mormons did not look on this with any acceptance. I assured her she would need to do something far worse for that to happen, though I honestly don't know what my child could ever do that would make me not love her.

Still, I found myself crying every time I thought of the situation. I reviewed my life in raising her and wondered what I had done that would have caused this. I had done what I thought parents should do. I taught her to be independent. I loved her. I gave her opportunities. What had I done?

I consulted with two therapists. Both, after laying out possible theories, agreed that we don't really know much about the cause. My second therapist gave me a paper from the LDS Church which was sent to church leaders. It said that it is not known why homosexuality occurs. Everyone falls somewhere on a spectrum of sexual attraction, homosexual at one end and heterosexual at the other end. There is much misinformation out there because we just don't know. The Church encourages love and a great deal of patience with our homosexual family members.

After a great deal of therapy, I was satisfied that homosexuality cannot be explained and just is what it is. But what was clear was that I loved my daughter with all my heart, and I needed to know that Heavenly Father loved her *at least* as much as I did. From all I had heard, those who participate in this are horrible sinners.

I searched my heart for an answer. I prayed to the Lord to let me know he loved her. I went to the temple, listening every time for some assurance that he loved her. I knew that if I just knew he loved her, I could get through this. But I didn't find the answer.

One day while reading the *Ensign* [the Church's official magazine]—I don't remember which article or who wrote it—I found something that moved me. The author was seeking an answer for a child of hers, and she read these words from a child's Primary song. "Mother, I love you; mother, I do. Father in Heaven has sent me to you . . . " There was my answer. Of all the mothers who have ever lived on the face of the earth, I was chosen to be Keli's mother, to help her through this life with all the challenges it gives. He loved her so much that he especially selected me to be there for her though this situation and whatever else comes. I will not disappoint him.

But even before I felt that strong reassurance, during my time of real distress, we had to decide about the commitment ceremony. Would we go? *Of course* we would go! We were living in Utah, and the ceremony would be in New York. "What can I do to help?" I asked my daughter.

"Well, Mom," Kelly said hesitantly. "I'll tell you what would mean more to me than anything. Could you—make a wedding dress—for Elizabeth?"

Should I laugh or should I cry? Or should I just say yes? I said yes. Yes, I would make a beautiful wedding dress for the gay partner of my beautiful daughter. As I cut and sewed, if my heart was heavy now and then, it was from the weight of love, a deeper love than I had ever known.

My husband and I attended the commitment ceremony on July 19, 2003. Elizabeth looked lovely in my wedding dress, and my daughter wore a nice pair of slacks and a top that was from the same fabric as her partner's dress. I felt as though I was in a dream, that this wasn't real. Even though it was in a church, I did not sense much happiness. At the reception party after the ceremony, a family member of Elizabeth's told me that she feared God's wrath for them on judgment day. At this point I was still so unsure of the situation and was very emotional throughout the whole day. But fear of God's wrath? I had never felt that, for myself or for my children.

The time recently came to let extended family members know of Keli's situation. I was never going to tell Keli that she or her family were not welcome at our family gatherings. Members of our extended family could come or not come if she was going to be there, whatever they felt they needed to do. However, there has been nothing but an outpouring of love for Keli. She is welcome at any event, along with her family. In fact, some of our relatives said, "Family is family, no matter what."

Keli came to Sandy for her brother's missionary farewell and has been a great support to him. The turn in his sister's life has been a hard struggle for him, but I am confident that time will help, and wounds will be mended.

How is my daughter doing now? She is doing very well, and I am so happy for that. Keli and Elizabeth are responsible people. They are contributing members of society. For the last two years, they have been foster parents to two little boys, who have absolutely blossomed with them. Recently Keli called and told us, with deep emotion, that the judge has told them they may proceed with adoption.

I am so glad I let my daughter know that I love her no matter what. I am so glad I made the wedding dress and went to her commitment ceremony to show her how much I love her and love her partner. I am ready to be there when Keli and Elizabeth adopt the boys and make me their grandmother. I am so glad I am the one Heavenly Father chose to be the mother of this remarkable girl, who I love with all my heart.

It Has Become Our Universe

Carol Lynn and
David Hardy
Park City, Utah

"Carol Lynn, I need to apologize for something right off the bat."
That was the first thing David Hardy said to me as we began our
phone conversation. I had met him briefly a couple of years
prior, but we'd never really talked. "All my life I've been accused
of never showing emotion. But with everything I've been through
in the last seven years, sometimes I can't stop crying. I just
needed you to know that."

My heart went out to this sweet man, and I'm honored to be
able to share with you something of his story. David Eccles
Hardy is an activist. The Mormon Church does not routinely
produce activists, certainly not on matters that impact the faith.
Obedience, following the Brethren, are hallmarks of a good
member of the Church, and many parents of gay children that I
have spoken to grieve in silence, or perhaps they have probing
but guarded conversations with trusted others. Some throw cau-
tion to the winds and become activists, none that I know of
more publicly than David Hardy.

David was about as Mormon as a man can get. Both he and
his wife Carlie were of large and prominent Mormon families.

David had served as a missionary to France, had been a bishop, served on high councils five times, was father to a large family, and was a successful attorney in Salt Lake City. His trust in the Lord and in the LDS Church was absolute. But something uninvited turned a perfect world upside down. An unusual glimpse of the family's journey can be experienced in a letter, filled with frustration and heartbreak, that David wrote in 1999 to a man high in the leadership of the LDS Church. David gave me permission to share excerpts here.

⁓

Early on a Saturday morning six weeks ago, I watched as our car pulled away with my wife driving our eldest son [Judd] to a new city, a new community, and a new school to complete his senior year of high school. Ever since that morning, I have grown progressively angrier that to protect our son's life and sense of self-worth, we are compelled to send him away from our home and family. You see, this community of "Saints" we live in is so steeped in ignorance, fear, loathing, judgment, and qualified "love" towards our son and those who, like him, face the challenge of homosexuality, he twice arrived at the point where he was devoid of hope and felt he had no alternative but to take his own life. Fortunately, he did not succeed. My son is not manic-depressive, nor was he ever before suicidal. He simply . . . believed what his church teachers and priesthood leaders taught him about homosexuality. . . .

My wife and I are the parents of six children—two daughters and four sons—ranging in age from twenty-three to eight. Our oldest son at age thirteen had the courage to come to us with his growing fear that he had no attraction whatsoever to girls—the thought in fact disgusted him—but that he was very attracted to those of his same sex. That he would come to us without fear or shame, confide in us, and seek our counsel attests to the strong relationship my wife and I have both always had with our son. (This is ironic in light of the "parental causation" theories routinely hauled out by the Church's LDS Social Services counselors and Evergreen as the primary cause of homosexuality.)

This son was always spiritually mature for his age. He is the finest young man I have ever known—giving, loving, supportive, honest, reliable. Most definitely unselfish. A leader among his peers in his school and Primary classes and in his priesthood quorums. Since he was old enough to talk and walk, we were very much aware of certain differences that concerned us. He carried himself differently, walking and running. When we could get him to pick up a ball, he threw it differently. He spoke differently. He was not in the least interested in sports (in spite of countless practices and Saturdays we spent supporting him in sporting events that utterly disinterested him). He loved dolls and playing house. He loved music, literature, drama, and poetry. He made friends easily with girls but very rarely with boys. Carlie and I listened with hope to LDS counselors and leaders who dismissed or downplayed all of this as merely a "phase." We believed in and relied on them.

The years passed, but the "phase" didn't—this in spite of our doing everything recommended to us by LDS counselors, priesthood leaders and, of course, the teachings of the General Authorities. . . . [M]atters went from bad to worse. One evening in 1997, while I was out of town and my wife was being assured by our well-meaning stake president at his office that "if we just keep it quiet—the same as if someone in your family had committed adultery (our son had done nothing)—it will all be just fine, trust me . . . ," our son slit his wrists in his room at home. Earlier in the day, it had been the "Sodom and Gomorrah" lesson in seminary.

As bishop of a student ward at the University of Utah working with homosexual returned missionaries, I came to the painful realization that the "reparative therapy" practiced by LDS Social Services and organizations such as Evergreen (whose board of directors I then served on) was not merely ineffective, it was terribly damaging. In every instance I found that this "therapy" accomplished little more than driving these earnest brothers and sisters, desperate to believe that they would "change," deeper into self-loathing and despondency.

My experience as bishop of a student ward, the father of a homosexual son, and a friend and confidant to the many LDS homosexuals I have since become acquainted with would indicate to me that in some few cases, the terrible guilt associated with reparative therapy and the strong desire to remain in good standing with the Church and one's family has brought about an ability to *repress* one's homosexual desires—for a season. Usually just long enough to get married and ruin a family. . . .

By preaching [that homosexuality is not innate but a curable condition], you set the impossible goal of "cure" as the standard to which my son must hold himself responsible, as must his family and all other Church members. Until he chooses to do what he must to be "cured," he hasn't done enough. He will never have done enough. He will always come up failing in the most fundamental aspect of his entire existence as a child of his Heavenly Father. He is a pervert, an aberration, and an abomination. There is nothing left in this life or the next. . . .

Last week a dear friend (formerly a bishop) reassured us that he still loved our son "even if he has made a choice to be this way." *My son did not choose to be this way.* This type of "love" born of duty and pity for his abominable choice acts like a slow but virulent cancer on our son's self-esteem. It is for this reason we have found it necessary to send our son away from the community of the "Saints."

. . . I can't tell you how strange and difficult this is. It's like we woke up one morning on a different planet. In our greatest time of need as a family, the Church has failed us and abandoned us—and through the convenient but hurtful doctrine of parental causation, complicity, and guilt it directly promotes . . . it kicks us while we are down! I know this is only one of many issues that the Brethren deal with, and certainly not at the top of their list, but for us it has become our universe. We live in this issue twenty-four hours a day, seven days a week, and must raise our children through it by our best lights. And there are many more like us in the Church. Parents like us are ultimately forced to make a hopeless decision: abandon our homosexual children, or turn from the Church. . .

⌒

David's activism—in the above letter, in press conferences, newspaper articles, radio interviews—focused mainly on three Church pamphlets printed decades ago and still distributed that are foundational to the Mormon position on homosexuality. They use such language as:

> Homosexuality *can* be cured . . . . you should now make the super-human effort to rid yourself of your master, the devil, Satan . . . the sin is curable, and you may totally recover from its tentacles . . . the cause, when found, will turn out to be a very typical form of selfishness.

It was rhetoric like this that David attributes to his son's attempts on his life. And clearly young Judd agrees, acknowledging that the act was more from duty than despair. He had done everything possible to "change," even asking his parents to disconnect their cable and Internet service so that he would not be tempted by any alluring images of men. "It felt to me as if I was in this loop that I couldn't end," he said. "The Church wanted me to change, and I couldn't get past that. And I couldn't change, and I couldn't get past that." The decision to take his own life was "a quick resolution before doing the damage of falling into a life of sin. I believed too strongly in the Church and the Church's values, and I placed those above my own life."

⌒

There are some Mormon families who manage to hold onto their loyalty to both church and child. The Hardys chose not to do that. The configuration of the community wagons did not hold a place in the circle for them. In the midst of the turmoil, their son James asked for a family meeting. He said, "I don't understand, you keep saying that Judd doesn't have to go to church because he's gay and that's an extenuating circumstance. But don't you think the fact that I have an older brother I honor, respect, and look up to, and this is a church that doesn't have a place for him—isn't that an extenuating circumstance? It is for me, and I won't be going back." That was a watershed moment for the parents, and they looked at each other and said, "You know what? We're not going either. If this is an organization that will not support this amazing individual who is our son, Judd Eccles Hardy, then we will not be going either."

In our lengthy telephone conversation, David had been very open about the extraordinary wounds incurred by his family in a variety of ways as they dealt with the stress around their son's unasked-for challenge and the subsequent issues that arose. But his last email made me smile:

> I am doing wonderfully. Life is new each day, and you have to make the decision to get up and be a part of it—put on the armor and perhaps go out and slay a dragon or two. It is also a choice just to give up. That way lies pain and self pity—and the slide down. I am so grateful for the hard learning experiences life keeps offering up, and to be able to see that it is all, in fact, a gift and a miracle. I now know what it feels like to feel happy to be alive and loved by friends. And to take my place again in making a difference.

The Blessing

Stephen Williams
Salt Lake City, Utah

Stephen has created a short film based on this story, which has been shown in numerous film festivals.

~

In the fall of 1999, my father suffered a heart attack and was rushed into surgery. My siblings and I gathered at the hospital. As we sat in the waiting room, my two brothers began talking with each other about giving him a priesthood blessing [a church ordinance performed by the laying on of hands]. Having left the Mormon Church years earlier on account of my sexuality, I was not included in the conversation. Though it was clear to me that they were not trying to be unkind, I had my usual struggle with painful feelings of being "left out."

Finally we were ushered into the room where my father was recovering from his surgery. He was understandably weak, his eyes half-closed, but he seemed to recognize each of us. As my younger brother anointed his head with oil and gave a short prayer, my two sisters and I watched from the other side of the room.

After the anointing prayer, both of my brothers began to place their hands on my father's head to seal the anointing and bless him. Suddenly, my father raised his hand into the air, stopping them. Surprised, we all looked at each other. His eyes scanned the room until they came to rest upon me. He motioned for me to come over to the bed. Not knowing what he wanted, I slowly approached him.

As I reached the bed, he took hold of my right hand. Without a word, he placed my hand firmly upon his own head, then did the same with my left hand. He then closed his eyes. After a brief, somewhat awkward pause, my brothers placed their hands on top of mine. My elder brother then gave him a blessing.

As I have pondered this simple gesture over the months and years that followed, I have come to the strong belief that my father did exactly what Christ would do. My father's instinct told him that, above all other consideration, he needed to let me know that he sees me as a worthy and lovable son, equal to my brothers, and that my sexual issues make no difference to him. It was a transformative experience, pivotal for my life.

Thank You for Not Leaving Me Out

Craig Watts
Shanghai, China

Gary and Millie Watts are leaders in Family Fellowship, and the story of their family can be found on that organization's website. Their gay son, Craig, was student body president at Provo High School, served an LDS mission to Texas, earned a PhD from Osaka University, and currently resides in Shanghai. His parents have become actively involved in gay causes, and Gary served on the national board of PFLAG for seven years.

January 20, 1991
New York
Dear Gary and Millie,

You probably get a lot of thank-you notes like this, but this one is from your real son (not one of your many surrogates that you've helped—though the feeling is similar to the one they must feel).

I went to church here today, and though I kept calm and composed, it was a deeply emotional experience. Though you have to ride an elevator to get to it, the chapel with its rows of benches, podiums, budget pipe organ, and sacrament table looks a lot like ours in Provo. And though it's an "older" singles ward with more than its share of "diversity" and difficulties, the people look and act Mormon familiar. I sat at the right of the chapel, near the windows that look out on the streets of Manhattan. The whole ward scene is such a familiar one that I didn't feel nervous or embarrassed, just anxious to see whether I would know anyone there, wondering whether I would feel welcome there. I remembered that part of the reason I had been staying away was not to become dependent in any way on an organization that I felt had betrayed me, and one that would betray me again if it ever came to exchanging confidences.

We sang a hymn, had an opening prayer to our Heavenly Father—it could have been a meeting anywhere in the Church. When the sacrament came around, I couldn't take it—but I knew before I went that I couldn't take it. I thought of Mom crying at that part of the meeting because I am left out.

And that's what I'm writing to thank you for. Thank you for not leaving me out. If both the Church and the family had abandoned me, I would be a sad, lost person. Nothing cuts deeper than a parent's rejection of a gay son. I see it like ghosts in the faces of other people, sense the humiliation. It seems a miracle to me that you have been so supportive and positive about this from the beginning. When I think where you are now and of all that you do, I think I must be the proudest man in America.

When I look at the bishop and people in the Church who might be disgusted if they knew that I love men, I don't feel threatened or dependent on their acceptance of things they can't deal with. And it's because I have parents and a family that, despite all the troubles we drag along, is stronger than I ever knew and has ties like great roots.

People at church were friendlier than I expected—they must have people constantly drifting in and out. A friend from Provo High told me in the foyer that it was only her third time in seven years that she had come to church. She asked me if I planned to attend at all regularly, almost like she were looking for a friend to come back with. I told her that I didn't know because it's more difficult for me because I had been excommunicated for having a boyfriend. I told her that I wasn't angry but that I thought they were wrong to do it and that it was a shame that they had because it makes it more difficult for me to want to participate—having to explain circumstances that I feel like keeping private. She has been a dancer in New York for seven years, and I saw the look that caught the pain of it all. And she knew they were wrong to do it. It's hard to meet people who only knew me at Provo High before all this trouble, when I was so confident and full of life. It just reminds us of how the reality of our lives can be so much more difficult and disappointing than we imagined.

The bishop interrupted our conversation to introduce himself. He suggested that I talk to Brother So-and-So to fill out a form they have for new members. I told him in a steady voice that I had just arrived and hadn't decided how active I would be in the ward, that I wanted to wait to see how I felt.

When I was a deacon in Oak Hills passing the sacrament, I never could have imagined the path my life has taken. But looking back, it has been a path with love, honesty, friends, a family path. More than anything, a family path. That is the miracle I am writing to thank you for.

Love,
Craig

~

A poem written by Craig:

Coming Out to Grandma

I went alone, two hours in my sister's car
Not without a sense of duty.

A house so solid, lived in, at once familiar
Date bread and milk.

The old photos she pulled from drawers and walls
To bring to the table.

Her twilight world relayed to me in
Patches of tragedy, and shining humor.

And I have come to tell her who I am.
I am a family tragedy.

The crevassed blue veins in her hand
Holding Kleenex, the big ring.

Tears only whispered across to me like prayers
For our whole surrounding patchwork.

Warm eyes brimming
Quilting into the crocheted gloaming.

~

From Craig's father Gary:

Some have asked me how my then 89-year-old mother responded to Craig's "coming out." She didn't miss a beat. "I don't understand," she replied, "but I still love you." In a few short weeks, she became one of his greatest advocates.

A short time later, I had the opportunity to introduce her to a neighbor of ours who had been called to be an LDS mission president and was soon to depart to England.

"I'm happy to meet you," she said, then quickly added, "What are you doing about *our* problem?" Fortunately we had previously discussed our family issue with him. He gave her a big hug and said, "I will do everything in my power to make the world a better place for our gay brothers and sisters."

You Just Have to Love

Elona Knighton Shelley
Orem, Utah

This piece is adapted from a talk the author gave at an LDS stake Relief Society conference in 2005 in Orem, Utah. She has established a website for parents whose children take unexpected paths, www.ourfamilysaga.byu.edu

~

Among my earliest childhood memories was a strong desire to go to the celestial kingdom. It was a natural part of being raised in an active LDS family, and I tried hard to be "really good." However, as I grew older and learned more about what was required, I began to worry. What chance did I actually have of attaining such a lofty goal? I mean, you had to be perfect to go there!

After serving a mission, I met my husband at BYU, and we married in the temple. I had always wanted to be a mother, but I hadn't anticipated the overwhelming love I felt for our first little son, David. He filled our lives with delight and wonder. His bright mind and charming ways promised a happy future. I urgently desired to help him get to the celestial kingdom, too.

Over the next nine years, I gave birth to five more precious children. Meeting their needs created a stressful world for me, but I loved them more than I had ever dreamed possible. I tried desperately to make them do everything right so we could all go to the celestial kingdom together. Sometimes I met with stiff resistance, but I diligently persisted. We attended all our church meetings and activities, paid generous offerings, had family prayer and scripture time, and I over-magnified my callings. Unfortunately, I was also buried in guilt because I often caught myself yelling at my children. But what could I do? I was sure we would never be happy if we didn't do everything right. My fears intensified as I envisioned myself approaching the doors to the celestial kingdom and watching them slam in my face because in the end, I just wasn't quite good enough.

By the time David reached his mid-teens, he had become defiant and secretive. Most mornings, I had to drag him out of bed and take him to school. On the way, I usually reprimanded him angrily for the inconvenience he was causing me and for the problems he was creating for himself. Occasionally we shared a loving moment, but most often we were engaged in bitter conflict. He sought refuge with his friends.

One day David nervously approached me and said, "Mom, I want to tell you something before you hear it from someone else. I'm gay. I've known it for a long time. All my friends are gay. I just wanted you to know because I'm tired of hiding it." With that, he ran out the door and hopped into his friend's car. They sped away, leaving me in a total twilight zone.

My mind raced wildly as I tried to comprehend David's words. "What am I going to do? I can't tell anyone. We have to move away and not let anyone know where we are. We won't be able to tell anyone we are Mormons. I've failed the Church, and I've failed my family. I'm not even worthy to be a member of the Church because I have a gay son." I desperately wanted to pray, but I couldn't. What could I possibly say to God? I had failed

Him miserably, and I was sure He was terribly disappointed in me. I wished I could die.

I had known many dark days, but at that point my world went totally black. I cried endlessly and constantly asked myself what I had done wrong. How had I let this precious little boy's life turn into such a tragedy? Maybe if I hadn't been so cross, maybe if I hadn't been so busy with my church callings, maybe if we hadn't let him get a job, maybe if I had listened more, maybe if I had been more understanding. The questions and self-accusations never ended. I felt desperately lonely, but I was too ashamed to share my pain. I stopped writing in my journal because I felt if I wrote anything down, it would become permanent.

As the tearful days dragged into months, I realized I had to get some help. I made an appointment and cautiously discussed my situation with our doctor. He was kind, but I continued to be miserable. Finally I gathered the courage to tell my sister and also my walking partner, Margaret. What a relief it was to share my secret with them and feel their outpouring of love and support!

One day I was on the phone with Margaret discussing a mutual friend's plans to donate a kidney to her fifteen-year-old son. "They say the surgery is usually very hard on the donor," I told her. "She's making a huge sacrifice, especially considering all the younger children she has to care for." My words surprised Margaret. "Sure it would be hard," she said, "but I'd do it in a heartbeat for one of my kids, and so would you." Without thinking, I said, "I would for any of them but David."

Instantly, I was frozen in time, stunned as those words echoed repeatedly through my mind. I clumsily ended the phone conversation as new words clearly came to me. "In the last days the hearts of the mothers will turn cold." I crumbled to my knees in anguish. "Heavenly Father, please help me!" I begged. "Have I actually become a cold-hearted mother? I can't believe I said I would let David die!" My heart was truly broken, and I wept bitterly.

I remained on my knees for a long time, pleading for some kind of solace. Finally, words of comfort came, laced with a gentle reproach. "You are not a cold-hearted mother. You are just hurt. But think how much more David is hurting. You have friends and family who stand by you and support you. He has no one to turn to. He feels rejected by his family, by his church, and by everyone who has known him." As I pondered this new insight, a penetrating sadness crept over me—this time for my son instead of for myself.

"But Heavenly Father," I cried, "what can I do? I don't understand anything about homosexuality! How can I possibly be a good mother for him?"

"You don't have to understand. You just have to love."

"Well, I can do that!" I responded. "I can love!" I had loved many troubled kids over the years—nieces, nephews, children of friends, young people from church. My burden lifted, and for the first time in a very long time, my heart knew hope. I lingered on my knees, rejoicing in God's pure love for me and for David. I arose renewed, filled with gratitude for my new perspective.

At first, David was suspicious of my change of attitude. We still had many conflicts, but I constantly prayed for guidance and for the ability to retain the feelings of love I had been given. I encouraged him to bring his friends home, and I embraced them all, whether they had purple hair, nose rings, spiked leather jackets, chains, black lipstick —or all of it together. It was difficult for me to stop nagging about school, but when David explained how unsafe he felt there, I realized it was not a good place for him after all. He withdrew from high school and completed the requirements for an alternate diploma.

Though we continued to encounter a variety of challenges, the change in our relationship was remarkable. I had no idea what lay ahead, but I was optimistic. Several months later, however, as I was sitting alone at my kitchen table, this thought sprang into my mind: "But you can never be *truly* happy because all of your children will never be married in the temple." Suddenly I was drowning in a pool of despair as the thought repeated relentlessly, "I'm never going to be happy. I'm never going to be happy. I'm never going to be happy." Complete hopelessness consumed me, and it seemed all my progress had been swept away forever. But then just as suddenly, something deep inside me snapped. I sprang from my chair and shouted, "Oh, yeah? I can't live if I can't be happy! I'm just going to have to be happy no matter what!"

My unexpected outburst shocked me, but in that instant I knew without question that my happiness was in my own hands. It didn't depend on my children, my husband, or my external circumstances. This new knowledge burned in the very core of my being. I was finally able to allow myself to be happy! I was finally free!

A profound peace filled my soul. It strengthened and comforted me when David, still only seventeen, decided to move to Salt Lake City. Loading his bed, dresser, and personal belongings into our van tugged at my heart. Depositing them in a cheap, barren apartment with dusty pipes running everywhere was even harder. He had no job, a questionable roommate, and far more freedom than I would have preferred. As I tearfully embraced him to say our final farewell, he seemed nervous and un-settled, but he insisted it was what he wanted to do.

We didn't see David often, and after a few years, he moved to Texas to stay with a friend, who soon became his partner. Two years later they moved to New York City. David called sporadically to share his experiences. When he and his partner argued, he would often seek my advice. I always tried to be loving and supportive, but sometimes I found it quite difficult. I was especially challenged during the few occasions when he came home to visit. He was generally edgy and easily upset. I felt guilty that I liked having him live far away. I was afraid I was losing the gift of love God had given me.

About five years after David's move to New York, I learned a new way of studying the scriptures. I quickly came to understand what it means to truly "feast upon the words of Christ." I accepted Christ's invitation to "come unto me, all ye that . . . are heavy laden," and I joyfully received the promised rest. Sometimes I felt so overcome with gratitude that I would hold my scriptures and tenderly stroke the columns of words or lift them to my cheek and gently rest my face on the open pages. As I earnestly studied and prayed, the Spirit continually bore witness to me of Christ's pure love for me and for each of God's children, regardless of where or how they live. I realized that Christ offers us a straight path to Him, but that He also freely allows us to take whatever path we choose, so we can learn by our own experience. As I recorded my thoughts and feelings in my journal, an abundance of love and guidance flowed into my life. Looking back, I clearly see that the Lord was preparing me for what was coming next.

I got a call from David a few months before the World Trade Center attack in September 2001. We talked about his recent health problems and his declining business. He wasn't anxious to return to Utah, but we discussed the possibility of him coming home just long enough to regain his health. "It wouldn't be easy for you," I warned him. "Grandma is now living with us, and she is pretty vocal about homosexuality." We made no definite plans, but after the Trade Center attack, David's business collapsed completely. "I have a couple of relocation possibilities that look promising," he said, "but could I come home and recuperate for just a few weeks while I decide what to do? Grandma and I can survive for that long, and I will be fine sleeping on the floor." Though I wondered what "a few weeks" might mean, the Spirit undeniably directed us to welcome him back into our home.

Coming home proved to be an extremely difficult adjustment for David. It brought up a lot of anger about his past and about how my husband and I had parented him. There was constant hostility between him and my mother. He needed to talk through a lot of things, and we spent many long hours engaged in intense conversation. Sometimes he'd push me to defend myself, but I found I could calmly flow with his barrage of emotions as long as I maintained my new pattern of consistent prayer, scripture study, and journaling. I listened to his accusations without feeling attacked and was often prompted to offer an apology and ask for forgiveness.

While living in New York, David embraced Tibetan Buddhism, and I was delighted to find we had many common beliefs. However, we still strongly disagreed on many political and religious issues. I was blessed with an ever-present feeling of peace and love as we continued to hash things over, and we gradually developed a strong mutual respect. Months later, during one of our discussions, David paused and gazed at me for a moment. Then he thoughtfully said, "Mom, you practice your religion differently now."

"I understand my religion differently now," I replied. I have had countless opportunities to know the joy of practicing my religion differently. Besides being blessed with calmness in the face of criticism, I have also often been blessed to release my desire for control. It has taken so much stress from my life. For example, David picked up a smoking habit while he was gone. I know I would have felt distraught and compelled to lecture him before, but not anymore. He always went outside to smoke and was careful to see that I wasn't around. One night when I knew he was feeling deeply troubled, I stepped outside just as he lit a cigarette.

"Mom," he said through the darkness, "I'm smoking. I don't want you to see me smoking." I slowly walked over and sat next to him on the swing. I put my hand on his knee and leaned my head on his shoulder. After a brief hesitation, he poured out his grief to me. As I listened, I felt honored that he trusted me enough to share his heartache. He rarely smokes anymore. He knows I think it's a bad habit, but more importantly, he knows I love him whether he smokes or not.

Another example would be dealing with David's language when he is angry. Before he left home, we had numerous heated arguments about his inappropriate word choices. Although he generally respects my standards now, I recently made a comment about an event from his teenage years which triggered fierce emotion and a stream of foul language. It was obvious that heavy fear and pain still surrounded the event as it replayed itself in his mind. He raged on for several minutes before finally allowing me to put my arms around him. "I'm sorry you felt so abandoned and vulnerable when that happened," I said. His language was simply a non-issue. The following day he talked to me about his explosive response. He said he watched himself like a runaway train as he heard his angry words spew forth.

So much healing has taken place as David's time at home has extended from "a few weeks" to more than four years. These years have given him the opportunity to develop a loving relationship with each of his siblings and with his nieces and nephews. One of my favorite miracles has been the transformation of his relationship with my mother, which only happened once I quit trying to resolve the tension between them. I never cease to be thrilled by their frequent hugs and playful teasing.

I'm sure I don't yet recognize all the goodness that has come into my life because of this journey. I only know I wouldn't change it even if I could. It has taken me from a place of fear to a place of trust. I no longer feel compelled to "herd" my family to the celestial kingdom. And I no longer worry about those celestial doors slamming in my face. I'm on the path, and I can walk forward in peace and joy as I honor my children's agency, for "I know in whom I have trusted." How worthy He is of that trust! Indeed, as Nephi [in the Book of Mormon] said, "My God hath been my support; he hath led me through mine afflictions." He will lead each of us as we invite Him into our hearts. We do not have to understand all things. Sometimes we just have to love.

Our Children's Vows: Ben and Clare, Brett and Jeff

Marge and William Bradshaw
Orem, Utah

In June it was a wedding. The bride was a radiantly lovely young woman, Clare; the groom was a strikingly handsome young man, our son, Ben. The ceremony itself was one of solemnity and joy. The words that were spoken committed the couple to the highest and noblest of human aspirations—fidelity, responsibility, work, patience, kindness, sacrifice, happiness. It was not hard to imagine that among his silent resolves was thoughtfulness, as in getting up in the middle of the night to take care of her if she were ill. Her unspoken list surely must have included earning the title of best friend with tenderness and material gifts of her own design and execution. After the ceremony, in another place, there was food, laughter, and dancing. The groom with his mom, the bride with her dad. The bride's parents danced, the groom's parents danced; then they traded partners. Wives danced with husbands. Boyfriends danced with girlfriends. It was a gay occasion. We are convinced that everyone present found that there was more human goodness in the world than we had been aware of, and that the Heavenly Father of us all was pleased.

In October it was a commitment ceremony. Each of the two there to speak their vows was a tall, athletic-looking, affable young man. One was our son, Brett; the other was his partner, Jeff. All the parents were there, supportive, honoring their sons. Parts of the extended families and many friends were there, too, an expression of loyalty to loved ones. Some families consisted only of women. Some families consisted only of men. There were lots of exchanges between those who cared about him and those who cared about the other him. We were separate parts of a complex web of relationships made intimate because of love. But there was also a certain wistfulness accompanying the realization that occasions like this one are not always family gatherings—there's frequently a lot of deliberate absenteeism.

The vows that were spoken committed the couple to the highest of human aspirations—fidelity, responsibility, work, patience, kindness, sacrifice. It was not hard to imagine that each was making silent resolves, like getting up in the middle of the night to take care of the other who was ill, or earning the title of best friend by being supportive, encouraging, and honest. The content of the vows and the spirit that accompanied them were good, legitimate, and important. We were made to wonder: which of these very moral sentiments was inconsistent with applying legal sanction to such a covenant?

After the ceremony, in another place, there was food, laughter, and dancing. Each groom danced with his mom. The parents of each man danced together, then traded partners. Some men danced with men. Some women danced with women. Boyfriends danced with girlfriends. Grandpas danced with granddaughters. It was a gay occasion.

It seemed to us that everyone present found that there was more human goodness in the world than we had been aware of and that the Heavenly Father of us all was pleased.

Rod's Other Family

One of the best things about the Mormon Church is that it can serve as a "larger family" to those who have none or to those whose family of origin has failed them. This doesn't always work. We are imperfect, programs are imperfect, time and resources have limits, people fall between the cracks, but frequently someone who would otherwise be quite alone finds a loving family at church. And the Mormon Church is not just a "Sunday church"; it is part of the fabric of one's daily life.

I read that Iraq's minister of state for women's affairs, Azhar Abdul Karem al-Sheikhly, recently visited the U.S. specifically to spend a week in Salt Lake City studying the Church's organization for women, the Relief Society, founded in 1842 to relieve the poor and the needy. Iraqi women have been "searching for a way to build a network that could harness their collective strength, and they discovered a remarkable model in this Mormon organization." For example, the Relief Society has "visiting teachers," pairs of women assigned to visit each woman in the ward monthly and to be aware of her well-being and available to assist as needed. Azhar said, "I wish I could do this visiting teachers in my country. I wish to tell how families are strong in this country, how families take care of each other. . . . This is the way to build a new Iraq."

I give that example as prelude to the story of "Rod."

About nine years ago, I was sitting on the floor in the family room playing Scrabble with one of my children when the phone rang. "Sister Pearson?" The voice was very flat. "I'm calling to ask you why I should not commit suicide." I ended the game.

Rod was calling from Colorado. He was a gay Mormon man in his late thirties, was also a diagnosed schizophrenic, suffered from extraordinarily painful fibromyalgia, and had already made a couple of suicide attempts. He lived alone and survived on government social services. He had been celibate for fifteen years, loved and believed in the Church, but was in extreme pain because of its teaching on homosexuality. That pain, along with his physical pain, prevented him from being a regular church attender. His parents had disowned him, written him out of the will, and I heard from him a chilling statement I will never forget. His mother had said to his sister—the sister who still calls him—"I suppose I should be better to Rod, but he's not going to be with us in the next life anyway."

Rod called me when he was especially suicidal, in extreme physical pain, and even once when his cat was dying; and I called him from time to time. Sometimes when I called, he would start to cry that someone would call just to see how he was. Eventually I told him I would put him on my visiting teaching list, and he would know that he would get a call on the first Sunday of every month.

March 23, 2000
Just hung up from talking with Rod. . . . He is so fractured, so beaten down. . . . I had told him the other day to reach down into his core and find a place where he could get through this difficult time. Last night he said, so honestly and sadly, "You told me to go inside and find my core. I tried, and I don't have a core." Tonight I told him to visualize his angels around him.

"Do I have angels?" Of course. "I feel cut off from God." I told him God had not cut him off, just the words that he has heard so often. I asked if he thought I would condemn him. No. Well, God has to be at least as loving a being as I am, twenty billion times more. Just be brave enough to assume it, insist on it. But I know without a core all this is virtually impossible. . . . But a good thing. My insistence that he call PFLAG led to a man getting in touch with him, a good formerly Mormon man, a *psychotherapist*—how lucky can we be? . . . So glad there is someone there for Rod. One of the angels.

I learned of other angels that were there for Rod, and I was delighted to find that many of them were members of his own Mormon ward. I imagined they were puzzled, to be sure, about how to deal with a gay man, albeit a celibate gay man, but I listened and blessed them as I heard Rod's stories. Recently I called to have him remind me of the people in his church experience that have done their best to circle their wagons around him.

There was the stake patriarch, who had given Rod his "patriarchal blessing" when he was 18 and who had stayed in contact with him until the man's death just last year, becoming something of a grandfather to him. He knew Rod was gay, knew the family well, and said to him, "Rod, I'm afraid that your parents are among those who should not have had children in this lifetime. I'm sorry for them. They will have to account to the Lord for the way they have treated you." Rod recalls this man saying to him, "Heavenly Father loves you a great deal, and what you are doing is very important, just meeting your daily challenges and enduring to the end and being an example to others."

There was the bishop who showed up at the hospital three hours after one of Rod's suicide attempts. This man had a gay brother, knew that Rod was gay, and was very understanding of

his despair over his physical pain and especially the hopelessness of "living alone all my life, never able to have someone to
love." He invited Rod to spend Thanksgiving with his family,
paid his rent twice from the "fast offering" fund, and saw to it
that food was constantly brought to him from the "bishops'
storehouse."

There was the Relief Society president, who also knew Rod
was gay and, in fact, told him once she wished he could find a
companion whom he could love. They live in different wards
now, but she still calls him and takes him out for ice cream. He
remembers that when she and her family had him over for
Christmas Eve, her husband insisted that Rod sit in his special
chair because he was their honored guest. "They treated me just
like family," he told me. "They asked me questions and listened
to me like I was someone very important."

There is the family who picks him up for church because recently Rod has wanted to take the sacrament. "It helps me to
make amends and to make my life a little better, but I can't manage to sit any longer than that." And there is the couple who sit
with him, drive him home and then come back to finish the
service.

There are the men and women in the ward who sign up to
drive Rod to his many medical appointments and on other er-
rands.

I like to listen to his stories. Sometimes they make me smile,
and I think, bless those good people. A schizophrenic gay man
whose limited budget does not include food and who can't sit
through church because of physical and emotional pain does
present some challenges to the congregation. Bless them for giving him a better family than the one he was born into.

He Just Cried with Me

Julie Mark
Portland, Oregon

Dear Carol Lynn,

I remember my mother being so moved by *Goodbye, I Love You.* I was only 19 at the time, but little did we both know how close to home the "issue" would hit. Your goal to assist in healing relationships is desperately needed.

My name is Julie Mark, and I'm a 39-year-old woman, born and raised Mormon, who happens to be a lesbian. I was fortunate to experience a truly loving, close, nurturing family life growing up. My parents were crazy in love and adored their five children. As I grew up, my father was a bishop, stake president, and temple sealer and recently returned from a two-year mission in Russia. I have felt the effects of both failure and success within my family in their attempts to deal with my sexuality. I know the devastating effects of being alienated by a family member, but I would rather focus on the unconditional love I've received.

Being in the arts, I had a few gay friends growing up, but it never crossed my mind I was "one of them." I was a young single woman, happily pursuing her music dreams. I fell in love for the first time at age twenty-eight, to my utter horror and surprise, with a woman. Even though I had personally removed

241

myself from the Mormon Church, I knew the shame it would bring on my very conservative family. I will never forget calling my father from graduate school, sobbing, telling him that I had done something I couldn't believe and needed his support. I'd always been close to my father, and I knew I could trust him with my desperation. (Not only did I have sex before marriage, which I thought I didn't believe in, it was with a woman, and worse yet, I enjoyed it and didn't want it to be a one-time thing! The guilt I felt was indescribable.)

Before I even said anything, he just cried with me because his daughter was in pain. The love, concern, and warmth never wavered during that conversation or since. He reassured me of his great love, my worth, and of God's love for me. At the end of that conversation, I told him that mornings were the hardest for me, just facing another day. He asked if he could call me every morning for a while, just to make sure I was OK. I welcomed and looked forward to his reassuring, loving calls each morning as I woke to the most ruptured sense of self I ever hope to experience.

That call was eleven years ago, and we had a few conversations after that about my sexuality, all very honest and respectful. Long ago we agreed to disagree about certain things. What we both agreed on, strongly, was *unconditional love.* That love is what we focus on and cherish deeply. My mother had a little harder time "accepting things," but I know my father was instrumental in helping her see the big picture, and it didn't take her too long. Before her early death, eight years ago, she told me her wish for me was to be happy. She may not have understood (that made two of us at that time), but the unconditional love for her daughter rose above everything. Isn't that the message Christ/Buddha and all the great teachers taught? Unconditional love that we can't even fathom the magnitude and brilliance of? It's that simple, yet difficult for many.

I hope some day the gap between religion and this "issue" will drastically narrow, and people will recognize the unbelievable irony of how people are treated, all in the name of religion. How lucky I am that my parents already knew that.

Love,

Julie

P.S. I just closed on my first home, beautiful, with the love of my life. I'm a step-mom to her darling five-year-old daughter. I'm very happy!

Tumbling Down

Tracy Duvalis Kriese
Dripping Springs, Texas

And Joshua commanded, "Now children, shout!"
And the walls came tumbling down.
"Joshua Fit the Battle of Jericho"
—American spiritual

The woman who had just been introduced stood to take the microphone. Applause gave way to a hush as the crowd of teenagers awaited her first words. It was a quiet that honored her loss, that paid tribute to her courage in the face of great pain. Karen's daughter had committed suicide the year before, unable to endure one more insult, one more beating, from a community that could not accept who she was. Tiny little Rockdale, Texas, had not understood Tesia, a transgender teen, and so tiny little Rockdale had killed her almost as surely as if they had hung the rope around her neck themselves.

Tesia was dead, and for her there would be no more taunts hurled through school hallways, no more abuse shouted from passing cars. For her mother, there would be no more of Tesia's radiant smiles, no more of her free-spirited dances, and yet here was her mother, standing before us—before other people's children—wanting to tell them the same thing she had told her own child: you are beautiful, you have dignity, you have worth. You are loved, just the way you are.

I stood at the back of the crowd with other adults who were there to lend support to these kids and their fight for protection in school. The Dignity for All Students Act was once again before the Texas legislature, and we were determined that this time the bill would not die in committee. These students were there on the capitol steps to tell their stories of the insults that teachers did not seem to hear, of the threats that principals did not want to take seriously, of the awful burden of trying to learn in an environment that was dehumanizing and threatening. Tesia could no longer speak for herself, but her mother was there to share her story.

As she spoke, tears began to fall from my eyes before my heart even realized that they had been loosed. Immediately my breathing quickened, and my stomach clenched. Oh, no . . . no! . . . I could not cry! With tears came pain, and I *would not* feel that pain again! I knew that it lived somewhere in me still, but I had so successfully confined it behind thick walls of anger and activism that I could forget that it was there, that it had ever existed. Now those walls were under siege, and they were falling with every word Tesia's mother said. I wiped the stinging tears away with suddenly trembling hands, but it was no use; I could not hold them back. In desperate retreat, I turned away from the woman whose voice was pulling from inside of me this shaking, melting person I did not want to be. Panicked at how quickly, how inescapably the tears were coming, I searched the familiar grounds of the capitol for some sort of cover. There were the manicured green lawns shaded with oaks, wide walkways stretching to the street, bronze statues of fallen Texas heroes—monuments to courage?—but I could barely see them through my own fear. I was terrified of this pain that was pouring from me. I'd survived this feeling when it had first been born, had carried it with me day and night as a mother must so that her child's burden is lighter. Why did I have to feel it again now, in such an overwhelming rush that I might fall to the pavement if I gave in to it?

I stepped back farther away from the crowd, still well within the reach of Karen's voice. Her words were unintelligible now through the pounding of my own heartbeat, but I did not want to hear them anymore. Pain, heartache, grief. How could a mother bear it, the loss of her child? How does a parent survive a child's death?

Standing there that day, I knew that I might have been her. I had almost lost my child. Eric had wanted to die. And oh, hadn't he died in a way? A thousand times, over and over, as the world told him he was not normal, as we told him that he could change, that he must fight to change, as he told himself that God did not love him! The killing of his spirit had been so nearly complete by the time he was fifteen that the death of his body seemed not far behind. There were the nights of sleeping outside his door, of taking turns with my husband staying awake through those dark hours when our son might take that desperate step he seemed to long for more and more. In the stillness of a house asleep—fitfully, finally asleep—I would lie down at his door and listen for him—listen, too, for my daughters, anxious to keep them safe from the awful intruder, fear, that had moved into our Mormon home.

The house was heavy with its presence, especially in those hours before dawn. Moonlight through windows, light that once would have brought serenity with its quiet glow, now cast shadows in the corners. Dark and ominous, those shadows crept across the floor towards me as the hours crawled by. Haunting my thoughts were their whisperings of easy Sunday School lessons about heaven and hell, of memorized scripture references about sin and repentance, exaltation and damnation. Nothing was easy now. Nothing would ever be easy again.

Daylight brought no answers, and the shadows held only more questions, but still my husband and I took up our posts, night after night. Behind my son's bedroom door was a struggle with pain and despair which we did not understand and could not fight for him, but in the darkness outside his door we remained watchful, vigilant—believing that if we just listened hard enough, if we just *waited* hard enough, we could somehow save our child from the agony that was killing him.

And it was killing him. I saw it gaining hold in his once bright eyes, now dull and empty, in his body that no longer seemed to walk but rather was forced to move through his days. I heard it in the laughter that no longer rang. Joy had been Eric's gift since infancy. He had been blessed with a soul that delighted in life and that sought expression of intense feeling in whatever form it might come. Now those highs and lows had become one unrelieved surface, a depression of spirit that had left him empty of everything except its own aching void. I felt again the utter helplessness of holding him as he sobbed for release from this thing that he was, as he collapsed under the terrible burden of being a gay boy in a Mormon family, in a straight world. We and that world had taught him well: homosexuality was unnatural and unholy. It was not of God. Later he would tell me of the torment that haunted him during those dark nights: if God did not make gay people, then who made him? The nightmarish answer that came into his mind placed him so far outside the circle of creation of which we had taught him that he despaired of living. Eric would rather be dead than gay, but in my arms he sobbed all the harder because he lacked the courage to kill himself. His self-loathing extended even to that: he was a faggot, *and* he was a coward.

Now, hearing Tesia's mother speak of her loss, I was confronted again with that fear of five years ago. Washing over me and out of me was the pain of the knowledge that my own child had almost chosen death in the face of his unbearable suffering. Flooding my senses was the weight of that burden, of that five years of heavy lifting as our family had worked to free our son and thereby ourselves from the crushing lies that we had all been taught by the Church about homosexuality, from the heavy shame of being born gay in a society that declares there is no such thing.

Where was Eric now? I had to find him, had to hold him! These tears were for my son, and I needed to cry them while hugging him. I had to tell him again that I was so sorry for those first two years of misunderstanding and ignorance, two years of not seeing, of not hearing the truth, letting him fight the darkness alone for much of his life. I had to tell him how grateful I was that he was alive, that he had endured our struggle and our fear. He needed to know how thankful I was that on the other side of that bedroom door, he had waited, too, had waited for us to understand.

I found him, seated toward the back of the crowd. He was there that day not as a high school student—he had graduated the year before—but as an ally to support the kids who were carrying on the fight for dignity in the public schools. At Lake Travis High, he had founded the school's Gay Straight Alliance. At nineteen, he was an experienced speaker at congressional hearings, at rallies and marches, with newspaper reporters and television interviewers. His voice was now that of a young adult rather than a high school teen, but he knew he wanted to be there that day listening to others who were continuing the work.

I stepped carefully over the rows of teenagers and placed my hand on Eric's shoulder. He turned, his quick glance becoming a look of worried surprise at the unfamiliar sight of Mom's tears, and followed me away from the crowd.

It was right and fitting, then, that I would fall into his arms and find my tears giving way to quiet sobs. The boy whom I had held through so much heartache was now a young man holding me. "I'm so sorry, Eric—so sorry!" Words broken with emotion spilled from me as I told him how grateful I was that we had not lost him to the death he once thought would be his only freedom. He was here, he was whole, he was my beautiful child to embrace in all his awesome creation. He was holding me now, reassuring me with his words, healing my heart with his amazing compassion.

"Mom," he said with quiet insistence. (That voice! How close had we come to losing the sound of that voice forever?) "Mom, you don't ever have to apologize for loving me the way you did."

On the Inside

Guy Berryessa
San Francisco, California

When I met Guy Berryessa's mother Janet at a meeting of Family Fellowship, she said, "My husband isn't here because this is his temple night and nothing interferes with Max's temple night." Then she hastened to tell me, "But also nothing interferes with his love for his son." I met their son Guy and his partner Trey when our mutual friend Trevor Southey drove me to their charming home in San Francisco, where we spent Mother's Day with these two fathers and their daughter, and I convinced Guy to write his story for me.

A few weeks ago, my sweet niece got married in the Salt Lake Temple to a wonderful young man whom she met when they were both missionaries. My partner, our precious daughter, and I flew to Utah to be there for the celebration, just as my niece had traveled to San Francisco for our commitment ceremony some eight years earlier. As our four-year-old daughter Emma and I stood outside the temple, waiting for the newly married couple and the rest of the family to emerge, Emma asked me an innocent yet profound question, "Daddy, why are they on the inside and we are on the outside?"

I had no ready answer then, but someday she and I will talk about it. We both have histories that have placed us "on the outside," in church and in society. She is African American, and I

250

am gay. But I think when we do talk about it, we'll both be able to honestly rejoice that many walls have come down. I've seen so many crumble already.

Like so many gay men in religious families, I didn't acknowledge my sexual orientation to my family or to anyone until my mid-twenties. I was terrified and traumatized by what I'd been taught in the Mormon Church about being gay or anything like unto it. I didn't want to face the rejection I was sure would be mine, as well as the pain, sorrow, and shame it might bring to my family. I buried my awful secret for as long as I could beneath a very busy life of school, with scholarships and honors; of work, including teaching at BYU, the Provo School District and the Missionary Training Center; of service to church and community. Filling my time with good work made me feel perhaps just a little less unworthy.

Finally at the age of 26, I met the first gay man I'd ever known, and as he told me his story, I felt the dam break inside of me. The well of tears I'd held inside for so many years began to flow. I cried for the first time in many years and then most every night for the next several months as I dealt with what this meant for me and my family. I had to tell them. I was about to leave for Africa for a year as a volunteer health care worker, and I decided to tell my beloved father—on Father's Day, no less. He was the one I thought could bear it best.

My father is a wonderful, truly Christian man, very loving, very kind, perhaps a bit naïve. He was then serving as bishop in a BYU ward. I asked him to go for a walk with me, and told him as carefully as I could what I was experiencing. He responded gently that we all have a cross to bear and it will all work out somehow in the next life, never imagining that I might ever *act* on those feelings. Not another word was spoken about it, but when I arrived in Nigeria and unpacked, there lay a page copied from the bishop's handbook, instructions about dealing with homosexuality.

Later, when I returned from my service abroad, my mother took the news with more difficulty. I had begun an intimate relationship with my first partner, and the experience was life-changing for me. I knew that my purpose for being on this earth was not to be shut down emotionally, physically, and spiritually as I had been, but to be fully present and fully giving and loving in a committed relationship. I knew that there was no going back, no matter how difficult it might be. And I knew that what I had been taught about my homosexual feelings was wrong.

The memory of my first conversation with my mother about this is still wrapped in pain. The very thought was to her so unthinkably awful that she immediately left the room and threw up. I believe we both thought we might die, it was so painful. For a while I wasn't sure our relationship would survive, but my mother and my father both refused to let their love for their son be destroyed. They immediately started reading all they could find on the topic of homosexuality, attended a conference with me in Salt Lake City, met with various experts, locally and nationally, in order better to understand this phenomenon. And, most importantly, I think, began meeting with a group of other parents of gay children, a godsend for us. Also at that time, *Goodbye, I Love You* was published, and for the first time that I remembered, the topic of homosexuality was being discussed in the Utah Mormon community. All in all, my parents have been fantastic. Once I overheard my father telling someone how grateful he and my mother are to have had a gay child because they have learned and grown so much from it and have met such wonderful people.

My siblings' response has been mixed, but primarily it has been positive. Some family members seem to struggle more now than they did ten or twenty years ago. As the Church seems to get more politically involved in fighting gay marriage, gay adoption, etc., some members of my family have become more at odds with us over these issues. Some have said they will never accept our "lifestyle," though it is nearly identical to their own—raising kids, trying to make ends meet, being a good neighbor. One family member sent emails encouraging others in the family to vote for the anti-gay marriage amendments, and when others replied back with letters asking them not to send such things and giving us their support instead, the response was a letter saying all family members supporting us or not calling us to repentance would be damned, that the prophet has clearly spoken about this and they "have to draw the line." Yes, the line has been drawn by some, keeping us "on the outside," but I'm so grateful for the many whose hearts are large enough to invite us in.

My life partner, Trey, and I first met at BYU, both of us involved in a student peace and human rights advocacy group. I found him very likeable and honorable, but we never became close friends. Years later, when he was visiting Utah from New York, where he was finishing his PhD, we met again, acknowledged we both were gay, and found a bond developing. When Trey sent me an email asking if I would consider long-distance dating, I thought: This is perfect—I want to go very slow on this, really get to know this wonderfully calm, spiritually centered, kind person. Our emails became voluminous. Our phone conversations sometimes lasted until the sun rose in New York, and we still had more to say! Soon we knew we were going to be together: life companions, soul mates, partners. Our commitment ceremony was held in December 1997, with most of our family members present. Though the ceremony had no legal significance, it seemed to cement in the minds and hearts of others that we were, indeed, a couple. The overwhelming support of family and friends was something we'll forever cherish.

I had gone through the long, difficult process of giving up hope of having children, but gradually Trey and I decided we wanted to extend our family, to bring a child into our home to love and nurture. As there are so many unwanted children in the world, we decided to try to adopt, now that finally it was possible for a gay couple to do so. But we were living in Germany at the time, and it was difficult to find an adoption agency that both would work with a gay couple and had a social worker in Europe who could do a home study for Americans living there. Once we were very close to success with a California adoption, but it fell through as the birth mother reconsidered immediately after the birth and kept us waiting for a month in Barstow before she decided against the adoption. It was devastating for us, both emotionally and financially. We went back to Germany with heavy hearts and empty hands and pockets. We'd decided we'd have to start saving up and try again in another year. But then we got a call, just a few days after flying back. "There's a baby available in Seattle," we were told. "She's seven weeks premature and in the ICU. She's African American. In Washington, the mother has just 24 hours to change her mind after birth. Shall we show her your portfolio?"

Trey and I had little hope that the mother would choose us, a gay couple, but we told the agency to go for it. We spent a restless night. What if . . . ? We couldn't allow ourselves to think of it. The next day, the agency called back, and I could hardly believe what I was hearing. "She's yours if you want her." Trey and

I looked at each other dumbfounded. "Of *course* we want her!" I think at that moment we were both in tears.

"We'll come right away!" I said. We'd have to figure out some way to borrow the money and trust in God that it would all work out, but immediately I flew to Seattle. Coincidentally, on the same day and for completely different reasons, Trey's parents flew to Seattle as well, so we went together to the hospital to meet our little Emma. I could hardly believe it as I held her for the first time: so tiny, so beautiful, and ours.

Later Trey joined me, and we both stayed with her until she was strong enough to go home with us. What an overwhelming, wonderful experience! The fulfillment of a dream. And, of course, a frightening responsibility. Some people thought we were crazy, but we felt then, and we feel now, that we are so blessed to have the privilege of having her in our lives and in our family. Every day we pray that we will be worthy of her and be able to provide her with what she needs and deserves. Emma is deeply loved, by us, by our families and our friends. I hope I can be as good a parent to her as mine have been to me. As I look around at other gay and lesbian parents, I know their children, too, are truly wanted and truly loved. In most ways, we're just another family, though it took us longer to become one.

Years from now, when Emma and I have our conversation about who is invited in and who is left out, I will have so much to tell her. And one story that pleases me is this:

Recently Trey and I bought a condo in Provo, Utah, within the boundaries of the ward in which my family was living when I went on my mission. One of the priesthood leaders announced in ward council meeting that I and my partner and our African American daughter were moving into the ward, and would everyone please welcome us and especially reach out to and include our daughter! When we heard this, we choked up and very briefly pondered a move to Provo just to experience such a warm welcome.

I'd like to believe that someday there will be more and more places in which I and my family will be found safely "on the inside." I hope and pray that will happen.

Gary's Protectors

Eugene Kovalenko
Los Alamos, New Mexico

Eugene Kovalenko was born and raised a Mormon in California and Arizona. Retired from a career as scientist and singer, he has been a school bus driver for seven years.

~

"Gary" is a big kid, a gentle, soft-spoken giant, who towers over his 9th grade contemporaries. He used to dye his long hair various colors: sometimes red, sometimes jet black. Now he's cut it all off and is growing sideburns.

Some months ago, while on my afternoon school bus route home with middle school and high school students on board, I noticed Gary being harassed in the center of the bus by both middle and high school boys. "Hey Homo!" one of the 7th grade boys yelled at him. The older boys had started it and now were eager to escalate the taunts.

I stopped the bus and walked back to the pack attack. "What's going on here?" I growled.

"Aw, we were just talking to him," replied one of the toughs.

"Didn't look like 'just talking' to me," I said. "I want it to stop now!" I could see they were rankled and resented giving up their prey.

Just before Gary got off at his stop at the end of the route, I asked him: "Does this kind of thing happen to you often?"

"Every day of my life!" he whispered and sadly walked away.

That woke me up.

The next afternoon, after picking up the middle school kids and before getting to the high school, I pulled the bus over, stopped and faced the students. They had become quiet.

"How many of you know the meaning of the word 'phobia'?" I asked.

Immediately several students, including the earlier attackers, gave the correct definition.

"How many of you know the meaning of the word 'compassion'?" I asked again.

Immediately the same students gave the correct answer.

"Do you know the meaning of 'homophobia'?" No answer this time. It was clear everybody suddenly got my purpose. "The reason I stopped here is because I want to say something before we get to the high school. You remember what happened to a young man here yesterday. Yes?"

Many students had downcast eyes and sheepish expressions on their faces.

"I don't want that ever to happen again on my bus. I want our bus to be safe for all of you and for you all to experience it as a welcoming and pleasant place, not a ride to dread. And I want to tell you something about me and my family. My youngest son is gay, and I love him dearly. He is talented, smart, and popular with both girls and boys. He has five older brothers who also love him dearly and are proud of him. No one would dare to hassle him as was done on this bus yesterday, lest they face one or more ferocious protectors." I made eye contact with all who would look at me. "I expect every one of you to behave yourselves when we pick up at the high school."

When we arrived, Gary was there. I asked him to sit in the front seat on the right side. In the seat just in back of him were the two tough 7th grade jocks who had given him such a hard time the day before. These boys were both on probation from earlier infractions on the bus, and they knew their days were numbered should they misbehave again.

When we came to the getting-off stop of the first boy, I climbed out of the bus with him and asked his companion to get off and join us for a minute. I said, "I've got a plan, guys, and I want you to listen carefully. I'm asking you to take an important assignment. I want you to be Gary's protectors. Don't let anybody mess with him. You'll sit directly behind him and watch out for troublemakers. Can you handle it?"

They looked at each other. "Yeah, sure," said one.

"We'll get some points—against that other stuff we did?" asked the other.

"Absolutely."

Gary's protectors have done a great job in the ensuing weeks and months. *Nobody* has messed with Gary. Just this afternoon, as the last boy got off the bus, he pounded fists with Gary, an affectionate goodbye gesture for boys these days.

As I look at Gary now, he is relaxed, joking, laughing, and enjoying the ride. He has two new friends in the seat right behind him. And hopefully a better future in front of him.

My Son Is More Important
Than My Prejudice

Carol Lynn and
Diane Palaski
Walnut Creek, California

A good friend in my ward, Diane Palaski, occasionally invites me over for dinner, along with whichever child or grandchildren happen to be around. About a year ago, she said, "I really want you to meet my nephew, Erin. He's a gay man and is going to be here on Sunday with his partner. Can you come?"

I told her I would love to meet her nephew. "He's the sweetest guy," she went on. "When he was a child he really enjoyed playing with my daughter and doing feminine-type activities. Eventually he 'came out' and told his family that he was gay. It didn't surprise me a lot. His parents—especially my brother—were devastated and felt very uncomfortable with the situation. It made me sad because—that's just who he *is*, and I love him."

We had a pleasant Sunday evening together. Erin grew up in northern Michigan and lives now in San Francisco, where he is in charge of women's clothing for a large department store. Occasionally after that I asked Diane about her nephew, and the other day she said, "Oh, Carol Lynn! I have something fantastic to tell you about my brother! The last few times we've all been together, I noticed that he was treating Erin more warmly and seemed to be more comfortable with him. I asked him about it, and he said, 'Well, not long ago I attended the funeral of the gay son of a friend of mine. He had committed suicide. As I sat at that funeral, I realized just how much I really do love Erin, and I said to myself, this is never going to happen in my family. My son is more important than my prejudice.'"

Life Is a Song

Carol Lynn and
Sikoki Layton
Reseda Heights, California

"Sikoki" is an odd name for a Mormon boy. Scott Layton is his birth name, but when he went on a two-and-a-half-year mission to the Samoan Islands, he was given the name Sikoki and liked it so much he kept it. Sikoki tells me he "came out" to his mother when he was four. "I said, 'Mom, when I grow up I'm going to have a boyfriend and a little boy named Todd.'"

He tried his best to conform to expectations, especially the expectations of his church, but when the inevitable clash came, he chose his belief in himself over his belief in his religion. In my experience of Mormon gay men, Sikoki holds an enviable place. He is one who has come through it all with very few evident scars, with no bitterness, and with a personal presence of confidence, warmth, and enthusiasm. I am so glad I get to place his story here and not in the suicide section. Sikoki told me he considered attending BYU, but two gay men he knew had gone there, and both of them had committed suicide. And I am so glad I don't have to place his story in the ill-fated marriage section. Numerous smitten women pursued him, but Sikoki was clear-headed enough to know that he couldn't make them happy nor could they make him happy. Two years after they met in the Gay

Men's Chorus of Los Angeles, Sikoki and Richard knew they wanted to be life partners. Richard's Lutheran parents found it hard to believe they were actually going to have a *commitment ceremony*, but once his mom knew they were serious, she insisted they choose china and Waterford Crystal patterns, so she could buy them as a wedding present just as she had for her other children.

Sikoki wrote me this about his parents' response:

> Despite the fact that my *very* Mormon Relief Society and Young Women's president mom and my stake patriarch dad would have hoped I would have chosen a "virtuous daughter of Zion to raise a righteous posterity to the Lord," they accepted Richard like another son and with unconditional love were there on the front row to witness our union. Our commitment ceremony was held in the elegant Los Angeles Westin Hotel, and after the ceremony we went into the ballroom, where Richard and I had the first dance. And a memory I will cherish always is seeing our two sets of parents joining us in the second dance.

I love to picture the entire chorus, who were present a couple hundred strong, singing that evening for two of their own. But most of all, I love to picture the parents, the siblings, the aunts and uncles, the cousins, the nephews and nieces, the grandparents—especially that large Mormon family—gathering together to circle the wagons around two men that they loved so dearly, building a fire of warmth and light that would tell them, now and forever, "You are not alone. We are with you now, and we will be with you always. We love you. We bless you. And we will protect you."

The video camera recorded all four parents' responses that night:

Sikoki's Mom: Congratulations to you both. We feel honored to be here for your ceremony, which was very nice.

Sikoki's Dad: We pray that you will both do well and be happy. We support you and love you very much.

Richard's Mom: We wish you luck, happiness, and all the love in the world. The ceremony was beautiful.

Richard's Dad: Ditto to what Mom said. Lots of luck, and God bless you both.

We can imagine, however, that especially in 1990, the parents of both the groom and the groom would have wondered how this relationship was going to turn out. Our society has little in place to support such unions and a great deal to discourage them. Many of us believe these arrangements are doomed to fail and actually *ought* to fail because they're simply wrong. Perhaps we feel a smug sense of satisfaction when they do fail.

I had lost touch with Sikoki after those early years when the publication of *Goodbye, I Love You* brought him into my life. So when I began writing this book, I knew I had to find him, and I knew what my first question was going to be.

"Sikoki! How are you and—*quick*—are you and Richard still together?"

A big laugh. "Of course! It's better and better and better all the time! Eighteen years now. Of course we're together!"

I sighed in relief and settled down to a great hour of catching up.

It is my belief that this relationship has succeeded in part due to the welcoming arms of both families. As I look at the Christmas letters that I filed away year after year, the highlights always included Sikoki's adventures as a flight attendant and Richard's as an occupational therapist specializing in brain injuries, but also, more importantly, time spent with both families—touring Egypt with a sister and her roommate; welcoming into the family a niece, little Rachel Erin, just a few hours after her birth; visiting Sikoki's parents on their LDS mission in Oregon and later for his dad's heart surgery; hosting family reunions at their place in Reseda Heights, California; making "Optimus Prime" and "Megatron" (two six-foot-tall "Transformers") for nephew Ryan's robot-themed eighth birthday party. In one Christmas letter, along with a great photo:

> We decided we wanted to do something special for each of our nieces and nephews as a college graduation present—so we came up with the idea of each one picking a destination somewhere United flies around the world—and we'd take him or her there on our companion passes. Larisa is the first one to graduate, and she chose Rio. We had a blast, and Larisa went hang gliding for the first time off one of the mountains!

In fact, Sikoki and Richard were so busy with family involvements that Sikoki was not available to attend the church court that led to his excommunication. He told me, "I hadn't been to church in twenty years. Every once in a while someone from the Church would come by and we'd invite them in, and we were always gracious when the missionaries came by. I remember once when a missionary left our home, he spoke to us so sweetly—'I sure do hope Heavenly Father changes his mind about you guys soon so you can come back to church.' Anyway, two years ago two men in suits knocked at the front door. I thought they were from the IRS, but they handed me a letter saying I was called to appear at a church court to consider my conduct. I told them I was sorry, I couldn't make it on that date as I would be out of town with Richard for the eightieth birthday celebration of his father. So they had the court without me.

They sent me a letter saying I was excommunicated and recommending that I read Spencer W. Kimball's *The Miracle of Forgiveness* and a book on reparative therapy. It's sad. I still love the Church. It gave me so much. The good far outweighs the bad. And I gave them such great road shows [short, amateur musical productions]! After the excommunication, my sister and my two brothers wrote and had their names taken off the records of the Church. My sister said she would not raise her children in a church that teaches them their favorite uncle is unworthy because he loves and lives with their other favorite uncle. It's so unfortunate for everyone."

Obsessive historian that I am, I kept the copy I received of the commitment ceremony that Sikoki and Richard wrote together and had read by various family members and friends that night. Here are snippets:

> Today's celebration of human affection is the outward sign of a sacred and inward commitment—which religious societies may consecrate and states may legalize—but which neither can create or annul. Such union can only be created by loving purpose, be maintained by abiding will, and be renewed by human feelings and heartfelt nurturing.

They acknowledged having been "born of goodly parents," and thanked them

> . . . for always taking the time to listen and offer advice, to cheer in our times of victory and console in our moments of defeat. Thank you for your wisdom, your patience, your understanding, your support, your faith and prayers, and your always unconditional love.

After the readings and the songs by the chorus, Sikoki and

Richard exchanged rings and vows. Encircled by family and friends, they each spoke this promise:

> With continued love, friendship, and trust—
> I take joy today in committing my life to yours.
> I pledge to face the future by your side, as a
> friend—who will understand you, as a
> partner—who will support you, as a
> confidante—who will share your secrets, your hopes,
> and your dreams, and as a
> companion—who will unconditionally love and honor you,
> and care for you with tenderness
> and affection always.

A few months ago, Sikoki and Richard, who happened to be in my area for a friend's birthday, spent a Sunday afternoon with me. Still handsome. A bit older, a touch of gray even. So happy together after eighteen years. No couple I've entertained enjoyed each other more, were more alive, delightful, grateful for leftover taco soup.

A few days later, I received a note from Sikoki and Richard, thanking me for "the delicious meal and goodies and the nourishment of the soul" and telling me I am "very loved." But what really made me smile were the words on the seal on the back of the envelope:

"Life is a Song—Sing It!"

My Family Is Not Like That

Teressa Nielson
New York City

November 30, 1996
Dear Grandma and Grandpa:

   I just wanted to say thank you for your letter. I got it last week, and it was definitely good to hear you say the things you did. I have always been so afraid to tell anyone that I'm gay. I even waited until I was 30 years old to tell my own mother and father. But what I've found is that I needn't have been so afraid at all because everyone has accepted me without any reservations, including my gram and gramps. I thought maybe you'd have a harder time with the news because you are older and maybe hadn't known any people in your lives who were "out." But all of us should have given you both more credit.

   These last few years have been a time of renewed appreciation for my family. I have been able to get a lot closer to my parents and sisters, especially to Mom, who has been so wonderful. She has shown me how much she cares about me by opening her mind so that she is able to truly understand and accept things. I know it is not easy for most people to do this, and that this is not the type of news parents or grandparents expect to hear. It's hard to go through years of your life not allowing people to know your sexual orientation. I realize that the constant efforts I felt I had to make to hide my true feelings and to "put up a front" for so long really exhausted me emotionally and affected my ability to have relationships with others that are honest and satisfying. I often regret that so many years of my life were spent this way—it seems like a real waste. I have had to learn so many things in adulthood that I wish I could have experienced sooner. I'm sure Uncle Clair feels the same way. He is probably relieved now and excited to now be able to let his parents and the rest of the family know him more fully.

I am lucky to have a family that truly loves and appreciates each other. I think this is why the news about me and Uncle Clair has met with such positive responses from everyone. I think families that really care about each member will make great effort to understand and accept each other. So many of my gay friends have had bad experiences coming out to their families—some have parents who don't even talk to them any more; many have families who, while they still speak, never discuss homosexuality or don't welcome the son or daughter's partner into their home. I am so glad I don't have to deal with anything like that. Many of my friends are shocked when I tell them how great my family has been—since they know my family are Mormons, they assume that I would be rejected, but I just tell them that my family is not like that.

Thanks again, you are both wonderful and I love you very much.

I can't wait to see you at Christmas!

Love,
Teressa

6
THE ROAD AHEAD

The real voyage of discovery consists not in seeking new landscapes but in having new eyes.

—MARCEL PROUST

Filling Our Wagons

It is Easter morning, 2006. Is it breaking the Sabbath to begin this section? *Master, is it lawful to heal on the Sabbath?* I have been so looking forward to writing the end of this book, even though by pages I'm not there yet. I often like to jump ahead and write the ending. It helps me to know where I'm going. And so I am going to write of healing on this Sabbath, this Easter morning, before I go to church.

Sometimes I like to climb up in what I call my "spiritual helicopter" and look down at life on the earth, my own life, the life of the human family. I like to see where we've been, imagine where we're going, get a little perspective on today. The journey is one of consciousness, I'm very clear on that. Years ago, Gerald, ever the philosopher, quoted to me something I can't repeat quite correctly, and I don't know who said it. "The only battles that count are the battles fought on the field of consciousness."

A few mornings ago I read in Eckhart Tolle's *A New Earth*:

> There is only one perpetrator of evil on the planet: human unconsciousness. That realization is true forgiveness. With forgiveness, your victim identity dissolves, and your true power emerges—the power of Presence. Instead of blaming the darkness, you bring in the light.

We can track consciousness from this high helicopter, you and I. We can look down at the landscape, watch history as it goes back and back and back. We can see the darkness of unconsciousness illumined from time to time by the light of consciousness. Look! There—hard to believe—we thought the gods appreciated human sacrifice—we thought it just fine for one man to own another in slavery—we accepted the idea that women did not have souls—we were indifferent to the genocide of millions of Native Americans—large numbers of us accepted that Hitler's ethnic cleansing was a fine idea.

Looking down at that slowly moving demarcation, that border of "now," we see the ongoing birth of higher consciousness. It's not a straight climb, but surely it's three steps forward for every one back. Where, then, will our consciousness be ten years, thirty years, fifty years from now, assuming our world lasts? You have your list of hopes, I am sure. I have mine. I hope and believe there will be more consciousness of our human family being part of the larger creation, part of the environment. The feminine principle, both mortal and divine, will have established a stronger presence. We will be closer to a cease-fire over who owns God. Our religions will have remembered that each has deeply embedded in its platform a version of the Golden Rule. We will have stopped creating divisions and will instead celebrate our common humanity and divinity. We will be more reverent of the place and power of sexuality. Our heterosexual majority will have ceased reviling and persecuting our gay brothers and sisters, and we will look back and shake our heads and say, "Can you believe that in the name of religion we drove these people to suicide?"

Not an impossible dream, I think. I know the human family, and I say with Anne Frank, "I still believe, in spite of everything, that people are really good at heart." I know the Mormon heart. It is a good and great heart. It is a heart that opens wide whenever a need is seen. It is the heart of Sister Spencer, my visiting teacher that I wrote about in *Goodbye, I Love You,* who called me when she learned I had Gerald at my home dying. "I'm not calling," she said, "to tell you to let me know if you need anything. I'm calling to tell you to put by the phone a list of things that need to be done. I'm calling every morning at nine, and you're going to read the list to me, and the things will be done." It is the heart that sent a couple dozen of the ward brethren to my home on a weekend to paint the entirety of my large and weathered house. It is the heart that brought over 500 people in my stake to contribute and record children's books to send to schools in Afghanistan in a project I headed for our stake Public Affairs Council. It is the heart that moved our humanitarian services in Salt Lake City, hours before Hurricane Katrina hit, to put on the road to Louisiana fourteen semi-trailers filled with water, tents, sleeping bags, tarps, generators, canned food, and hygiene kits.

When we see a need, we respond. When we are conscious, we act. That new pioneer journey I spoke of in the first part of this book is a journey of consciousness. Now that you have read the stories of anguish and of healing, have met our gay loved ones and the parents, sisters, brothers, and friends who have circled the wagons around them, you have journeyed in consciousness and have, I believe, arrived at a new place.

Now you *know.*

I began with a Mormon pioneer image, and I want to end with another one. Many of us have heard this story. I expect to type through tears today, as some of you may read through tears.

It was 1856. The last handcart companies were on the plains headed for Utah. Anxious to join the body of the Saints and fueled by an unrealistic zeal, they had started late in the season and were ill prepared for an early Wyoming winter. The

Martin Company of six hundred found themselves stopped at the Sweetwater, unable to go further in the snow. They waited, they died. One morning, thirteen were buried in the hard ground. Riders reached Salt Lake City on Saturday, October 4, to tell of their plight. The next day was the Church's General Conference, and twelve thousand had gathered to hear the words of their leader, Brigham Young. Brigham rose and addressed the congregation, saying,

> I will now give this people the subject and the text for . . . the Conference. It is this: On the fifth day of October, 1856, many of our brethren and sisters are on the plains with hand-carts . . . and they must be brought here; we must send assistance to them. The text will be—to get them here!
>
> . . . I shall call upon the bishops this day—I shall not wait until tomorrow . . . for sixty good mule teams, and twelve or fifteen wagons . . . ; also twelve tons of flour and forty good teamsters. . . . I will tell you all that your faith, religion and profession of religion, will never save one soul of you in the celestial kingdom of our God, unless you carry out just such principles as I am now teaching you. *Go and bring in those people now on the plains . . .*

Today I have ridden in with a report that I feel is an urgent one. I am not the only rider, but I am the one you are hearing now. There are large numbers of our homosexual people who are safe and warm, who have the highest self-esteem and have healthy relationships with their families and friends and with God. For many of them, that well-being has been purchased at a high price, and their scars are deep. But I speak to you now of those who are suffering today, a group of our own who have been caught in a fierce winter, a winter that is largely of our own making. Some of them are dying. You have read in this book about only a few, but across the human family there are millions. I am asking you to look beyond your prejudice and your judgment and see the human beings who have been left in the cold.

It is too late for Stuart, who lived in constant torment and self-hatred and developed calluses on his knees from constant prayer until he shot himself on the steps of the chapel.

It is too late for my dear Brad, who took pills and went to the Provo Temple to die, hoping that some kind angels would be there to receive him, and who wept as he told me, "To be rejected by something so wonderful as the Mormon Church is nearly more than a person can bear."

But it is not too late for thousands who struggle in the cold of misunderstanding. Today there is a despondent gay man somewhere who has checked to see if his father's gun is still where it used to be. Tonight there is a lesbian who again cries herself to sleep over her awful alternatives, "You may choose between being gay or being a member of this family." Today there are parents whose tears are for the pain of their loved gay child, for the lack of support they receive from their church, for the condemning rhetoric they continue to hear, and for fear that the members of their congregation might find out the family secret. Today there takes place a marriage ceremony for a young, gay man, anxious to please God and his church, and an eager starry-eyed young bride who believes her groom's romantic restraint has come from his righteousness. Today a child cries before going to school, terrified that a classmate may learn that his father is gay and start calling him names.

These people are still on the plains. I am asking you to load up the wagons. You can do it without fully understanding, even without fully "approving." You have the supplies, parcels of love, compassion, encouragement, respect, good information, and humility in knowing that there is much we have yet to learn. You have the words of Jesus: "Inasmuch as ye have done it unto one of the least of these, ye have done it unto me." And you have the words that still echo across a century and a half: *Go and bring in those people now on the plains.*

The call goes out not only to the Mormon part of God's family, but to every other Christian, to Jews, to Muslims, to Buddhists, to Hindus, to all our cousins everywhere. Just now, as I wrote again and put in italics those pressing words mobilizing the rescue party, I realized I am speaking not only of those who have been harmed, but also of those who harm. All of us who have, in our arrogance, judged one another unkindly, looked at each other through the eyes of fear rather than the eyes of love—we, too, are out on the plains in a harsh winter, cold and without nourishment. And so I have to issue the same call to our gay friends and to their families, and to every other group of people who have been misunderstood and abused. I ask you also to fill your wagons, fill them with courage, with forgiveness, with patience, with exemplary behavior, and with unwavering insistence that we can, we must, and we will move to higher ground.

We take turns, then, don't we? When you are caught on any plain where love is not, I will gather what I have and bring what I can. And when I have used up all my love and am stranded in the cold, I will watch for you to appear with fresh supplies. That way we can make it, I think, all of us. We can be sufficiently creative and sufficiently kind that we will draw circle upon circle upon circle, bringing each other in, leaving no one out, joining, linking, enlarging, until the pattern of the whole human family, seen through the eye of God, is complete.

Endnotes

1. FIRST STEPS

This New Pioneer Journey

"Rafe, we're circling the wagons around you":
Vince Horiuchi, "Gay Mormon gets real on 'Survivor,'" *Salt Lake Tribune*, December 1, 2005.

An Enemy Is Someone Whose Story You Do Not Know

"The Science of Sexual Orientation," *60 Minutes*, March 12, 2006.

"Receive truth, let it come from whence it may":
Alma P. Burton, ed., *Discourses of the Prophet Joseph Smith* (Salt Lake City: Deseret Book, 1977), 199.

Statements from BYU professor on biology of homosexuality:
Brittney McLaws, "Professor claims scientific evidence of homosexuality," *BYU NewsNet*, March 26, 2004.

Statements on genes influencing sexuality:
Duane E. Jeffery, "Genes and Human Behavior," *The Provo Herald*, June 14, 21, and 28, 1993.

"Timing and amount of testosterone released in utero by the developing embryo":
R. Jan Stout, "Sin and Sexuality: Psychobiology and the Development of Homosexuality," *Dialogue: A Journal of Mormon Thought* 20 (Summer 1987): 29-41.

450 species exhibit homosexual behavior:
Bruce Bagemihl, *Biological Exuberance: Animal Homosexuality and Natural Diversity* (New York: St. Martin's Press, 1999), 12.

Ray and Silo, gay penguins:
Gersh Kuntzman, "An Unusual Love Story," *Newsweek*, March 2, 2004.

Religions as "divisive rather than unifying forces":
Eckhart Tolle, *A New Earth* (New York: Dutton, 2005), 15, 74, 75.

"Have mercy on one another":
Alma P. Burton, ed., *Discourses of the Prophet Joseph Smith* (Salt Lake City: Deseret Book, 1977), 88.

"Everything that comes from love is a miracle":
A Course in Miracles ([s.l.]: Foundation for Inner Peace, 1975), 1.

Goodbye, I Love You: *Then and Now*

"Crime Against Nature":
Spencer W. Kimball, *The Miracle of Forgiveness* (Salt Lake City: Bookcraft, 1969), 77-89.

"President Kimball's strongly negative attitude toward homosexuality": Edward L. Kimball, *Lengthen Your Stride: The Presidency of Spencer W. Kimball* (Salt Lake City: Deseret Book, 2005), 85.

President Gordon B. Hinckley and Larry King:
Larry King Live, December 26, 2004.

"We realize there may be great loneliness in their lives":
"First Presidency Statement on Same-Gender Marriage," October 19, 2004, http://www.lds.org/newsroom.

Recent official statement on position of LDS Church by Elders Oaks and Wickman: "Same-Gender Attraction," 2006, http://www.lds.org/newsroom.

"Spencer later seemed to wish he had adopted a gentler tone":
Edward L. Kimball, *Lengthen Your Stride*, 79-80.

1.6 million copies of The Miracle of Forgiveness *sold:*
Edward L. Kimball, *Lengthen Your Stride*, 79.

2. THAT FINAL, DESPERATE ACT

Driving Them to the Brink

Utah suicide statistics:
Lucinda Dillon Kinkead and Dennis Romboy, "Deadly taboo: Youth suicide an epidemic that many in Utah prefer to ignore," *Deseret Morning News,* April 23, 2006.

National suicide statistics for gay youth:
Report of the Secretary's Task Force on Youth Suicide (Rockville, MD: U.S. Department of Health and Human Services, Public Health Service, Alcohol, Drug Abuse, and Mental Health Administration, 1989).

Suicide statistics in LDS Church publication:
"Suicide rates increasing—Church members not immune," *LDS Church News,* January 15, 1994.

Suicide of Anna Wallner:
Mary Lou Wallner, *The Slow Miracle of Transformation* (Cabot, AZ: Teach Project, 2003), 138.

Suicide of Bobby Griffith:
Leroy Aarons, *Prayers for Bobby: A Mother's Coming to Terms with the Suicide of Her Gay Son* (San Francisco: HarperSanFrancisco, 1995).

Suicide of Stuart Matis in Newsweek:
Mark Miller, "To Be Gay—And Mormon," *Newsweek,* May 8, 2000, 38-39.

Story of Stuart Matis by his parents:
Fred and Marilyn Matis and Ty Mansfield, *In Quiet Desperation* (Salt Lake City: Deseret Book, 2004).

Letter of Stuart Matis to cousin:
"Letter to a Cousin," February 2000, http://www.affirmation. org/suicide_info/letter_to_a_cousin.shtml.

Suicide of Clay Whitmer:
Mark Miller, "To Be Gay—And Mormon."

Suicide of Brian (DJ) Thompson:

"Brian DJ Hyer Thompson (1967-2000)," http://www.affirmation.org/suicides/dj_thompson.shtml.

"From too much love of living":
Algernon Charles Swinburne, "The Garden of Proserpine," in *An Anthology of Famous English and American Poetry*, ed. William Rose Benet and Conrad Aiken (New York: Random House, 1944), 359.

3. STAR-CROSSED LOVES

I Speak for Romantic Love

Deepak Chopra, *The Path to Love* (New York: Harmony Books, 1997), 65, 133.

Thomas Moore, *Soul Mates* (New York: Harper Perennial, 1994), 136, 146, 187.

Nathaniel Branden, *The Psychology of Romantic Love* (Los Angeles: J.P. Tarcher, Inc., 1980), 163.

Sad Harvest

Lyla White, foreword to *Stranger at the Gate*, by Mel White (New York: Simon & Schuster, 1994), 5-7.

When It's Your Daughter

Ruth Muir Gardner, "Families Can Be Together Forever," *Children's Songbook* (Salt Lake City: The Church of Jesus Christ of Latter-day Saints, 1989), 188.

There Are So Many Kinds of Love

Trevor Southey, *Reconciliation* (Salt Lake City: Signature Books, 1997), 17-25.

Planning the Wedding

Article on Russ Gorringe:
Deborah Bulkeley, "Commitment Expo 2006 reaches out to gays," *Deseret Morning News*, May 11, 2006.

Choosing and Keeping the Star-Crossed Love

"Why should we mourn or think our lot is hard?":

William Clayton, "Come, Come, Ye Saints," *Hymns of the Church of Jesus Christ of Latter-day Saints* (Salt Lake City: The Church of Jesus Christ of Latter-day Saints, 1985), 30.

"Deviations from the optimal path of development":
Ken Carey, *The Third Millennium* (San Francisco: HarperSanFrancisco, 1991), 44.

I'll Walk with You

Navajo "Two Spirit People":
Sue-Ellen Jacobs, Wesley Thomas, and Sabine Lang, *Two-Spirit People: Native American Gender Identity, Sexuality, and Spirituality* (Urbana: University of Illinois Press, 1997).

Statistics on autism:
The Contra Costa Times, May 5, 2006.

Carol Lynn Pearson, "I'll Walk With You," *Children's Songbook*, 140.

4. CIRCLING THE WAGONS (ONE)

When There's Love at Home

"When there's love at home":
John Hugh McNaughton, "Love at Home," *Hymns of the Church of Jesus Christ of Latter-day Saints*, 294.

"Keep your families close together and love and honor your children":
Gordon B. Hinckley, "First Presidency Message: Family Home Evening," *Ensign*, March 2003.

Rabbi Harold Kushner on children disappointing parents:
http://www.newmorningtv.tv/rabbi_kushner106.jsp.

Catholic statement on parents not rejecting gay children:
Always Our Children: A Pastoral Message to Parents of Homosexual Children and Suggestions for Pastoral Ministers (Washington, DC: United States Catholic Conference, 1997), http://www.nccbuscc.org/laity/always.shtml.

"Some of the parents don't love their children anymore":

Eddie Sarfaty, "I Make My Grandmother Cry," in *When I Knew*, by Robert Trachtenberg (New York: Regen Books, 2005), 65.

"Through Heavenly Father's plan":
Ruth Muir Gardner, "Families Can Be Together Forever," *Children's Songbook*, 188.

Mormon families' fear of losing children in the afterlife:
Carrie A. Moore, "Bridging the Divide," *Deseret Morning News*, January 21, 2006.

"Families are strengthened, not weakened":
Gayle Hayes Castleton, "Support and acceptance are the true family values," *Salt Lake Tribune*, June 25, 2006.

I Drew a Circle That Took Him In
Martin Luther King on loving your enemies:
Clayborne Carson and Peter Holloran, eds., *A Knock at Midnight: Inspiration from the Great Sermons of Reverend Martin Luther King, Jr.* (New York: IPM/Warner Books, 1998), http://www.stanford.edu/group/King/publications/sermons/5 71117.002_Loving_Your_Enemies.html.

You Don't Know Him
Statements from Lowell Bennion:
Mary Lythgoe Bradford, *Lowell L. Bennion: Teacher, Counselor, Humanitarian* (Salt Lake City: Signature Books, 1995), 248, 295-97.

Pieces of Eugene: Navajo, Mormon, and Gay
Article on Eugene Tachinni:
Peggy Fletcher Stack, "Taped together: A passionate pastiche," *Salt Lake Tribune*, February 25, 2006.

Snapshots for the Family Album
Story of NFL football player:
Esera Tuaolo, *Alone in the Trenches: My Llife as a Gay Man in the NFL* (Naperville, IL: Sourcebooks, 2006), 177-78.

My Voice Will Not Be Silenced
"If by a still small voice he calls":

Mary Brown, "I'll Go Where You Want Me to Go," *Hymns of the Church of Jesus Christ of Latter-day Saints*, 270.

Hatred Saddens Mom of Gay Son

Newspaper column on Christine and her gay son:
Cathy Free, "Hatred saddens mom of gay son," *Deseret Morning News*, March 30, 2006.

5. CIRCLING THE WAGONS (TWO)

I Never Would Have Dreamed

Newspaper article on Bruce Bastian and Gene Robinson:
Amy Choate, "Religion called important in lives of gays, lesbians," *Deseret Morning News*, July 1, 2006.

It Has Become Our Universe

On the Hardy family:
Katherine Rosman, "Mormon Family Values," *The Nation*, February 25, 2002.

Rod's Other Family

Iraqi women on Relief Society:
Peggy Fletcher Stack, "Relief Society intrigues Iraqi women," *Salt Lake Tribune*, May 26, 2006.

6. THE ROAD AHEAD

Filling Our Wagons

Tolle on human unconsciousness:
Eckhart Tolle, *A New Earth* (New York: Dutton, 2005), 160.

"Go and bring in those people now on the plains":
LeRoy R. Hafen and Ann W. Hafen, *Handcarts to Zion* (Glendale, CA: The Arthur H. Clark Company, 1960), 120-21.

Resources

GENERAL

GLSEN (Gay, Lesbian & Straight Education Network): "Focused on ensuring safe schools for ALL students." 212-727-0135 www.glsen.org

HRC (Human Rights Campaign): "Working for lesbian, gay, bisexual, transgender equal rights." www.hrc.org For religious support, link to "Faith and Religion."

PFLAG (Parents and Friends of Lesbians and Gays): "Promotes the health and well-being of gay, lesbian, bisexual and transgender persons, their families and friends." www.pflag.org For religious support, link to "Education and Support" and "Welcoming Faith Communities."

SPECIFICALLY FOR MORMONS

Some organizations formed by LDS or formerly LDS people to address the needs of gays and lesbians and their families are:

AFFIRMATION: GAY AND LESBIAN MORMONS: "Serves the needs of gay, lesbian, bisexual, and transgender LDS and their supportive family and friends through social and educational activities." 661-367-2421 www.affirmation.org

DISCIPLES2: "Those whom we serve are attempting to obey the laws of the Lord, including the law of chastity." www.disciples2.org

EVERGREEN: "For people who want to diminish same-sex attractions and overcome homosexual behavior." www.evergreeninternational.org

FAMILY FELLOWSHIP: "A diverse collection of Mormon families engaged in the cause of strengthening families with homosexual members." 801-374-1447 www.ldsfamilyfellowship.org

GLYA (Gay Latter-day Saint Young Adults): "Provides safe and healthy social activities and events for gay, lesbian, bisexual and transgender young adults ages 18-30 who share the similar cultural and religious background and/or heritage in Mormonism, and provides resources and information for their physical, mental/emotional well being." www.glya.com

GAMOFITES: "Men united in the joys and challenges of being fathers, gay, and Mormon." www.gamofites.org

LDS RESOURCES: "Presents material that evidences a collective, responsible, spiritual concern for homosexual Latter-day Saints and their families and a desire to find more constructive, gospel-centered ways of dealing with what, for many, is a painful and often divisive issue." www.ldsresources.info

RECONCILIATION: "Affirms the spirituality of gays and lesbians and seeks to provide a safe haven for individuals with a Latter-day Saint background to discuss the gospel of Jesus Christ." 801-296-4797 www.ldsreconciliation.org

WILDFLOWERS (Co-founded by my daughter Emily): "To support the beauty, strength, courage and rebirth of women who have been or who are currently married to homosexual men." www.wearewildflowers.com

---

SUICIDE HELPLINE, TOLL FREE

If you are thinking about suicide or just feeling down and need someone to talk to, call the Trevor Helpline for gay/lesbian/questioning youth:

24 HOURS A DAY, 7 DAYS A WEEK

866-4-U-TREVOR (866-488-7386)

About the Author

CAROL LYNN PEARSON lives in Northern California and has authored more than forty books and stage plays. Many of her poems have been widely reprinted in such places as the Ann Landers column and *Chicken Soup for the Soul*, as well as college literary textbooks. In addition to *Goodbye, I Love You*, the story of her life with her husband, her books include *Consider the Butterfly*, a finalist in the Inspiration/Spiritual category of the 2002 Independent Publishers Book Awards, *The Lesson*, *A Stranger for Christmas*, and a one-woman play, *Mother Wove the Morning*. A complete list of her books and plays can be found at
www.clpearson.com

A stage play by Ms. Pearson, *Facing East*, tells the story of a Mormon couple dealing with the suicide of their gay son. To purchase the book or to learn about current productions or production rights, see
www.nomoregoodbyes.com/facingeast

~

To read or submit comments about *No More Goodbyes*, to share your own story, or to put your name on Ms. Pearson's personal mailing list, visit www.nomoregoodbyes.com. At that website you will also find information on additional services Ms. Pearson offers on the subject of this book, such as speaking, workshops, private retreats and individual consulting. Contact her directly at
clp@nomoregoodbyes.com

Note

To see photos of many of the individuals and families whose stories appear in this book, go to www.nomoregoodbyes.com/photos

Quick Order Form

(*CD read by the author)

INTERNET: www.nomoregoodbyes.com OR www.amazon.com

POSTAL SERVICE: For postal orders send this form to:
Pivot Point Books
1384 Cornwall Ct.
Walnut Creek, CA 94597

Please send:

quantity		total cost
_____ No More Goodbyes, the book, $14.95 each		_____
_____ No More Goodbyes, on cd read by the author, $24.95 each		_____
• 7.75% sales tax (California residents)		_____
• shipping: $4 first item; $2 each additional item		_____
• outside U.S. see www.nomoregoodbyes.com		_____
• TOTAL		_____

Name_____

Address _____ State _____ Zip _____

check attached _____   charge credit card _____

Visa _____   MasterCard _____   Discover _____   American Express _____

Card #: _____ Exp. month _____ yr. _____

Name as it appears on card: _____

Phone (in case of problem only)_____

Email: _____

Please include me on occasional, related email updates by Carol Lynn Pearson

BOOKSTORES, GROUP SALES: see www.nomoregoodbyes.com